Charting For D...

MW01108315

Fifteen Rules to Beating the Market

- **Treat technical trading and investing as a business.** You *can* beat the index averages. And you *can* make extraordinary profits in securities markets. But you have to treat technical trading and investing as a business (and remember, a majority of new businesses fail).

- **Succeed in trading on technicals by being more observant, more thoughtful and more careful than the other guy.** Excellence in technical trading and investing is like excellence in any field of endeavour. You have to take it very seriously and work at it very hard. Trading is a competition, and the other guy wants to win (in other words, take your money).

- **Trade and invest to make money.** Don't do it for entertainment or to be right.

- **Use fundamentals to select securities, not trade them.** Get as much fundamental information as you need, but at the end of the day, use it to select securities, not to trade them.

- **Trade with the trend.** If you don't know what's going on, don't trade. Don't fall into the 'value trap' — that a high-quality security will come back after a fall. It may, but you may have to live a long time to see it happen. While you're waiting, you're missing opportunities to build capital.

- **Take the empirical approach.** *See* what you're *looking at* on the chart. Don't let wishful thinking skew your vision. Accept the evidence of your eyes.

- **Impose strict risk management controls.** Technical indicators give you an advantage — the 'trader's edge' — but no indicator is a crystal ball. Technical indicators are wrong — a lot — so you make up for imperfections in technical techniques by imposing strict risk-management controls.

- **Know what your indicators are measuring.** Understand the crowd sentiment underlying your technical indicators.

- **Use the confirmation principle — multiple indicators — to improve your odds.** No indicator is a magic bullet. But don't demand so much confirmation from so many indicators that you hardly ever get a signal — analysis paralysis. Use indicators that work well together without duplicating the ruling concept.

- **Acknowledge that you will take losses, and control them.** The biggest cause of losses isn't bad indicators; it's you. You can design a reasonable technical trading regime and still fail to make money if you don't control losses. If you can't tolerate any loss, you shouldn't trade at all.

- **Acknowledge that trading arouses emotion in you, and control it.** Establish rules when to remain unemotional to overcome bad decision-making. Reduce trading after a big loss and a big gain. Pace your trading to the amount of money you have. Don't overtrade. You can't control the market, but you can control yourself.

- **Plan every trade.** Establish your best-case profit as well as your worst-case loss. Trading isn't gambling — it's a business, with probable outcomes that you can estimate. Take money off the table once in a while and put it somewhere safe, and cut losses ruthlessly to preserve capital.

(continued)

For Dummies®*: Bestselling Book Series for Beginners*

Charting For Dummies®

- **Don't listen to gurus and experts, and don't take tips.** Do your own work. Nobody else understands your risk appetite and tolerance for uncertainty the way you do. Everyone trades the same indicator on the same security a different way, and no one way is the right way. If you do take guidance from gurus, learn their strengths and weaknesses, and verify their work with your own. Don't give tips, either, unless you're quitting your day job to set up an advisory business.

- **Diversify.** Trade several securities and types of securities to reduce the risk of a market catastrophe wiping you out.

- **Keep an honest trading track record and an honest trading diary.** They'll show you what techniques work and where your techniques fall short, and they give you information about your discipline that may or may not be welcome news.

The Basic Bar

The price bar is the basic building block of technical analysis. Most indicators are nothing more than an arithmetic manipulation of the four price bar components.

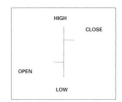

Anatomy of a Candlestick

Candlestick charting displays the price bar in a graphically different way from standard bars. Candlesticks are dramatic and visually compelling.

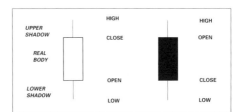

For Dummies®: Bestselling Book Series for Beginners

by Barbara Rockefeller

Adapted for Australia by
Ken Henderson, Larry Lovrencic and Peter Pontikis

Wiley Publishing Australia Pty Ltd

Charting For Dummies®

Australian Edition published by
Wiley Publishing Australia Pty Ltd
42 McDougall Street
Milton, Qld 4064
www.dummies.com

Copyright © 2007 Wiley Publishing Australia Pty Ltd

The moral rights of the authors have been asserted.

National Library of Australia
Cataloguing-in-Publication data

Rockefeller, Barbara, 1946– .

  Charting for dummies.
  Australian ed.

  Includes index.
  ISBN 978 0 731 40710 1 (pbk.).

  1. Investment analysis. I. Title. (Series : For dummies).

332.6

Cover image: © Imagemore

Wiley Bicentennial Logo: Richard J. Pacifico

Printed in China by
Printplus Limited

10 9 8 7 6 5 4 3 2 1

About the Authors

Barbara Rockefeller is a writer specialising in international economics and finance, with a focus on foreign exchange. She is the publisher of a daily newsletter on the foreign exchange market, 'The Strategic Currency Briefing'. Her newsletter combines technical and fundamental observations and features a daily report on trading FX futures, which is technically based. Barbara has a BA in economics from Reed College in Portland, Oregon, and an MA in International Affairs from Columbia University. She teaches economics at the University of Phoenix Online.

Barbara is the author of *How to Invest Internationally*, published in Japanese in 1999 (Franklin Covey), *CNBC 24/7, Trading Around the Clock, Around the World*, published in 2000 (John Wiley & Sons) and *The Global Trader*, published in 2001 (John Wiley & Sons). She also writes articles from time to time for *Futures, Active Trader* and *Stock, Futures and Options* magazines.

Ken Henderson is a private investor who works in the IT industry. He is currently the Secretary of the Australian Professional Technical Analysts (APTA) group and was a founding member of APTA. Ken is also a member of the Australian Technical Analysts Association (ATAA) and a former Treasurer and President of the ATAA board of directors. He believes that experienced traders should share their skills so that investors may understand the art of trading successfully.

Larry Lovrencic is an Executive Director of First Pacific Securities Pty Ltd and Delta Capital Markets Pty Ltd and is editor of the *Institutional FX* publications. Larry is co-author, with Alex Douglas and Peter Pontikis, of the book *FX Trading: An Australian Guide to Trading Foreign Exchange*, published by Wiley Publishing Australia Pty Ltd.

Larry has more than 20 years' trading experience, and lectures and examines Technical Analysis for tertiary students and financial institution employees in Australia, Singapore and Vietnam. Larry is a Senior Fellow of the Financial Services Institute of Australasia (FINSIA).

Peter Pontikis has worked in financial markets for almost 25 years and is an institutional treasury strategist for a large Australian banking and insurance group. Peter is the treasurer of the International Federation of Technical Analysis as well as a past president of the Australian Technical Analysts Association. He has authored books on foreign exchange as well as producing Mandarin-speaking CD training programs for the Chinese financial markets.

Dedication

This book is dedicated to the grand old men of technical analysis who came before us, who blazed a trail by establishing the theory of *technical analysis* as a discipline of financial markets analysis. The work done by Charles Dow, Richard Schabacker, Robert D Edwards and John Magee have stood the test of time and have built a solid foundation on which our analytical techniques are based.

Authors' Acknowledgments

Barbara acknowledges *For Dummies* editor Mike Baker, 'who caused much suffering. I'm wrung-out, but you, dear reader, have a better book.'

Ken, Larry and Peter tip their hat to *For Dummies* acquisitions editor Charlotte Duff, who envisaged an Australian version of *Charting For Dummies*, as well as editor Giovanni Ebono, for his patience and ability to quickly absorb and understand a very technical subject.

Charts have been prepared using Metastock charting software by Equis (data courtesy of eSignal and Reuters), and AmiBroker software.

Publisher's Acknowledgments

We're proud of this book; please send us your comments through our Dummies online registration form located at www.dummies.com/register/.

Some of the people who helped bring this book to market include the following:

Acquisitions, Editorial and Media Development

Project Editors: Giovanni Ebono, Maryanne Phillips, Mark Baker

Acquisitions Editor: Charlotte Duff

Technical Reviewer: Daniel Chesler (US), John Jeffery (Australia)

Editorial Manager: Gabrielle Packman

Production

Layout and Graphics: Wiley Composition Services, and Wiley Art Studio

Cartoons: Glenn Lumsden

Indexer: Karen Gillen

Contents at a Glance

Table of Contents

Introduction

• •

*T*iming is everything.

Timing is critical in cooking, romance, music, politics, farming and a hundred other aspects of life on this planet. Putting money into a securities market is no different — you need good timing to get the best results.

Technical traders all over the world, amateur and professional alike, earn a living using technical analysis to time their trades. They not only earn a living, but they're still standing after a market crash. In this book, we try to explain how they do that, and how you can do it, too.

Beating the Market

Charts and the application of technical analysis to charts have been around for over 100 years, but until the personal computer came along, they were mostly confined to professionals who had access to live prices and the sound of the crowd on the trading floor. From professionals arose the study of price itself, independent of what people know (or think they know) about the fundamentals of securities. Technical analysis is about making extraordinary gains — beating the market — and if you think that isn't possible, you haven't looked hard enough.

Many people try to beat the market and fail. Well, many people fail in every endeavour. Everyone knows the story of the hapless day traders of the 1990s who deluded themselves into thinking that they possessed trading secrets when all they had was a roaring bull market. A few survived — because they adapted their trading techniques to the market. To trade well is a skill that takes training, practice and learning from mistakes, just like any other business. You wouldn't open a restaurant without knowing how to cook, but somehow people think they can trade securities without understanding how and why prices move.

Whether you just want to get out ahead of another crash, sharpen your trading skills or aspire to become a self-supporting trader, use your noggin: This is going to take some sweat. And some hard choices. You may be disappointed to discover that technical analysis doesn't offer a single, coherent path to market wisdom. You'd think that after 100 years of development, traders would have a rulebook with a single set of steps to take and processes to go through. But we don't.

Why not? For the same reason that there are ten equally delicious ways to cook an omelette. Each cook selects a different pan, whisking and stirring techniques, amount of salt, amount of heat and so on. Likewise in trading, each trader sees a different amount of risk on any particular chart, chooses one set of indicators over another, and has a taste for taking a certain amount of profit (or loss) for the capital at stake. Just as no-one can dictate a single right way to cook an omelette, no-one can name the single best way to trade a particular price situation. Theoretically, you could say that the best way is the way that makes the most money, but that fails to take into account the trader — his experience, goals, personality — and how much money he has to risk.

To blend technical methods with your own personal risk profile isn't the work of one day. It's a lengthy and difficult process that requires some soul-searching. To keep the process manageable, confine your conclusions to what you can observe and verify — the empirical approach. Be careful to avoid the error of composition, like reading that one set of technical traders believes in magic numbers and concluding that all of technical analysis involves magic numbers. (It doesn't.) It's astonishing how many otherwise smart people misjudge technical analysis these days in exactly this manner, and in widely reviewed books, based on an incomplete understanding of the field. Many critics take one technical idea, fail to integrate it with their personal risk profile, and then blame the charts and the use of technical analysis for their losses. This is like putting the eggshells into the pan and blaming the eggs for an inedible omelette.

Another error to avoid is the overly scientific approach. Like the expert who proved that the Bernoulli principle is mathematically wrong and therefore airplanes can't fly, probability experts say they can prove prices are random. Random numbers do throw up patterns, the argument goes, so technical analysts are deluding themselves that apparent orderliness can be exploited for profit over any length of time. And yet you do see orderliness, and you can exploit it (at least some of the time). Traders have been profiting from technical methods for over a hundred years — longer, if we count 17th-century candlestick charting.

Finding Order

Much of the time you can see order in the way prices evolve, even though securities prices develop in an infinite variety of configurations and each chart is literally unique. Technical traders attribute that orderliness to the swings of market sentiment. Prices form patterns because the traders in the market behave in regular and repetitive ways. We can identify, measure and project prices because we can identify, measure and project human behaviour. We can do it only imperfectly, but we can do it.

Probably the most intriguing thing about technical analysis is that ideas and insights about price behaviour from 1900 are as fresh and valuable today as they were then. Technical analysis never throws anything out — it just finds more efficient ways to capture price moves. Since the personal computer came on the scene, technical analysis has become more maths-oriented, but the essence of technical analysis is still to grasp the underlying human behaviour that makes the price move.

In the grand scheme of things, technical analysis is a fairly new field of endeavour, and is still changing. We have a long way to go. The few things we know for certain are:

✔ No technique works all the time.

✔ No technique works on every security.

✔ Something mysterious is going on that we don't yet understand. A famous trader named Bernard Baruch said

Have you ever seen, in some wood, on a sunny quiet day, a cloud of flying midges — thousands of them — hovering, apparently motionless, in a sunbeam? . . . Yes? . . . Well, did you ever see the whole flight — each mite apparently preserving its distance from all others — suddenly move, say three feet, to one side or the other? Well, what made them do that? A breeze? I said a quiet day. But try to recall — did you ever see them move directly back again in the same unison? Well, what made them do that? Great human mass movements are slower in inception but much more effective.

This is what technical analysis seeks to explain.

About This Book

The use of charts as a means of trading and the application of technical analysis to these charts is positively blooming. Go to an Internet search engine and type in **technical analysis**, and you get 31.8 million responses. The phrase **support and resistance** gets 7.12 million hits. Okay, everyone knows the limitations of Web searches, but even after weeding out the mismatches, that's still a huge amount of material. Don't be intimidated. In this book, we include core concepts, some of which you can apply *today* with no further research.

We want you to grasp the mindset of the chartist/technical trader/investor: To think independently, to take responsibility for actions, and most of all, to act on observation rather than conventional wisdom. Try to leave your preconceptions about trading and investing behind. For example, a core technical concept is that the technical trader cuts losses and lets the winning trades run. Chances are you think that, after taking a loss, you should continue to hold the security, because if it's a true value investment, it'll come back.

But try to think like a 10-year-old as you read this book. In fact, go find a 10-year-old, if you have one handy, and ask, 'Which is better to hang onto, a thing that has already let you down (losses) or a different thing that's delivering exactly what you wanted (profits)?' See? Technical analysis is subversive that way.

It's fun and rewarding to beat the system. The market doesn't know your age, gender, ethnicity, good looks or lack of them, singing talent, or anything else about you except whether you're a successful trader. The market is blind. In fact, the market is indifferent. It's one place you can go to be judged solely on your merits.

Conventions Used in This Book

To help you navigate through this book, we use the following conventions:

- *Italic* is used for emphasis and to highlight new words or terms that are defined.
- **Boldfaced** text is used to indicate phrases you'd type into search engines, keywords in bulleted lists or the action part of numbered steps.
- Monofont is used for Web addresses.

Foolish Assumptions

Authors must make assumptions about their audience, and we've made a few assumptions that may apply to you:

- ✔ You've never put a cent into a security but you plan to, and when you do, you intend not to lose it.
- ✔ You're reasonably well versed in the trading game, but you're looking for new tools to become a more effective trader.
- ✔ You're tired of the buy-and-hold approach in which your returns seem unrelated to the supposed quality of the security you bought.
- ✔ You want to find out how to sell. You know how to buy, but timing your sales ties you up in knots.
- ✔ You've experienced some setbacks in the market, and you need an approach to make that money back.
- ✔ You want to know whether technical analysis has any basis in reason and logic or we're all crackpots.

If any of these descriptions fits the bill, then you've picked up the right book.

How This Book Is Organised

We've organised *Charting For Dummies* into six parts. Part I introduces you to the field of charting and its relationship to the market, Part II introduces you to the basics of reading price charts and what the patterns you find might mean. Part III and IV introduce other ways of analysing price movements and Part V puts it all together to gives you an overview of different ways you can apply this knowledge. What's that leave? Only the famous *For Dummies* Part of Tens — Part VI.

Part I: Defining Technical Analysis

The point of technical analysis is to help you observe prices and make trading decisions based on reasonable expectations about where 'the market' is going to take the price. This part shows you how to view security prices as the outcome of crowd psychology.

Part II: Observing Market Behaviour

The price bar and its placement on the chart deliver a tonne of information about market sentiment. It doesn't take much practice to start reading the mind of the market by looking at bars and small patterns. You have to be patient, imaginative and thoughtful, but the payoff is cold, hard cash. With a little practice, you can quickly start throwing around technical jargon like *support and resistance* with the best of them. Better yet, this part provides the concepts you need to start making informed decisions.

Part III: Trading on Trends

This is the part that deals (mostly) with maths-based indicators. Relax — it's only arithmetic. Maths indicators are the workhorses of technical analysis. Especially since the introduction of the personal computer, these indicators are as easily read as the lines on a chart. They help you identify whether your price is trending, the strength of the trend and when the trend is at a reversal point. Applying these indicators carefully and consistently is the key to trading success.

Part IV: Dynamic Analysis Using Indicators

Indicators based on mathematical calculation have the advantage that they can detect underlying patterns that are not readily visible on a chart. This part focuses on the indicators that show the strength of trends and the momentum in price moves. Another technique, point and figure charting, can also help you predict when a trend is ending, faster than you may be able to using a conventional chart layout.

Part V: Using the Tools of Technical Analysis

Before you plunge into risking hard-earned cash on securities trading, you have to realise that it's not the security that counts, it's the trade. Each trade has two parts: The price analysis and *you*. With price analysis tools (indicators) you have to select the ones that match your personality and preference for risk. But most people don't know their risk preference when they start out in securities trading (which changes over time, anyway), so you have a chicken and egg situation. By studying the kinds of profit and loss outcomes that each type of indicator delivers, you can figure out your risk preferences.

And if you're mathematically competent, you can take a giant leap into system building, and remove most of the day-to-day judgemental decision-making that trading involves.

Part VI: The Part of Tens

As we say in Part I, there's the trade, and then there's you. You can be merely competent at using indicators and still achieve excellence as a trader. We show you how in this part, by sharing ten rules that every top trader follows and ten technical things you can do that help you make money trading. Finally, we include a brief listing of the top resources to follow up on.

Icons Used in This Book

When you see this icon, you don't want to forget the accompanying info — pretty subtle, huh?

This piece of art clues you in on hands-on advice that you can put into practice. In many cases, this icon tells you directly how to conduct a trade on a technical principle, usually an indicator crossing something, breaking something or dancing a jig.

Ignore this information at your own financial peril. We use it to warn you about mistakes, missteps and traps that can sink even the most hardened professional.

This icon flags places where we get really technical about technical analysis. Although it's great info, you can skip it and not miss out on the subject at hand.

What You Need to Get Started

If you don't already know trading basics, you need to get a few things under your belt to get the most out of this book — things like what a securities exchange is, exchange hours, what trades in after-hours, what brokers do (and don't do), trading conventions like 'bid and offer' and types of orders, how to read a brokerage statement, and oh yes, the nature of the security you plan to trade.

After that, all you really need is a newspaper that publishes securities prices, a sheet of graph paper and a pencil. Fortunes have been made with nothing more than that. But these days a PC, an Internet connection and at least one piece of software that allows you to collect data and draw charts are also standard issue. You can also do charting directly on technical analysis Web sites without buying software

Don't skimp on tools. Buy data, books, magazines and software. Pay for lessons. Get a trading coach. You wouldn't try to make a *cordon bleu* dinner on a camp stove with three eggs and a basil leaf, so don't try to make money in the market using inadequate tools. Your first task when you're ready to take your technical knowledge out for a trial run is to earn back the seed capital you put into the business, the business of technical trading.

Where to Go from Here

For Dummies books are designed so that you can jump in anywhere and get the information you need. Don't feel like you have to read every chapter — or even the entire chapter. Take advantage of the Table of Contents and Index to find what you're looking for, and check it out. But, if you're new to charting and technical analysis, take a close look at Parts I and II for the scoop on the field.

Part I
Defining Technical Analysis

Glenn Lumsden

'I'm all for using crowd psychology to turn the market bullish or bearish. Just as long as we don't turn brokish.'

In this part . . .

*G*et ready to suspend belief in everything you think you know about trading and investing. In technical analysis, you look only at what prices are doing, not at what some theory says they should do. In this part, we explain how the price behaviour of securities is the outcome of crowd psychology, which may be based in part on the fundamentals you're already familiar with — but often isn't. In technical analysis, you observe how prices actually move, and try to use past regularities in price movements to predict future regularities.

Chapter 1

Opening the Technical Analysis Toolbox

So you're interested in charting, which, for you, may be a new way of looking at stocks and other securities. Simply put, charting is the graphical approach to technical analysis. Whether you take a visual or a mathematical approach, technical analysis is a set of forecasting methods that can help you make better trading decisions.

You may be thinking that technical analysis is all about reading charts full of squiggles and lines, and although we give you plenty of material in this book about these squiggles and lines, technical analysis is also about managing market risk. In this chapter, we take you on a quick tour of key technical concepts and review why these work (and why sometimes they don't).

Does that sound a bit too grand? Well, building a house isn't chiefly about hammers and nails, although you need them. Squiggles and lines are just tools. Think of tackling technical analysis as a project to build better trading practices. Yes, you need the squiggles and lines, but your goal is to use those tools to make money.

Understanding the Lingo

Technical analysis, of all sorts, focuses on prices. Many technical traders think the price reflects all the useful information they need to make a trading decision. But how you *analyse* prices can take many different forms — from drawing lines on a chart by hand to using high-powered computer software to calculate the most likely path of a price out of a million randomly generated paths. Charting is also called *technical analysis, market timing* and *trend-following.* All the terms are used interchangeably by the press, the public and even technical analysis authors.

When you see these terms in this book and elsewhere, don't fret over a strict interpretation — and don't accept or reject a technical idea because it has a particular label. You could put ten technical traders in a room and get ten definitions of each term. The following sections are our interpretation of these terms and their nuances.

Technical analysis

Technical analysis is the broadest of the terms, covering hand-drawn lines as well as grand theories of price cycles. But many people associate technical analysis with statistics-based graphic indicators that use price data in one way or another to represent the direction, strength or some other characteristic of the trend. Instead of counting on your eyes, you count on maths, which is a breakthrough and a curse. You can have a textbook-perfect trend with ten confirming indicators, but maths cannot overcome the inconvenient fact that behind the numbers are other human beings who often behave in irrational and inexplicable ways. Technical analysis (so far) remains an art, not a science, even when it uses scientific methods.

If you really want to sink your teeth into technical analysis, consider joining an association or undertaking courses in technical analysis. In Australia, a good starting point is the Australian Technical Analysts Association (ATAA) at www.ataa.com.au. The ATAA meets monthly in most capital cities, has a bimonthly journal and a video library, and holds an annual conference each year with international speakers attending. The New Zealand equivalent is the Society of Technical Analysts New Zealand (STANZ), at www.stanz.co.nz.

Charting

Charting is probably the oldest generic term used for technical analysis. Charting refers to reading supply and demand into bars and bar patterns. Some technical analysts may reject the term charting because it harkens back to the days of coloured pencils and rulers. They see charting as subjective, while viewing statistics-based indicators as 'objective'. We started out this way, preferring a moving average to a support line, for example. But charting conventions developed over many decades are widely used by many traders, and they *work*. Today, personal computers do the hard work of calculating mathematical indicators and displaying the results on-screen, taking charting to new levels of sophistication.

Market timing

Market timing is another term used in place of 'technical analysis'. All technical trading involves timing, but to our way of thinking, the term market timing refers to statistical analysis that goes beyond a single chart. Market timing encompasses many techniques, such as sentiment indicators and calendar effects, that many self-described chartists would say aren't charting and some technical analysts would say aren't technical analysis. We cover these and other tools in Chapter 3.

Technical analysis is about both time and price. Sometimes, prices can move too far, too fast and as a result, either reverse and correct sharply or move sideways in a clearly defined range, marking time until both price and time are said to be in equilibrium. Only then will the primary trend continue.

Trend-following

Because so much emphasis is put on the presence or absence of a trend, technical analysis is sometimes named *trend-following*. Parts III, IV and V contain techniques that are 'trend-following'. Some analysts object to the term because you aren't always following, but often anticipating a trend, as when you use momentum indicators (as we describe in Chapter 11).

Different Ways to Trade

You can apply charting and other technical analysis methods to trading in a variety of ways. The following sections discuss how to develop your own trading style and hone your timing.

Trading or investing: The many faces of technical analysis

Both traders and investors use technical analysis. What's the difference between a trader and an investor?

- A *trader* holds securities for a short period of time.
- An *investor* holds securities for a long time.

Okay, what's the difference between these holding periods?

- A short holding period is anywhere from one minute to one year.
- A long holding period is anywhere from six months to forever, depending on who you ask.

Notice that we overlap the holding period of the trader and the investor. Actually, the dividing line between trader and investor isn't fixed (except for purposes of taxation). We use the word *trader* in this book, but don't let it distract you. People who choose to call themselves *investors* use technical methods, too.

You can use technical methods over any investment horizon, including the long term. If you're an expert in Blue Sky stock, for example, you can add to your holdings when the price is relatively low, take some partial profit when the price is relatively high, and dump it all if the stock crashes. Technical analysis has a tool for identifying each of these situations. You can also use technical tools to rotate your capital among a number of securities depending on which ones are delivering the highest gains these days. At the other end of the investment horizon spectrum, you can use technical analysis to spot a high-probability trade, and execute the purchase and sale in the space of an hour.

Setting new rules

You may have the idea that because technical analysis entails an active trading style, you're about to embark on a wild and risk-laden adventure — like that one-hour trade we just mentioned in the last paragraph. Nothing could be further from the truth. Executing the one-hour trade has less inherent risk of loss than buying and holding a security indefinitely, without an exit plan, based on some expert's judgement of its value.

Preventing and controlling losses is more important to practically every technical trader you meet than outright profit-seeking. The technical analysis approach is demonstrably more risk-averse than the value-investing approach.

That's because to embrace technical analysis is to embrace a way of thinking that's always sensitive to risk. *Technical trading* means trading with a plan that identifies the potential gain and the potential loss of every trade ahead of time. The technical trader devises rules for dealing with price developments as they occur in order to realise the plan. In fact, you select your technical tools (from the many available) specifically to match your trading style with your sensitivity to risk. We talk about this in Chapter 14.

Using rules, especially rules to control losses, is the key feature of long-term success in trading. Anybody can get lucky — once. To make profits consistently requires you not only to identify the trading opportunity, but also to manage the risk of the trade. Most of the 'trading rules' that you hear about, such as 'Cut your losses and let your winners run', arise from the experience of technical traders. (We come back to this rule and the subject of managing the trade in Chapter 17.)

Making the case for managing the trade

To buy and hold securities for a very long period of time is a well-documented path to accumulating capital, but only if your timing is good — you're lucky enough to buy the security when its price is rising. If your timing isn't so hot or you're unlucky, it's a different story all together. Consider the following examples.

✔ Using the United States stock market as an example, if you had bought stocks at the price peak just ahead of the 1929 Crash, it would've taken you 22 years to get back your initial capital.

✔ Since the end of World War II, the Dow Jones Industrial Average in the United States has fallen by more than 20 per cent (a *bear market* — see the 'Keeping your bulls and bears straight' sidebar in this chapter) on 11 different occasions.

✔ In Australia, the All Ords has fallen more than 20 per cent on at least four separate occasions since 1984.

More recently, from January 2000 to October 2002, the United States S&P 500 index fell by 50 per cent. If you owned all the stocks in this index and held them throughout the entire period, you would have lost 50 per cent of your stake, which means you would now need to make a gain equivalent to 100 per cent of your starting capital to get your money back, as Table 1-1 shows. Ask yourself how often can anyone makes a 100 per cent return on investment.

Table 1-1	Recovering a Loss
Loss	*Gain Needed to Recover Loss*
10%	11.1%
20%	25.0%
30%	42.9%
40%	66.7%
50%	100.0%
60%	150.0%
75%	300.0%

Timing your entry and exit from the market is critical to making money and controlling losses. The central part of the book, Chapters 4 through 16, covers technical methods that aim to improve the timing of your entries and exits.

Talking like a trader

Traders use language a little differently from the bulk of humanity. You've probably heard many of the terms, such as *selling short* and *going long*. We explain a few of these technical terms here because you need them as you draw your rule-based trendlines. If you know this stuff, just skip ahead. If not, here are the terms:

- ✔ **To have a position in the market:** This means that you have either bought the security or sold it short. (To buy a security is self-explanatory, but to sell short may not be — see the definition in this list.)

- ✔ **To go long:** This is the trader's term for buying a security you don't currently own. It's the most straightforward way to take a position in the market.

- ✔ **To sell short:** This means to sell something you don't own in the expectation that you'll be able to buy it later at a cheaper price so that you can make money when you deliver on the sale. When you sell short you reverse the normal order of the buy-sell equation. It carries the same sort of risk as in going long, the only difference being if prices go up after you short sold, you stand to lose money buying back your short position. Conversely, you make money if the price falls after you sell (so you can buy it back later at a lower level).

- ✔ **Entry:** This means to initiate a position in a security. Usually, this entails using cash to buy the security, but as described in the description on short sales, sometimes it means selling first and buying afterwards, reversing the normal order.

- ✔ **Exit:** To exit means to get out of a position in a security. Usually this involves selling the security for cash, but in a short sale, where you have sold securities you do not yet own, to exit the position means to buy the securities you have already sold, to cover the short sale. In this case, where you've bought the securities that you have already sold, the transaction is complete and you have exited your position.

- ✔ **Square (or flat):** These terms mean you're neither long nor short — you have no position in the security. Another synonym is *neutral*.

You're probably most familiar with stock market trading, where for most people to initiate a position is to buy the security and to exit a position is to sell the security. In Australia, as in the United States and the rest of the world's markets, traders have a semantic bias towards understanding *entry* to mean buy and *exit* to mean sell. But don't forget that short sellers, in contrast, understand *entry* to mean sell and *exit* to mean buy. Commodity traders almost always specify *enter long* or *enter short* or come right out and say buy or sell on a case-by-case basis, because it's easy to make a mistake.

The lingo of technical analysis is no more difficult or silly than the lingo of fine cooking. But it does have some additional problems. Not everybody agrees on word usage. A *bearish market* is one in which prices are falling. It rises to the status of *bear market* (no -*ish*) when it has fallen by 20 per cent or more from a peak, for a sustained period. A *bull market* is one that has risen at least 20 per cent from a major low, again for a sustained period. Some writers, even experts, call *any* big move a bull or bear market when they should use a more careful phrase, such as 'the market has a bullish tone'. In short, market commentators are prone to exaggeration and the sloppy use of language.

Keeping your bulls and bears straight: A word about words

A *bullish market* is one that is rising and a *bearish market* is one that is falling. A *bull* is an optimist who thinks prices will rise and a *bear* is a pessimist who thinks prices will fall. Visualise a bull throwing the market into the air with his horns, causing it to rise, while the bear rises up and pounces upon the market driving it down towards the ground.

A lot of people don't like these words. They find them to be coarse, undignified and often inaccurate. When you buy a security for an expected long-term holding period, you feel positive about the security, but the word 'bullish' sounds emotional and doesn't describe the deeply intellectual process you went through in selecting the security. When you sell a security, you may not appreciate being named a bear. You may not have had a negative attitude towards that security — you just wanted the money from the sale for some other purpose.

Bull and bear are oversimplifications. But those are the words commonly used in discussing securities markets. Accept them. The word 'bull' applies to the long-term holder as well as the in-and-out quick-trade artist. The point is that bull and bear, or bullish and bearish, are useful shorthand words that summarise market players and market sentiment as either positive and optimistic (prices will rise) or negative and pessimistic (prices will fall).

It's All about the Trend

You can look at most charts and see that in the big-picture sense, securities prices tend to move in trends, and trends persist for long periods of time. A *trend* is a discernible directional bias in the price — upwards, downwards or sideways.

The trend is your friend. If you identify trends and trade with them, you can make more money trading securities. Trend identification gives you an advantage and helps you perform two functions near and dear to the heart:

- ✔ **Create capital:** As a general rule, you want to buy securities only when their price is rising, called an *uptrend*. Buying into an uptrend makes money, providing you can figure out where to sell.

- ✔ **Preserve capital:** You make fewer mistakes and preserve capital by not buying a security when the price is falling (a *downtrend*) — no matter how charming the salesperson or fascinating the story — and by selling a previously rising security when it starts downtrending. You don't know where or when a downtrend might end.

Successful trading is all about confirming the direction of the primary trend and trading in the same direction. Very few people can trade against the primary trend and be successful in the longer term. Many have tried, but we don't know any who have been successful.

Checking that the price is right (and respectable)

Securities prices are the product of the collective decision-making of buyers and sellers. Prices incorporate (or *discount*) all known information about the security, and prices change as new information becomes available. *All known information* consists of hundreds of factors ranging from accurate facts to opinions, guesses and emotions — and previous prices. They all go into the supply and demand for a security and result in its price. We talk about supply and demand in Chapter 2 and environmental factors that affect the price in Chapter 3 as well as Chapter 8.

Charles Dow, one of the founders of *The Wall Street Journal,* observed around the turn of the 20th century that whatever the true facts are about a security and whatever people say about it, the price neatly cuts through all the clutter of words and is the one piece of hard information you can trust.

Note that prices on a chart don't tell you anything about the underlying *value* of the security. Where the price 'should' be is a totally different subject, named fundamental analysis. Most technical traders use both forms of analysis. Technical analysis isn't antithetical to fundamental analysis, as some critics think. The two can be used together. You can choose to trade only the highest quality securities on a fundamental basis, but time your purchases and sales according to technical criteria. This, by the way, is the basis of one of the top charting software packages (see the Appendix for the names of software and other valuable resources).

Technical analysis and fundamental analysis are compatible. The core ideas of technical analysis aren't some new and crackpot flash in the pan, but rather, they came into being over 100 years ago. Technical ideas have a respectable origin and have been embraced and explored by some very brainy and successful financial figures. To give you just a taste of the basic observations underlying technical analysis, Dow said:

✔ Securities prices move in trends much of the time.

✔ Trends can be identified with patterns that you see repeatedly (covered in Chapter 7) and with *support and resistance* trendlines (covered in Chapters 7 and 8).

✔ Primary trends (lasting months or years) are punctuated by secondary movements (lasting weeks or months) in the opposite direction of the primary trend. Secondary trends, today called retracements, are the very devil to deal with as a trader. See Chapters 2 and 14 for more on retracements.

✔ Trends remain in place until some major event comes along to stop them.

These ideas, and many more attributed to Dow (sometimes wrongly), are called *Dow Theory* and still cited today.

Charting your path

Prices and trends rule, so you have to be able to track and identify them. And to identify prices and trends, you have to see them. So here it is, the price chart (see Figure 1-1). This chart shows a classic uptrend following a downtrend.

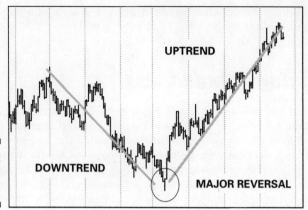

Figure 1-1:
Uptrend and
downtrend.

UPTREND

DOWNTREND

MAJOR REVERSAL

At the most basic level, your goal as a technical trader is to shun the security shown on the chart while it's downtrending and to identify the major reversal point — which is the best place to buy (shown in the circle) — as early as possible. Figure 1-1 is a good example of the kind of chart with which you spend most of your time. A chart is the workspace of technical analysis. Technical analysts have developed numerous indicators based on price and volume that can be expressed as statistics, tables of numbers and other formats, but the core method remains a graphic display of prices in a chart.

You absolutely, positively must become attuned to looking at charts and trying to figure out what the prices are telling you. In Figure 1-1, for example, is this price going to make a new high — or is there evidence that the rally is over? (Yes, it did make a new high and no, the chart shows no evidence of the trend coming to an end.) By the time you finish this book, you'll know that at a glance, too.

Looking at the Many Faces of Trendedness

Trend means different things to different people. Trend is such a wide and flexible concept that a large variety of definitions is possible. In fact, to be pragmatic, you can say that a trend is a price move that your indicator identifies. In other words, you can define trend according to technical measures that appeal to your sense of logic and what works for you. In this book, definitions of trendedness are spread out under various technique headings so that you can choose which definition of trendedness suits your personality and trading style.

Quantifying trendedness

Creating a chart like the one in Figure 1-1 is easy. To illustrate classic trend behaviour, we could've taken any security out of thousands in our databases and found some period of time over which the security's price looked like this chart. However, we could also have found many periods of time when this same security was not trending. In fact, some securities are frequently in a trending mode and others seldom trend, or their trends are short-lived. To complicate matters, some securities exhibit a 'habit' of tidy trending while others trend in a sloppy way (with high variability around the average).

Charles Dow may have started the ball rolling in technical analysis over 100 years ago, but in the grand scheme of things, we're still in frontier days. Ask a group of technical traders, 'What percentage of time are securities trending and what percentage of the time are they non-trending?' We guarantee that nobody can give you a single correct answer. Actually, most technical traders tell you that securities are typically in a trending mode about 30 per cent of the time, but that statistic isn't based on hard facts. It's a guess because of two factors — the definition of trendedness an individual chooses to use and the time frame he or she looks at.

Choosing a definition

Say we trade foreign exchange and we say the pound, the euro and the yen are trended about 60 per cent of the time. We say that because 60 per cent of the time, we can draw a linear regression line with a directional slope (up or down) around which currency prices cluster. (We discuss linear regression lines in Chapter 9.) Someone else may say currencies are trended only 40 per cent of the time — using a different and equally valid definition of trendedness.

Only one thing is certain — no security is trending all the time. Even the best-behaved security spends some time going sideways (non-trending) while the people who trade that specific security make up their minds what they think about it. So no trend-identification technique is going to work all the time.

We give you the key definitions of trendedness in Parts II through IV. Chapter 4 describes it as a series of higher highs together with a series of higher lows (for an uptrend). In Chapter 10, trendedness is defined as the price rising above a moving average, or a short-term moving average rising above a long-term moving average (also an uptrend). The rest of the chapters contain other definitions, like the linear regression slope we mention at the beginning of this section. No single definition of trendedness is the universal gold standard on which everyone agrees, so it's hardly surprising that no-one can say, 'Securities are trended *x* per cent of the time', with any authority.

Picking a time frame

If you're looking at ten years of daily prices, you get a different view of trendedness than when you're looking at only two years of data. Further, a security that trended in the 1990s may not trend in the 2000s. Or a security may have trended highly in the 1970s, trended by a different extent in the 1980s, and only sometimes trended in the 1990s. You can blend the trendedness rates over the three decades and get a number that doesn't represent any of them, much less tell you the degree of trendedness in the current decade. Markets are dynamic. They change (then they change back). Accept it.

You also need to consider the periodicity of your data. A security may display a trend on data captured every hour but appear to be non-trending when you look at daily data. Some securities may trend in the morning and not in the afternoon. To go to the other extreme, you may not be able to detect a trend on daily data but a weekly or monthly chart shows a trend.

Accept the spirit of empirical investigation embodied in technical research: When you're drawing charts, experiment with different time frames.

Identifying your definition of trendedness

Trendedness can be defined in various ways, but as a practical matter, you need to choose the definition of trendedness that suits you. You don't have to be statistically rigorous as long as you have rules for defining trendedness and apply them consistently. We discuss how to choose your definition — which is the same thing as how to choose indicators — in Chapter 14.

To you, a trend may be a series of higher highs with higher lows over seven bars (we describe bars in Chapter 4). To the next trader, a trend has to have a moving average crossover that has lasted a minimum of 20 bars (see Chapter 10 to find out about the moving average — the workhorse of technical analysis). Some traders insist that to be identified, a trend has to qualify on a daily chart and a weekly chart as well.

Selecting a time frame to trade is just about the hardest thing you do as a technical trader, because you have to discover within yourself your tolerance for retracements, those minor pullbacks that occur in every trend. Tolerance for temporary pullbacks is a central aspect of your personal attitude towards risk. Psychologists and trading coaches make a good living helping traders find their comfort zone with respect to risk.

Why Technical Analysis Does and Doesn't (Always) Work

 Technical analysis works because people consistently repeat behaviours under similar circumstances. To give just one example, after a security makes a big move up, some market participants choose to take a profit by selling the security. Sellers temporarily overwhelm buyers and the price falls even though the trend is still in place. Technical analysis offers many tools to identify when a price dip is just profit-taking versus when a dip signifies a possible end of the trend.

As we show in many chapters in this book, technical methods do work to enhance your timing if you're *careful* and *consistent*. As we explain in Chapter 14 (and illustrate in Chapter 15), if you follow the buy/sell trading instructions embedded in your technical indicators, you should make gains that are higher than your losses over a sufficient period of time. It's not fair to try out an indicator, take a few losses and throw away all of technical analysis as worthless. Technical trading does entail taking losses. The point is to have gains that are bigger than losses.

We say at the beginning of this chapter that technical analysis is a forecasting method. Like all forecasting, it uses past and current behaviour to predict future behaviour. To say that technical analysis is merely 'looking in the rearview mirror' is to be uninformed about the art and science of forecasting. All forecasting takes information from the past and stirs it up within a set of statistical constraints, but the answer doesn't always come out as expected because

- ✔ At any moment, thousands of factors are potentially able to affect the price of a security, and you can't hope to account for all of them.

- ✔ Human behaviour is somewhat predictable, but not 100 per cent predictable.

For example, CBH Resources — a mining company listed on the Australian Securities Exchange — experienced an unforeseen rock fall in its Endeavour mine in October 2005. The fall was so significant that mining operations were suspended for six months. The impact on the share price was even more significant, with the price falling approximately 50 per cent in a short period of time.

 We discuss the constraints on technical analysis as a forecasting technique in Chapter 3. You need to understand the limitations of technical analysis as a forecasting tool to avoid mistakes. The biggest mistake that beginning technical traders make is attributing too much reliability and accuracy to technical methods. Every experienced technical trader knows that no technique works all the time.

Understanding why no technique works all the time helps you overcome doubts raised by critics who say that the whole field of technical analysis is not worthwhile because techniques are not 100 per cent reliable. Because a method doesn't work all the time, or even a high percentage of the time, isn't the right criterion for evaluating it. Just because the meteorologist is wrong 50 per cent of the time doesn't mean you should take off in your aeroplane when he's forecasting a violent thunderstorm in the next hour.

 In financial markets, the value of an analytical method is determined by whether it helps you to consistently make more money than you lose. Notice that this statement has two components — the method and *you*. A professional trader may use a particular method to generate high profits and low losses year after year. You may try to apply the same method, or what you think is the same method, but fail to get the same results. What works for someone else may not work for you. We discuss how to figure out what trading style works best for you in Chapter 16.

Chapter 2

Uncovering the Essence of Market Movement

*U*sing charts and indicators to analyse the behaviour of a particular security focuses on the price of the security rather than its fundamentals. Prices are set by the collective behaviour of buyers and sellers, also known as 'the crowd' or 'the market'. The market may be rational or irrational, but the market is always 'right' in the sense that it sets the price of a security. As minor members of the market, we don't get to set the price, no matter how intelligent our analysis and piercing our judgement.

In this chapter, we suggest one way of looking at the supply and demand dynamics of crowd behaviour that's consistent with the technical approach — the auction model of supply and demand. We also illustrate one technique used by a large group of technical traders who think that crowd behaviour fits a particular model based on a sequence of numbers called the Fibonacci sequence. At the end of the chapter, we address whether this is a useful way to work with technical concepts.

The eBay Model of Supply and Demand

Securities are not regular goods, and to apply orthodox supply and demand economics to securities trading can result in some silly conclusions.

In the biggest macroeconomic perspective, securities are indeed subject to the standard laws of supply and demand, but as a practical matter for your day-to-day trading, the auction model is more useful.

Securities aren't socks

Securities are different from cars, bread and socks. You don't buy a security for the joy of owning it and using it. You can't drive it, eat it or wear it. The only reason to buy a security is to sell it again, preferably for more than you paid for it. Unless you're a retailer, you hardly ever buy anything with the idea of selling it again — except securities.

In classical economics, demand for an item depends on its price, which is a function of scarcity. If something is rare, it's expensive. At higher and higher prices, demand falls off. At some point, the high price induces suppliers to produce more of the thing, whereupon the price falls. *Equilibrium* consists of buyers and sellers finding the mix of quantity and price that they both can live with. This process is called *price discovery,* and it can be lengthy.

In securities trading, the pricing process is more like an auction than like the traditional price-discovery process of classical economics. For one, things move a lot faster. Plus, in an auction (such as the online auction eBay), demand for the item in question often rises as the price rises. If you've ever participated in an auction, you probably paid more than you should have. Every time someone else outbids you, you want the item more than ever and you become determined to be the winner. The intrinsic value of the item doesn't matter.

Demand creates demand

In an auction, what gets your blood running is that someone else wants to buy the item in question, too. Visible demand begets more demand. Auction economics are contrary to what traditional economics teaches — that demand will *decrease* as the price rises. In the auction situation, demand *increases* as the price rises. The item may or may not be actually scarce in the real world — it doesn't matter. The immediacy of the auction is what skews prices, sometimes to absurd levels. Later, when suppliers see the high prices, they may indeed be able to find or produce more of the item — but by then, the specific demand created by the dynamics of that particular auction is gone.

Creating demand from scratch

When you decide to buy a security, it's because you think the price will rise. When you decide to sell, it's because you have a juicy profit that meets your needs, or because you have taken an intolerable loss. You seldom think about the true supply, or even fundamental value, of the security.

Although, technically, the supply of any security is limited by the number of shares outstanding and the like, supply may be considered infinite for all practical purposes. If you really have to have 100 shares of True Blue Widget stock, some price you can offer will get you those shares. Turn it around and you can easily see why. A price exists at which you can be induced to sell the stock for which you paid $1. It might be $2 or $20 or $100 — but rest assured, some price will force you to part with it, and *right now.*

In technical trading, think of demand for a security as rising on rising prices, not falling ones. Similarly, the supply of a security dries up on rising prices, at least in the short run. (Later, when the long-term security holder sees how high the price has gone while he wasn't looking, he may say 'Holy Moley!' and call his broker to sell, making more supply available.)

Identifying Crowd Behaviour

Technical analysis is the art of identifying crowd behaviour in order to join the crowd and take advantage of its momentum. This is called the *bandwagon effect.* Here's how a bandwagon works: A fresh piece of news comes out, a majority of traders interpret it as favourable to the security, and buying overwhelms selling so that the price rises. You profit by going with the flow. Then when everyone is jumping off the bandwagon, you should jump, too.

Traders are people and people often behave in predictable ways. When it comes to emotions such as fear and greed, people today are little different from people 100 years ago or maybe even 1,000 years ago. People become reckless and irrational in a mania. They become overly cautious after a bubble bursts. A *mania* is a situation in which traders buy an object or security without regard for its intrinsic value or even whether they'll be able to sell it again later at a higher price. They fear being left out of an opportunity. They're caught up in the moment and are temporarily irrational. A *panic* is the opposite — people can't sell the thing fast enough and will accept ever-lower prices just to get any money back at all.

In economic history, a mania or a panic comes along only a few times in a century. In the technical worldview, mania and panic happen every day, in miniature. Emotional extremes lead to price extremes in the context of the hour, day or week — mini-manias and mini-panics occur all the time. Those aren't the words used in technical trading lingo but the emotion and the price effects are the same as in big-picture manias and panics. (We lead you through a technical terminology minefield in the section 'Identifying Crowd Extremes and What to Do about Them' later in the chapter.)

The individual versus the crowd

People behave differently when they act as individuals from the way they act when they're part of a crowd. Crowd behaviour encompasses fraternities, sports teams, political parties, gangs, religious sects, mobs, people attending an auction — the list goes on. A crowd is more than the sum of its parts. Otherwise sensible individuals can behave in the most extraordinary ways when they become part of a crowd. One famous case is how people in 17th-century Holland saw tulipmania, the trading of tulip bulbs for sums like $250,000, deflate overnight when someone mistakenly ate one, revealing how ridiculously far prices had diverged from any reasonable concept of value.

You know that if someone shouts 'Fire!' in a crowded theatre, people will trample each other to get to the exits. In markets, you see the same thing in the price of a security after bad news about it is released. Also, if someone shouts, 'Free ice cream!' people will fall all over each other to be first in line. The same thing happens to securities prices as they reach new highs, especially if an authority figure pronounces the security a gem and a bargain.

You shouldn't be surprised to hear that traders invent rumours to try to create a stampede — in either direction.

As a technical trader, you want to be sensitive to what the crowd is doing without succumbing to the ruling passions of the crowd itself. Technical traders work hard at not listening to chatter about securities, even from authority figures. You're unlikely to get useful information — and you may get *disinformation* (deliberately misleading information). All the information you need is embedded in the price. It's more practical to see the crowd reaction to information in the form of real prices than to guess how the crowd may react to any fresh news or opinion. When you do check the news for the cause of a price action, be sure to do it with a healthy dose of scepticism.

Playing games with traders' heads

The market is self-regarding — it watches itself. One behaviour begets another in a dynamic way. For example, many traders use an old rule that if a price falls by 30 per cent from a peak, it's prudent to exit the trade. Because the 30 per cent rule is so well known, many traders use it and cause the rule to be self-fulfilling. Traders know that others will exit at a level 30 per cent under the peak and will sell the security specifically to get everyone to exit, whereupon they're able to buy the security at a cheaper price. Activities like this shape the game-playing aspect of trading.

Game playing can become incredibly complex, replete with bluffing, cheating, feints and double-crossing. Note that many top traders are also top competitors in fencing, chess, backgammon, bridge or poker. Each security or class of securities has a different degree of crowd complexity. The crowd that trades the ASX 200 (SPI) or the overseas currency futures contract is different from the crowd that trades the China A50 Index or BSE Sensex futures contract, and that crowd is different in turn from the crowd that trades the Australian dollar and the one that trades resource or banking sector stocks.

Choose the securities you're going to trade with crowd complexity in mind. For example, in foreign exchange, some 70 per cent of traders use some form of technical analysis. To trade foreign exchange, you need to become skilled not only in the techniques that this crowd uses, but also the games they play.

Identifying Crowd Extremes and What to Do about Them

As market participants get excited about a security, they become increasingly bullish and either buy for the first time or add to positions, a phase named *accumulation*. When traders become disillusioned about the prospect of their security price rising, they sell, named *distribution*.

To buy 100 shares of a stock is to *enter a position*. To buy another 100 shares for a total of 200 is to *add to your position*. If you have 500 shares and sell half, you would be *reducing your position*. To sell all the shares you own is to *square your position*. When you're *square* (also called *flat*), you have no position in the security. All your money is in cash. You're neutral. We talk more about changing your position in Chapter 17.

After traders have been accumulating the security on rising prices, eventually the price goes too far. *Too far* is a relative term and can be defined in any number of equally valid ways. (We discuss using the trading range in Chapter 5, and dealing with breakouts in Chapter 9, to provide detailed methods for defining how much is too much.)

If you like to draw support and resistance lines (for more on support and resistance lines see Chapter 8), *too far* is a level beyond the lines, a *breakout*. If you're of a statistical bent, you will determine that *too far* lies just outside a band constructed from the average true range, two standard deviations away from a moving average (Bollinger band), or some other non-judgemental measure. See Chapter 12 for a description of those techniques.

Overbought and oversold

When a price has reached or surpassed a normal limit, it's at an extreme. In an upmove, everyone who wanted to buy has already bought. The market is called *overbought,* a term specific to securities trading. In a downmove, everyone who wanted to sell has already sold. The security is called *oversold.*

The concept of overbought/oversold is applied to market indices as well as individual securities. It's usually measured by the momentum indicators described in Chapter 11.

By the time most of the market participants have jumped on the bandwagon, it has become so heavy it can't move forward. Traders are tapped out. All their money is in a position. Traders have to square their positions just to put cash back into their pockets so they can conduct additional trades.

Position squaring is the closing of positions after a big price move. Position squaring doesn't necessarily imply market participants think a move is over. They may plan to re-enter the security in the same direction later on. Position squaring occurs because

- ✔ Traders think that the move is exhausted for the moment.
- ✔ Traders have met a price objective — profit or loss.
- ✔ Traders have met a time limit, such as the end of the day, week, month or tax period.
- ✔ Traders want to withdraw money from the security to trade a different security, or for a non-trading purpose.

Position squaring occurs when a large number of traders have big losses, too. Say, for example, a high percentage of traders believe in a particular price-move scenario that then fails to develop in the expected way. Eventually, some traders throw in the towel. The resulting change in prices causes bigger losses for the remaining traders, and they, in turn, throw in the towel. You get a succession of stop-loss orders being hit that turns into a runaway wagon — downhill. A *stop-loss order* is an order you give to your broker to sell your position if it goes against you too far and reaches the maximum loss you're prepared to accept. We describe stop-loss orders in Chapter 17.

Retracements

When a price has gone too far and traders deem the security overbought or oversold, the price stops rising or falling. It doesn't just stop, though, and hover at a particular level. As nature abhors a vacuum, traders abhor an unmoving price. Instead, the price moves in the opposite direction for a while, as traders take profits or cut losses, as the case may be. As we mention in Chapter 1, a move in the opposite direction of the main trend is named a *retracement*. It is also called a *correction,* which explicitly recognises that the security had gone too far and is now correcting course, like a ship. A retracement may also be termed a *pullback* or *throwback*.

Prices seldom move in one direction for long. Even a major trend exhibits retracements. When the market runs out of cash, traders have to close positions to get their cash back so they can put on new trades. If they've been buyers, they need to sell. If they've been sellers (shorting the security), they need to buy. Therefore, at the extreme outside limit of a price move, you should expect a temporary, minor reversal of the previous price move. In an uptrend, a retracement is always a drop in price. In a downtrend, a retracement is always a rise in price. Position squaring always causes a price move in the opposite direction of the trend.

Retracements can get out of hand and transform themselves into trend reversals, too. At the time a retracement starts, you don't know for sure that it is a retracement. For all you know, it could be a full reversal, with the price switching direction. This is one of the occasions when it pays to check the fundamentals, by which we mean the news and events pertaining to the security. An ordinary retracement caused by normal position squaring can suddenly turn into a full-fledged rout in the opposite direction if fresh news comes out that seems to support a reversal. But also remember that sometimes traders try to trick you into thinking they have interpreted fresh news in a particular way when all they're trying to do is push a retracement further, so they can stampede you into a trading action that is to their benefit.

In Figure 2-1, the chart shows a primary trend with several retracements, each outlined by an ellipse. In this instance, the retracements last only a day or two — but retracements can last a lot longer, several weeks on a daily chart, for example. They can also retrace over more ground.

Empiricists 1, Academics 0

Finance academics assert that the price of a security depends on forecasts of the security's underlying value in the future, such as a company's future earnings. The price today already contains market expectations about the price tomorrow. This idea is called *rational expectations*.

Rational expectations sound okay until you lift up your head and look around. You find many more price changes than you can find information about future earnings! In the 1990s, some dotcom stock prices represented 1,000 times future earnings — for companies that had no earnings. Finance academics said people knew the earnings expectations were absurd fictions, but they didn't care because they expected to unload the stock at a higher price to a greater fool.

Finance academics stopped at the greater fool theory. If you buy a security whose price is wildly divergent from some estimate of 'value', you're the fool. This is profoundly disappointing, because nobody has a certain way to attribute intrinsic value to any security. So how do you know when you're the last fool, the one who will get stuck with the security at its highest price? Even historical comparisons are iffy. To use the price-earnings ratio over the past 50 years, for example, is to assume that those traders knew the right way to merge price and value, so following this logic, there were no fools in 1950. And which earnings are you talking about, anyway? The definition changes.

Finance academics treat manias and panics as though they're inconvenient and rare exceptions to the rational expectations rule. In 2000–2003, most technical analysts escaped the appalling losses that accompanied the pricking of the dotcom bubble because to them, manias and panics are normal and familiar market behaviour — writ large.

Behavioural economics is just starting to define in exactly what ways people aren't rational. One key is that most people have a lousy understanding of probability. The gambler's fallacy is the most famous example — in a coin toss, after heads comes up 50 times in a row, just about everybody will bet on tails, ignoring that the coin doesn't remember which way it fell last time and the probability of heads is still 50 per cent. In fact, the probability of heads may be higher than 50 per cent, because the coin may not be a fair one.

But it's more complicated than misunderstanding probability. For example, people will give up a small certain gain for the chance to deprive their opponent of a larger gain. People go out of their way to avoid small risks but then take wild gambles on the word of a stranger. Most people feel twice as much pain at a loss than they feel pleasure at a gain. Behavioural economists, now winning a few Nobel prizes, are starting to grasp and quantify these 'irrational' behaviours. Eventually this work will lead to a coherent theory of crowd behaviour.

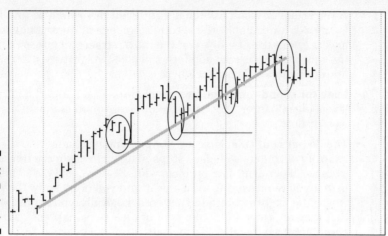

Figure 2-1:
Trend with retrace-ments.

The press often has it that every retracement is a profit-taking correction. This isn't accurate. If traders took profit on every correction, they'd all be rich. Remember, somebody bought at the high. If the correction goes too far against him, he must get out of the position at a loss. From this simple observation you should deduce that to stick to a position when it is correcting against you requires the courage of your convictions — and capital. (We talk more about managing money during retracements in Chapter 17.)

Catch a falling knife

To try to estimate where a retracement will stop is called 'to catch a falling knife'. In other words, no reliable rules exist to tell you *where* a trend correction will end or *when* the primary trend will resume. One of the chief uses of indicators and combined indicators, described in Chapter 15, is to get guidance on where and when a retracement will stop.

Your tolerance for retracements is the key to deciding what time frame you want to trade in. If the security you want to trade regularly retraces 50 per cent and the prospect of losing 51 per cent turns you into a nervous wreck, you need to trade it in a shorter time frame — or find another security.

Acknowledging that no-one can forecast a retracement hasn't stopped technical traders from trying to establish forecast rules. The following rules are generally helpful, but no-one can offer statistics to back them up, so take them with a grain of salt.

✔ **A retracement won't exceed a significant prior high or low.** In Figure 2-1, for example, the second retracement doesn't challenge the lowest low of the first dip, and the third retracement doesn't challenge the second. This is cold comfort, since knowing where it *won't* go doesn't help you figure out where it *will* go.

✔ **Look for round numbers.** Research shows that support and resistance levels (see Chapter 8) occur more often at round numbers than chance would allow.

✔ **The 30 per cent rule.** Measure the percentage change and assume that a majority of traders will place stops to avoid losing more than x per cent, such as 30 per cent. The problem with this idea, and it's a chilling one, is that you're measuring from a peak and you don't know the price level where the majority of traders entered. Logically, you should assume that they're protecting 70 per cent of their personal cash gain from their entry, not from the peak. To measure from the peak would be to say that traders make decisions based on opportunity loss rather than cash loss, and although this contains a germ of truth, it's not a reliable assumption about crowd behaviour. (The germ of truth lies in people feeling worse if they expected to get $10 and got only $1, compared to how they feel if they expected to get $5 and got only $1, as shown by behavioural economics — see the sidebar 'Empiricists 1, Academics 0'.)

Big-Picture Crowd Theories

Some important ideas about the extent of retracements come from theories about the cyclical nature of history. This section deals with these ideas as a stand-alone section because they're pervasive — and controversial.

When you start gathering technical analysis material, you inevitably run into big-picture crowd theories, a school of thought that is very popular today. Some people swear that the ideas are obvious. But just as beauty is in the eye of the beholder, theories about the ebb and flow of history are just that — theories. No big-picture theory has been proved by statistical measures. To be fair, no theory has been disproved, either.

Technical analysis is a sufficiently crowded field already, and offers a bewildering variety of tools and techniques. Why make things more complicated than they have to be? If you use the empirical evidence in front of you — clean and easy techniques like drawing support and resistance lines, for example — you can use technical analysis to make profits and avoid losses. Do you really need to know the secrets of the universe, too? Our heartfelt advice to the beginner is, don't go there.

But you need to know that these ideas are scattered throughout the field of technical analysis and some smart and successful people in the field believe them. Those who don't are mostly too polite to ridicule the ideas. You'll also run into critics who mistakenly think that all technical analysis involves big-picture crowd ideas. So buckle your seat belt.

Some analysts subscribe to the idea that in the ebb and flow of human affairs, they can perceive cycles, including market cycles. Some of these ideas contain mystical overtones and unproven claims about how the world works, such as the trading crowd is only the instrument of bigger forces at work.

Because these crowd theory ideas can never be verified, some critics unfairly colour the whole field of technical analysis with the charge of supernatural voodoo. Empiricists and skeptics cast doubt on these theories because they're not proven and by their nature, can't be proven. In particular, economics offers no theoretical basis for cycles that are fixed in size or duration. Economists do observe business cycles — several of them — but they overlap and don't appear reliably. It is undeniable, however, that retracements do occur sometimes near the levels forecasted by cycle theorists. As a result, technical traders are reluctant to level the charge of crackpot against cycle theories.

The Gann 50 per cent retracement

In the early 1900s, a trader named W D Gann discovered that retracements in the securities he was trading at the time tended to occur at one-half of the original move from the low to the high. To illustrate, say the price moved from $1 to $3. At $3, the crowd decided that the security was overbought, and started to sell. The ensuing price decline, the retracement, stops near 50 per cent of the original $1 to $3 move, namely $2. Figure 2-2 illustrates the 50 per cent retracement case, and Figure 2.3 shows a real-life example.

In fact, Gann said that the best retracement — the one that will make you the most money — is a 50 per cent retracement. The area around 50 per cent is a danger zone, because the price can keep going and become a full-fledged reversal around there (in which case you lose all the gains). But it's the best place to re-enter an existing trend (with an exit planned just below in case it doesn't work). If the trend resumes, it will then exceed the previous high, which gives you an automatic minimum profit target. This observation may be the origin of the phrase, 'Buy on the dip'.

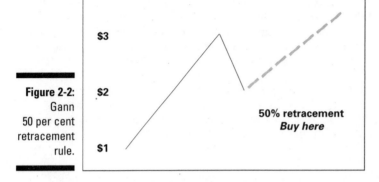

Figure 2-2:
Gann
50 per cent
retracement
rule.

$3

$2

$1

50% retracement
Buy here

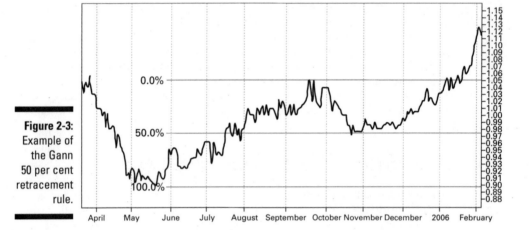

Figure 2-3:
Example of
the Gann
50 per cent
retracement
rule.

0.0%

50.0%

100.0%

April   May   June   July   August September October November December   2006   February

Gann also saw retracements occurring at the halfway point of a move, such as 25 per cent (half of 50 per cent), 12.5 per cent (half of 25 per cent) and so on. Statisticians can't offer proof that retracements occur at 12.5 per cent, 25 per cent or 50 per cent with more frequency than chance would allow. The absence of statistical proof in a field populated by mathematical sophisticates is puzzling at first. But when you ask a statistician why he doesn't just run the numbers and test the hypothesis, he points out that defining the low-to-high original move and then defining the stopping point of a retracement is a computational nightmare. No matter what definitions he gives his software, another analyst is sure to want to refine them in some other way. You may see studies, for example, showing that the actual percentage change of many retracements isn't precisely 50 per cent, but rather in a range of 45 to 55 per cent. Should you accept a minor retracement of 45 per cent but not a major one that correctly predicts a trend resumption at 44 per cent?

A critical point about the 50 per cent retracement rule is that you may think you want to exit to protect your profit at the 50 per cent level. If you bought the security at $1 and it rose to $3, but then it falls to $2, as shown in Figure 2-2, you want to sell at $2 to hang on to the gain you have left. But if the 50 per cent retracement rule works this time, you would be getting out exactly when you should by buying _more_ (adding to your position), because a resumption of the trend at the $2 level almost certainly means that the price will now go higher than the highest high so far, $3.

A 100 per cent retracement, a price that goes from $1 to $3 and back to $1, will often form a _double bottom_, a bullish formation (see Figure 2-4). When the price peaks twice at the same level, you have a _double top_, a bearish formation (as shown in Figure 2-5). See Chapter 7 for more details.

Figure 2-4:
A double
bottom
retrace-
ment.

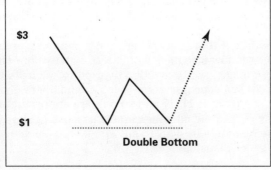

Figure 2-5:
A double
top
formation.

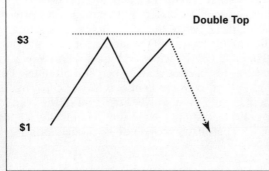

Magic numbers: 'The secret of the universe'

Another theory about how retracements should form is based on the Fibonacci sequence of numbers. This theory says that a retracement is most likely to stop at one of a series of numbers, with an emphasis on 38 per cent or 62 per cent of the original move. Where does this come from?

A 13th-century Italian mathematician named Fibonacci discovered a self-replicating sequence of numbers with curious properties. It starts with 1, 1, 2, 3, 5, 8, 13, 21, 34, 55, 89, 144 and so on to infinity. The sum of two adjacent numbers in the sequence forms the next higher number in the sequence. Most importantly, the ratio of any two consecutive numbers approximates 1.618 or its inverse, 0.618 (after the first few numbers).

Nature offers many examples of these ratios: Daisy petals, ferns, sunflowers, seashells, hurricanes, whirlpools and atomic particles in a bubble chamber. And many of man's works purportedly embody the Fibonacci ratios as well: The pyramids in Egypt, the Parthenon in Greece and Cézanne's choice of canvas shape, although some mathematicians dispute those claims.

Of course, critics point out that many other events in nature, architecture and human behaviour follow a sequence of 2, 4, 6, 8 and so on. The number 11 can be considered magic, not to mention *pi,* used to calculate the circumference of a circle. Prime numbers, which are numbers divisible only by themselves and one (3, 5, 7, 11, 17 and so on), are important numbers. In fact, many other self-replicating number sequences exist. In short, scientists say that to attribute human behaviour to any single number sequence is ludicrous, or at least not plausible.

A trader named Ralph Elliott believed that man's behaviour, including his behaviour when trading in the stock market, revealed the same characteristics as the Fibonacci sequence and could therefore be charted to predict future behaviour. Elliott observed that securities prices appear in a wave-like form on charts, hence the name of his forecasting method, the Elliott Wave. Elliott wrote that the Fibonacci sequence provides the mathematical underpinnings of the wave principle. Elliott Wave adherents expanded Elliott's use of the Fibonacci sequence and often use Fibonacci levels, with special attention to 38 per cent and 62 per cent (but also including 23.6 per cent, 50 per cent and 100 per cent of the high-low span), to predict the extent of retracements. Note that technically, 50 per cent isn't a Fibonacci number. It's customary to include it, though, possibly because of Gann's influence.

To make life difficult, some traders who like the Fibonacci sequence aren't strict adherents of the Elliot Wave principle and some Elliot Wave traders don't necessarily believe that price moves will stick to Fibonacci numbers. See the sidebar 'The Elliot Wave principle' in this chapter for more about the Elliott Wave, which goes far beyond the subject of retracements.

Seeing too many retracements

Fans of the Fibonacci sequence assert that the 38 per cent and 62 per cent retracement levels occur more often than chance would allow, although we have never seen statistical proof (perhaps because any statistical studies would degenerate into squabbling over measurement criteria).

Some traders embrace Gann's ideas, some embrace the Elliott Wave, some embrace Fibonacci numbers, and some embrace them all. If you were to put the main Gann retracement numbers (12.5, 25, 50 and 75 per cent) and the main Fibonacci retracement numbers (23.5 per cent, 38 per cent and 62 per cent) on the same chart of a trend, you'd have so many lines that the next retracement would be bound to hit one of them or a level near one of them.

Some advisers who like all the ideas choose to display the retracements that did work while conveniently not mentioning all the others that could have been shown on the same chart. In other words, they're going to be right no matter how the retracement turns out. You may see advertisements and solicitations claiming that the seller has 'objective' methods of forecasting securities prices, and these methods are often based on Gann or Fibonacci 'scientific principles'. Beware. By definition, all maths is science. If you're going to follow an adviser, put your faith in a consistently winning track record rather than in claims of an inside track to universal truth.

Like all technical methods, applying Gann and Elliott Wave ideas is an art, and constant revision is necessary as prices evolve. Statisticians scoff at magic numbers, but in any particular market or security, if a majority of traders believe that a retracement will stop at 38 per cent, 50 per cent or 62 per cent after a peak, they can and do make it come about.

The sensible approach to Gann and Fibonacci retracement ideas is to be aware of their influence over some traders. You don't have to believe in cycles, or the universal truth embedded in Fibonacci numbers, or that market prices follow a hidden system in order to take advantage of what the crowd is thinking.

Figure 2-6 shows a security with four waves and three corrections (69.2 per cent, 35.7 per cent and 78 per cent). Notice that none of the percentage retracements qualifies precisely as a Gann or Fibonacci number, although you might stretch the point and say that 68 per cent isn't all that far from 62 per cent (Fibonacci) and 78 per cent is fairly close to 75 per cent (Gann). Most traders acknowledge the wave-like movement of prices even if they don't try to count them according to the Elliott Wave principle.

TECHNICAL STUFF

The Elliott Wave principle

The wave idea became popular in part because one of its proponents, Robert Prechter, predicted a massive bull market in 1982 that did materialise — and then he called the top, just ahead of the 1987 Crash. That certainly got the market's attention! And prices do seem to move in waves on many charts.

The basic idea is that all price movements have two segments: Impulse waves and corrective waves. The *impulse* wave is the way the crowd wants to take the price in a trend. Considering that the right way to look at price developments is through the lens of crowd psychology, impulse is an excellent choice of words.

Each impulse wave has five parts: Three waves that go in the trend direction, alternating with two that go in the opposite direction. In a correction, each corrective wave has three parts: Two that go against the main trend and one that goes with it. If a bull market reaches a new high in five waves instead of three and also goes down in five waves instead of three, it's the beginning of a major bear market.

You will often see three clear waves up, although sometimes a move has more upwaves than three, as in Figure 2-6. The three-waves rule is only the model of how markets move, not a rigid orthodoxy.

Elliot Wave practitioners are the first to admit that calling corrective waves is tricky, much harder than seeing impulse waves. Experienced practitioners advise against straining to make a correction 'fit' the Elliott Wave model. A correction often just keeps on going, too, whereupon it isn't a correction but a true reversal and thus a new trend in the opposite direction. Counting waves can be an elaborate, time-consuming process, and miscounting as prices evolve can result in losses and having to start all over again. If the wave idea appeals to you, be prepared to devote a lot of time to it. If you choose not to count waves, you can still benefit from the observation that trends start with an impulse wave that then retraces in the opposite direction before the trend resumes. 'Buy on the dip' isn't bad advice when you are sure you have a trend.

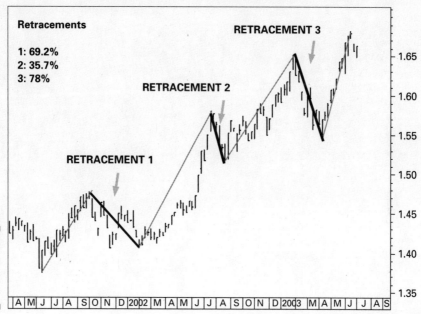

Retracements

1: 69.2%
2: 35.7%
3: 78%

RETRACEMENT 3

RETRACEMENT 2

RETRACEMENT 1

Figure 2-6:
Wave-like
appearance
of a trend.

Chapter 3

Going with the Flow: Market Sentiment

*Y*our goal as a technical trader is to identify what the crowd is doing and take advantage of it — without falling prey to the extremes of sentiment that can cause big losses when the market wakes up and realises it has gone too far. When just about every trader is either bullish or bearish, you need to stop following the crowd. Acknowledging that the balance of buyers and sellers can tip violently, analysts have devised sentiment indicators and volume indicators to help identify crowd extremes. Sentiment indicators identify extreme situations so you can catch the next wave or get out of the way.

Sentiment and volume indicators operate on the principle that 'the trend is your friend — until the end', meaning the crowd is wrong at price extremes. Some sentiment indicators apply to 'the market' in its entirety, and others apply to individual securities. In this chapter, we discuss a few of the 100 or so sentiment and volume indicators commonly used. We can't possibly cover all of them, and besides, new sentiment indicators are invented every day.

We start with volume because volume directly represents the extent of trader participation, and is a powerful indicator in its raw state, before you even manipulate the data to derive an *indicator*. The word *indicator* refers to a statistic comprised of data about the price or volume of a security that has been reorganised or rearranged to provide analytical insight. You can use just about any market data that takes your fancy to create an indicator.

Some indicators pertain to the entire market, like the day-to-day change in the volume on the Australian Securities Exchange, and some indicators relate to specific securities, like BHP stock. The purpose of an indicator is exactly what its name suggests — to indicate the upcoming behaviour of the price or volume. But remember, indicators only indicate, they do not dictate.

Defining Market Sentiment

In technical analysis, sentiment comes in only two flavours — bullish (the price is going up) or bearish (the price is going down). At any moment in time, a bullish crowd can take a price upward or a bearish crowd can take it downward. When the balance of sentiment shifts from bullish to bearish (or vice versa), a pivot point emerges. A *pivot point* is the point (or a region) where an up move ends and a down move begins (or the other way around). At the pivot point, the crowd itself realises that it has gone to an extreme, and it reacts by heading in the opposite direction. Another term for pivot point is *major reversal*.

As far back as the early 1900s, traders observed that if they were patient and waited for a pivot point to develop, they could trade at the right psychological time — just as the crowd is beginning a new move. When the crowd is reaching an extreme of emotion, it's usually wrong. A reversal point is impending. You should do the opposite of what the crowd is doing, or at least get ready to.

Tracking Volume

Volume is the term for the number of shares or contracts of a security traded in a period. Volume is the most powerful confirming indicator of a price move, and *confirmation* is a key concept in technical analysis. (See Chapter 15 for more on the confirmation concept.)

When you look at price changes, you imagine buyers demanding more of the security at ever-higher prices or sellers offering a greater supply at ever-lower prices, as we discuss in Chapters 4, 5 and 6. But a price can move on a single large purchase or sale, especially if the market happens not to have many participants at that exact moment, a condition named *illiquidity*. (See Chapter 4 for a description of liquidity.)

You can feel more confident that a price move has staying power if you know that many traders are involved in a price move and not just one or two.

In technical trading, you use volume to measure the extent of trader participation. When a price rise is accompanied by rising volume, you have confirmation that the direction is associated with participation. You're no longer imagining demand as being behind the price rise, as when you perform bar analysis (see Chapter 4) — you have outright, direct evidence of demand. Similarly, if you see a price fall by a large amount, but the change isn't accompanied by a change in volume, you can deduce that the price change was an aberration. Some trader made a mistake.

Leading the way with spikes

Volume sometimes leads price. The most obvious situations are when volume spikes. A *spike* is a volume number that is double or more the size of volume on the preceding days. Say volume has been running at 100,000 shares per day for several days or weeks and suddenly it explodes to 500,000 shares. If the price had been in a downtrend, this wild increase in volume means that the crowd is throwing in the towel and exiting *en masse*.

Guess what? You should be thinking — hard — about buying! When everyone has jumped off the bandwagon, it's time to get ready to jump back on. Nobody's left to propel the price lower. Conversely, the same advice is usually correct when you see a volume spike, because the price is making new highs. The underlying principle is the same — the crowd has exhausted its supply of cash. Think about taking profit if you already own the security. If you're considering a new position in a rising security that just had a volume spike, think again. Look at other indicators. Try to understand why so many people suddenly jumped on the bandwagon — does fresh news justify the increase in demand for the security, or is it just animal spirits?

A volume spike is one of the occasions when fundamental information is complementary to a technical observation. In the case of a price making new highs coupled with a volume spike where you discover that no fresh news or fundamental information prompted new buyers to come on the scene, be wary. Chances are the top is in. If the security has new, legitimately exciting news and you can reasonably deduce that it attracted new buyers, you have a non-technical reason to ignore the usual spike interpretation.

Tracking on-balance volume

On-balance volume (OBV) is a running (cumulative) total of volume, calculated by adding the volume on days the price is higher than the day before and subtracting the volume on days the price is lower than the day before. The logic goes like this: At the simplest level, when the price closes higher than the day before, demand was greater than supply at each price level. Buyers had to offer higher prices to get holders to part with their shares. You can attribute *all* the volume on a higher-close day to net buying and *all* the volume on a lower-close day to net selling. This isn't a realistic assumption, but hang in there for another minute. A market technician named Joe Granville devised the OBV indicator to display volume in just that way.

Figure 3-1 shows how the OBV indicator works. Daily prices are in the top part, volume (in hundreds of thousands of shares) is the centre of the chart, and the OBV indicator is in the bottom window of the chart.

OBV doesn't work all the time, but a change in the indicator often precedes a change in the price. You can see how to use the OBV indicator in two instances on the chart in Figure 3-1. Note the moves listed opposite.

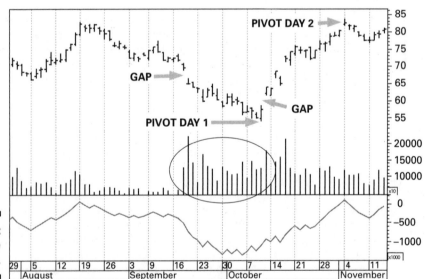

Figure 3-1:
On-balance
volume.

✔ **The down move:** In the section marked by the ellipse, notice how the price down move, already in progress, is suddenly accompanied by a big rise in volume. The increase in volume starts *the day before* the downward gap. We describe gaps in Chapter 5, but take our word for it: A falling price punctuated by a downward gap is a message to the market that the price is going to fall some more.

The OBV indicator forecasts the impending bottom. It starts to fall *ahead* of the volume spike and *ahead* of the gap. If you own the stock and see the OBV indicator start to decline and then you see spiky volume (like the area in the ellipse), you should sell. Holding on after the downward gap is to court a fat loss. In fact, the loss from the open on the gap-down day to the close on the day of the lowest low is $7.22. If you had sold the stock on the very day that volume spiked, the day before the gap, you would have saved another $4.75, for a total of $11.97.

It's true that this time, the stock did come back and put in higher highs a few months later. But you don't know that in advance. To hold on through the falling-price period is to give up the chance to save as much as $11.97 in cash against the day that the bottom comes in, or to put into a different security.

✔ **The up move:** OBV reaches its lowest levels about two weeks *before* Pivot Day 1, which features the lowest low in the series of lower lows, but a higher closing price and a gap upward the following day. (For more information on price bar components, see Chapter 4.)

Notice that OBV is already rising while the price is still falling, a divergence that is a critical clue to an impending change in the direction of the price.

The divergence of price and an indicator that normally rises and falls in tandem with it is itself a wake-up call. A change in volume often predicts a change in price. The indicator is telling you something you can't see with the naked eye — prices were putting in new lows, but prices weren't consistently *closing* lower than the day before. Buying and selling pressure, or supply and demand, was reaching a balance. Your eye can see the price down move, but the indicator can detect the exhaustion of the sellers (supply).

The term *smart money* refers to traders who see the exhaustion of a price move ahead of everyone else. They're alert to the moment when the crowd suddenly realises it has taken a price too far — and reacts violently in the other direction. Down around the price lows in the security in Figure 3-1, somebody had to be buying in order for the stock to be closing at higher levels than the day before (which is what changed the OBV indicator). These traders were the smart money.

Notice that after Pivot Day 1, the price puts in several gap days upward. This is a message to the crowd to buy, and they do, leading to Pivot Day 2 in Figure 3-1. If you had bought this security at the close on Pivot Day 1 and sold it one day after Pivot Day 2 (when the OBV indicator turned downward), this would be your profit-and-loss statement:

Buy	10/10/02	$57.58
Sell	15/11/02	$81.68
Gain/Loss		**$24.10**

The raw percentage return is 42 per cent for a holding period of a little over a month, or about 500 per cent annualised. This is an ideal example of how using an indicator for buy/sell timing is supposed to work.

Truth to tell, no indicator works all the time, and this one doesn't, either. The OBV indicator didn't forecast Pivot Point 2 on Figure 3-1, although it did fall right afterward. Therefore, you'd have to say it was not leading this time, but rather *coincident*. Granville, the inventor of OBV, famously missed a major bull market that started in 1982, and then persisted in saying it was a false bull for the next 14 years. Granville's personal woes with forecasting don't detract from the usefulness of his indicator, although it can be tricky to apply. OBV correctly predicted the crash of October 1987 — but in August, two months early.

Refining volume indicators

As noted in the section 'Tracking on-balance volume' earlier in the chapter, it's not realistic to attribute *all* of the day's volume to the accumulation column just because the close today is higher than yesterday's. OBV works (sometimes), but you have to wonder whether the reason it doesn't work more often is because it's too crude a measure. It makes more sense to attribute only a portion of the volume to the price rise. A technical analyst named Marc Chaikin figured that a more representative amount would be the percentage equivalent of the price that is above the midpoint of the day. A *midpoint* is calculated as the high of the day plus the low of the day divided by two.

If a security closes above its midpoint for the day, bullish sentiment ruled. The close over the midpoint defines *accumulation,* referring to buyers being willing to pay higher prices to get sellers to part with the security. The closer the closing price is to the high, the more bullish it was. If the price closed *at* the high, then you say that 100 per cent of the volume can be attributed to bullish sentiment. *Distribution* is sellers willing to accept lower prices to induce buyers to buy. Lower prices imply bearish sentiment. Distribution is calculated the same way — a close below the price midpoint means distribution, and the closer the closing price is to the low, the more distribution there was. If the close is exactly at the midpoint, then the indicator has the same value as yesterday — you have no reason to add or subtract volume from the running total.

Chaikin's version of accumulation/distribution is more refined than OBV, and you can use it as the basis for other indicators. We don't have the space to go into Chaikin's indicators here, but keep an eye peeled for them and for other indicators that use volume to confirm or reject price action. When you have low volume and/or low accumulation, for example, you should be suspicious of a seeming price rally. The rally doesn't have legs — real volume.

Thinking Outside the Chart

You may have the inside scoop on the best stock ever, but if the entire market has a case of the collywobbles, your best-ever stock is likely to fall, too. Conversely, when the market is in a manic phase, even the worst of stocks gets a boost (hence the old saying, 'A rising tide lifts all boats'). This isn't only because of individuals in the crowd buying or selling everything in sight, but also because money flows into and out of managed funds. Managed funds have latitude about how much money to keep in cash. In a mania, they get more fully invested, and in a panic, they pull a higher proportion of total funds out of the market and into cash.

Nobody knows for sure, but some percentage of any security's price move is attributable to changes in the market environment. Factors include not only the index to which it belongs, but also its size (large-cap or small-cap, for example) and sector (biotech, high-tech, no-tech). A guess is that about 25 per cent of a price move in any single issue should be considered a function of what is going on in its index (or other benchmark to which the issue belongs).

In parallel, some portion of the price move in a commodity is a function of the price move of the overall commodity indices, like the Commodity Research Bureau index (CRB). In currencies, the benchmark is something called the *dollar index,* a price average comprised of individual currency prices weighted by their countries' share of trade with the United States and published by the Federal Reserve. A different index blend is traded on a futures exchange. You may question whether you want to buy the dollar against a specific currency counterpart like the Japanese yen when the dollar index is falling.

Overall, the market environment has a magnetic effect on individual components. It goes without saying, however, that some individual securities escape the magnetic field. In a rally, some stocks just sit there. In a panic, some stocks flourish.

To get a handle on possible market effects on your specific security, you want to measure overall market sentiment. You do this by looking at market statistics. Strictly speaking, market statistics are not 'technical analysis', which is the study of how specific prices behave. Nevertheless, sentiment measures can be very helpful as a supplement and complement to work on your individual charts.

Sampling information about sentiment

Most sentiment indicators look outside the price dynamics of a particular security or index of securities for information about whether the trading crowd is humming along with expectations of normalcy or is willing to jump ship.

If you type **investor sentiment** into a search engine, you get over 1,3000,000 hits. Watch out! Nearly all of this material is talk, and in technical trading, the key principle is to study what people *do* (price and volume), not what they *say*.

Managed funds and technical analysis

The managed funds industry in Australia is quite large. In December 2006, Australian investment funds had $424 billion in equities under management, the fourth largest in the world. A managed fund's goal is to pick securities that together can return more than a bond or bank savings account. And they strive to do this without incurring undue risk. Most managed funds aim to match or beat an index, such as the S&P/ASX 300 Index. In the three years to 30 June 2004, retail managed funds underperformed the S&P/ASX 300 Index by 18 per cent. Technically oriented observers think that some managed funds fall short because managers jump on a trend just when it's about to peak, then exit just when a bottom is being reached.

On several occasions active fund managers have outperformed passive funds. Unfortunately, for active fund investors, the 'star' managed funds of the previous years don't tend to follow through as next year's stars. They're replaced by the new 'star' managed funds, but as an investor, you don't know who the next 'star' will be. Is this an argument for buying a *passive* fund that buys every stock in the index? If you're going to buy any managed fund, yes.

Asking advisers how they feel

In the United States, the Investors Intelligence Service (started over 50 years ago) measures the balance of bullish sentiment against bearish sentiment (which it calls the Bull/Bear Ratio), and claims an excellent track record in predicting turning points — major reversals come when the majority of advisers (60 per cent or more) are bullish or bearish. In other words, when everyone recognises the trend bandwagon and has hopped on board, it's over.

Note that other services have sprung up to measure bull/bear sentiment in general, in specialised sectors and in managed funds. In the United States, you can find the Bull/Bear Ratio and other indicators on hundreds of Web sites and in business newspapers. To get a specific bull/bear ratio from a specific supplier the minute it's published, you have to pay a subscription fee. Unfortunately, to the best of our knowledge, no similar service is available in Australia for Australian markets.

Following the money: Breadth indicators

Breadth indicators measure the degree of participation by traders in the overall market represented by an index, such as the S&P/ASX All Ordinaries Index. Breadth indicators include:

- **Ratio of advancing to declining issues:** This indicator measures the mood of the market. Stocks that are reaching a higher price today than yesterday are called *advancing issues*. Stocks that are reaching lower prices are called *declining issues*. When advancers outnumber decliners, money is flowing into the market. Bulls are beating bears. Sentiment is favourable. A buying frenzy is accompanied by a higher level of advancing issues to decliners. When the rally starts getting tired, the number of advancing issues declines while the number of falling issues rises.

  - If you chart the cumulative total of advancing issues minus declining ones, you get the advance/decline line.

  - If you chart the advancing issues divided by declining issues, you get the advance/decline *ratio*, usually abbreviated A/D.

- **Difference between issues making new highs and those making new lows:** The logic is the same as in the advance/decline case. If more stocks in an index are closing at higher prices than the period before, bullishness is on the rise. When a higher number are putting in new lows, supply is overwhelming demand and the mood must be bearish.

Figure 3-2 shows the S&P/ASX All Ordinaries index in the top chart and the advance/decline line in the bottom chart for the Australian market to June 2006. Notice that in May 2006, the All Ordinaries index continued to make new highs, as marked by the ascending line across the peaks, but the advance/decline line failed to make a new high. It actually made a lower high, as shown by the descending line across the peaks. This demonstrates that fewer and fewer stocks were participating in the bullishness of the index and served as a warning that the index was about to fail.

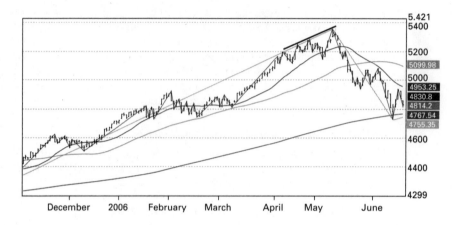

Figure 3-2:
Advance/
decline line
for ASX to
mid-2006.

Following the betting: Options

The Australian Securities Exchange (ASX) is the venue for options trading in Australia. The ASX publishes the ratio of puts to calls.

- **Put:** The right to sell at a set price in the future. Traders who buy puts are bears (pessimists) who think the index won't reach their set price.

- **Call:** The right to buy at a set price in the future. Traders who buy calls are bulls (optimists) who think they'll profit when the market rises to and beyond their set price.

The *put/call ratio* is calculated by dividing the number of put options traded by the number of call options traded. Accordingly, the *put/call ratio* is an indicator of whether sentiment is bearish or bullish. A high put/call ratio means bears are winning. By now, you should be able to recognise that an extreme of emotion like this is usually wrong and marks a turning point. You should start planning to do the opposite. The same line of thinking holds true for a low put/call ratio: When emotions are running strongly optimistic, watch out for an opportunity to take advantage of a change.

Figure 3-3 shows the put/call ratio for ASX options to 6 April 2007. You can see how the chart fluctuates from bullish to bearish sentiment. The spike of January 5 denoted extreme bearishness in the market and was a point where the All Ordinaries turned around from bearish to bullish.

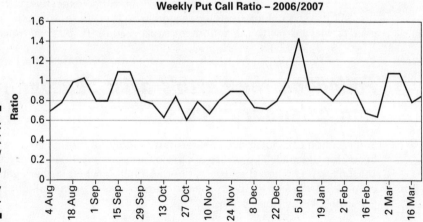

Figure 3-3: The ASX weekly put/ call ratio to April 6, 2007.

Viewing volatility with the VIX

In the United States, the Chicago Board Options Exchange (CBOE) publishes one of the most popular indicators used today: The volatility index (VIX). This index is calculated from the implied volatility of a range of S&P 500 index options. The details of its calculation are too complicated to get into here, but for information about volatility, see Chapter 12. Just accept that when the crowd is jumpy and nervous, it projects that anxiety into the future and assumes that prices will be abnormal. In other words, the crowd believes volatility will be high. When the price of VIX is high, options traders have been buying puts and selling calls on the index — they're bearish and think the market may fall. Actually, what they really think is that the *risk* of a fall is high and worth spending some insurance money on. When VIX is low, the market is relaxed and confident — too confident.

But we know that when the crowd is feeling an extreme emotion, like anxiety, it's usually wrong. Therefore, a high VIX value means exactly the opposite of what it seems to mean — the bottom isn't coming, it's already in! Conversely, when VIX is low, traders are complacent. They're projecting the same price levels, or nearly the same levels, into the immediate future with little variation and therefore little risk. When VIX is either abnormally high or abnormally low, you know it's the right time to trade against the crowd. If VIX is high, the market is readying for a lull. If VIX is low, the crowd is girding its loins for a big move. In short, VIX is used as a contrary indicator.

Theoretically, you can create a volatility index for any security in which options are traded, although it takes computational expertise. Unfortunately, the ASX doesn't calculate an index similar to the VIX in Australia, so you need to make do with the sentiment expressed in the *put/call ratio*.

Following the Earth's axis: Seasonality and calendar effects

You shouldn't be surprised to hear that heating oil futures go up as winter heads for Chicago. The prices of agricultural commodities often track the seasons, rising when the crop is poor and falling when farmers get a bumper crop. *Seasonality* is the term used for the natural rise and fall of prices according to the time of year.

Oddly — very oddly — equities and financial futures exhibit a similar effect: They change according to the time of year. The changes are regular and consistent enough to warrant your attention.

You have probably heard the United States adage, 'Sell in May and go away'. This advice comes from work on calendar effects by Yale and Jeffrey Hirsch, who tested the correlation of stock index prices with the time of year in their annual *Stock Trader's Almanac.* The economies of the northern hemisphere are so large compared to Australia's, that our seasonality almost completely follows the cycles of the United States and, to a lesser extent, Europe.

Hirsch discovered that nearly all the gains in the S&P 500 are made between November 1 and April 30. This isn't true without exception, but it's true for most years since 1950. It's also true for the Australian stock market. When April 30 rolls around, you sell all your stocks and put the money in government Treasuries. Come November 1, you re-enter the stock market. In the United States, if you'd followed this rule every year since 1950 and also modified the exact timing a little by applying the moving average convergence-divergence (MACD) indicator (explained in Chapter 10), a starting capital stake of $10,000 in 1952 would have ballooned to $1,308,304 by 2003. On average, you would've been invested only six and a half months each year — and remember, when you're not in the market, you're not taking market risk.

Contrarians and cranks

A true contrarian is someone who has a *fundamental* reason for thinking that a security is mispriced. In equities, a fundamental reason could be insider knowledge that an out-of-favour pharmaceutical company has secretly discovered the cure for some important disease and its price will shoot to the moon when the announcement comes out. In financial futures (stock indices, bonds and currencies), a fundamental reason to judge a security mispriced may be an in-depth analysis of a central bank interest rate change that nobody else can see coming. A true contrarian is quite rare, although lots of people fancy themselves contrarians when they're just cranks. When a contrarian is right, he becomes a zillionaire and is called eccentric. When he is wrong, he stays poor and is called a crackpot.

In contrast, technical trading is by its very nature non-contrarian. You want to go with the crowd, not against it (most of the time). Identifying when the crowd has gone too far isn't contrarian in the proper sense of the term. When you figure out that a pivot point is impending, you're a crowd leader. Confusion about the meaning of the word contrarian arises because some followers of sentiment indicators use it when talking about turning points predicted by indicator extremes. To recognise that at the top of a rally everyone is fully invested and no buyers are left is called *contrarian logic*. But to say that the crowd is wrong isn't contrarian — it's simply understanding crowd dynamics. Remember, a true contrarian has a fundamental reason to say that the crowd is wrong.

The sell in May rule is called the *best six months rule.* Other calendar effects include:

- ✔ **January Barometer:** When the S&P/ASX All Ordinaries Index is up in January, it'll close the year higher than it opened.

- ✔ **The US President's Third Year:** In the United States, since 1939, the third year of a presidential term is always an up year for the Dow. In fact, going back 84 years, the only big down year in the third year of a presidential term was 1931.

- ✔ **The US Presidential Election Cycle:** Wars, recessions and bear markets tend to start in the first two years in the United States, while prosperity and bull markets tend to happen in the second two years. Since the mid-1900s, the last two years of a president's term produced a cumulative net gain in the Dow of 717.5 per cent, while the first two years produced 227.6 per cent.

Many other calendar effects have been discovered, by Hirsch and by others. Hirsch's annual *Stock Traders Almanac* publishes the probability of any of the three major indices (Dow, S&P 500 and NASDAQ) rising or falling on any day of the year. The almanac bases this information on what has happened in those indexes on those dates since January 1953. Type **stock market calendar effects** into a search engine and you get 1.3 million hits, some of which are dense academic papers confirming and qualifying the effects.

Seasonality used to be a word applied to agricultural prices and *calendar effects* was applied to equities, but today they're used interchangeably.

Keep your eye on the United States markets. There's an old saying in the markets: 'When Wall Street sneezes, the rest of the world catches a cold'. Undeniably, there are strong inter-market linkages between Wall Street and the Australian stock market. Most traders pay attention to this correlation during times of market stress, but the effect that Wall Street has on Australian markets also exerts itself on a day-to-day basis. Normally, the tone on Wall Street translates to Australian stock markets. For this reason, you can usually use calendar effects, such as the United States Presidential cycle, to your advantage when trading Australian stocks.

Using calendar effects

Paying attention to calendar effects can help improve your timing. When you're sitting down to make a trading or investment decision, you can avoid a costly mistake by consulting the calendar not only for the specific security, but also for the index to which it belongs. If you receive a large sum of money in May and plan to put it in the market, you may want to see if the market is obeying the 'sell in May' sentiment this year. Remember that the big-picture calendar effects apply to the indices. Plenty of individual stocks defy the rule and go up.

Calendar effects are more than a curiosity, although a security on a wild rally isn't going to stop solely because it's May 1. But because so many traders and money managers know about calendar effects, it seems that to some degree they become a self-fulfilling prophecy.

Be aware that statisticians don't all agree on exactly how to measure seasonality effects. Seasonality statisticians quarrel with one another about matters big and small. If you have a talent for statistics and for judging among the available techniques, you can easily benefit by consulting seasonality studies or conducting your own. But people without a grounding in statistics find it easy to become overwhelmed and to spend unproductive time on the subject.

Blindsiding the Crowd

It's comforting to think that you can find regularity and orderliness in charts, using the technical methods that take up most of this book or the sentiment statistics pertaining to the market at large described in this chapter.

But don't get too comfortable. A big black hole in orderliness appears when markets puff up into manias and when they crash in panics. The art of technical analysis is to identify the crowd psychology underneath price moves. To the technical trader, just about any price move can be seen as a mini-mania or a mini-panic, as we say in Chapter 2. When they're small, they're forecastable and tradeable. But sometimes the market delivers a mania and an ensuing panic that are huge and all but define an era. Think of the Roaring '20s and the crash of 1929, which took 22 years to recover.

Searching for historic major reversals

One of the enduring mysteries of market history is that big major reversal points come out of the blue. Seldom can you find a specific event that triggers a rally taking off or a bubble bursting. Think back to the large correction of the Australian equity markets in 2002. Exactly what caused that? Experts can name a dozen contributing factors, but no-one can put a finger on a single defining factor. Technical indicators were very useful to exit not long after the bubble burst, but to be honest, this was a function of the risk management principles embedded in technical analysis far more than forecasting capability.

Does that mean that historic major reversals occur randomly? If so, then why shouldn't we say that *all* major reversals occur randomly?

Opinion is divided on the answer. One camp says that news causes prices to change and nobody can forecast the news. News is random. Therefore, prices must be random, too. But if prices were random, you wouldn't be able to see trends on a chart, and you do see trends on a chart. No amount of fancy theorising can overcome the evidence of your eyes. If prices were random, prices wouldn't go into trends. But unmistakably, they do.

Besides, *any* particular price may be random, but not *every* price can be random, or traders wouldn't be able to make a bid and an offer on the next price. The market would collapse — no trading would take place. Instead, traders remember preceding prices, and they put the current price into the context of those past prices. From past prices, they form an expectation of the future price. This isn't to deny that some prices are random. You do see inexplicable prices and it's fair to call them random. But how can one or two random prices turn into a major reversal when other prices, whether random or on trend, don't?

Nobody knows. So how should you think about it? Many people give up on technical analysis at this point. If you never know when a major turning point is going hit you over the head with a hammer, how can you trust technical indicators? The answer is that you can trust your indicators only up to a point, and then your survival as a trader depends on risk management, which we talk about in Chapter 17. In the meantime, it's important to have a useful way to think about randomness and not let it overwhelm you.

Enduring randomness

Technical traders acknowledge that random events can and do cause the occasional wild price departure from the norm, but the acknowledgement doesn't alter the expectation that prices will behave normally. As we explain in Chapter 5, for example, you sometimes see a price (named a *spike*) that is so far out of whack you don't know how to interpret it. Often you never find out why such a bizarre price occurred.

A price spike is the equivalent of a cyclone in weather forecasting. We know the conditions that cause cyclones — we just don't know exactly when an actual cyclone will develop.

Whereas it's virtually impossible for nature to deliver snow in Cairns, the equivalent does happen in markets. Sudden cataclysmic events aren't as rare as you may imagine. Who would have thought that the S&P/ASX All Ordinaries Index could fall nearly 25 per cent in a single day? Most market observers used to say it was impossible. But that's exactly what happened on the day following Wall Street's Black Monday in 1987. Most market storms, like Black Monday, give plenty of technical warnings ahead of time. The problem is that we often have those same warnings and don't get a Black Monday. This is an inconvenient fact of life that you have to accept.

Remembering the last price

Market panics and crashes on the scale of occasions like 1929 and 1987 are historic *events* outside the scope of the crowd's normal trading *process.* In normal trading, you can assume that a wildly erratic price has a low probability of occurring. But you can't attach a specific probability statistic to an event of historic proportions — partly because those events are so rare.

In weather forecasting, a low-probability event (like a cyclone) that happens today doesn't change the probabilities of the usual high-probability events happening next week, or next year. But in markets, a low-probability event does change the odds for the next period analysis. This is because traders *remember.* The clouds forming over the Pacific don't remember that their cousin cloud just dumped a cyclone on Innisfail. The dice don't remember that they came up double sixes on the last throw, nor the coin that it came up heads on the last toss. The probability of the next outcome in science and gambling isn't dependent on the last outcome.

But in technical analysis, you're counting on traders to remember the last prices and to form their trading plans on those prices. The next price is normally dependent on preceding prices.

Sometimes, all it takes is one or two abnormal prices to upset the apple cart and alter the expectations of the trading crowd. If before they were bullish, suddenly they become bearish. When you have only two modes of sentiment together with a few abnormal prices, sometimes determining which way the crowd will jump is like a coin toss.

The coin toss analogy raises the issue of the reliability of indicators, which we describe in Chapter 14. They're essentially forecasting tools that depend on past behaviours to predict future behaviours, but they fail near really big major reversals. And this is where most maths-based models fall short. For example, a basic rule of momentum, discussed in Chapter 11, is that a body in motion tends to stay in motion. But in securities, the price can hit a brick wall. Think of a pivot point (especially the historic ones) as the brick wall. Unlike physical substances, prices don't behave in predictable ways after hitting a brick wall, like particles in a chamber. To make matters worse, particles in a chamber are not savvy creatures who get and respond to feedback about how they just moved, whereas traders do get information about price moves. In short, technical analysis is not science, as its inability to capture historic major reversals ahead of time demonstrates.

Oddly, neither sentiment indicators nor standard technical analysis is much help in detecting the cataclysmic change from rally to crash.

Thinking Scientifically

Even in the absence of the occasional historic event like 1929, in regular trading even the best indicator fails to work all the time. In fact, some of the best indicators work less than 50 per cent of the time, and that's when conditions are normal! Critics use this awful statistic to say that charting is a waste of time. This is a failure to appreciate the benefits of risk management and also to appreciate the limits of applying maths in a decidedly unscientific context.

You may think that it's overkill to discuss 'scientific methods', but we can practically guarantee that this section will have a big payoff for you. That's because you're sure to see enticing advertisements for software or trading programs that are 'scientific' and 'objective'. Well, all maths is 'scientific' and 'objective'. That doesn't mean you can use it to make money.

Conditions and contingencies

When you hear someone say, 'Blue Sky Mining has a 75 per cent chance of rising,' it means that three out of the last four times when the technical method was applied, the security rose. Unspoken is the assumption that *conditions didn't change*. But the market is not a laboratory. Of course conditions changed.

Your forecast needs to be qualified because of the thousands of factors that may come along and influence the price. *Contingencies* are things that are possible but not expected, or not expected in any great number at the same time. You know what a contingency is — it's hitting every red light on the way to catch the express from Central Station. If you hit the average number of red lights, you can make it with time to spare. If they're all red and you have to slow down for construction, you miss your train.

Most technical traders hate to attach a probability to a particular outcome, such as 'Blue Sky Mining has a 75 per cent change of rising'. Reluctance to call a spade a spade is due to a realistic assessment of the contingencies. In statistics, when you want to calculate the probability of two events happening simultaneously (*joint probability*), you multiply their probabilities. If you have two remotely possible contingencies, each with a probability of 10 per cent, the chances of both happening simultaneously is ten per cent times ten per cent, or 1 per cent.

To calculate the effect of a 10 per cent probability contingency on your trade, you take the reciprocal of the probability, or 90 per cent, as the amount to modify the 75 per cent. In arithmetic notation:

75 per cent *times* 90 per cent = 67.50 per cent

Good grief — introducing one contingency reduced the probability of your outcome from 75 per cent to 67.5 per cent. It gets worse. If you have four contingencies and you attribute a 10 per cent chance to each of them, the same process reduces your 75 per cent odds to a mere 49.21 per cent, which is less than 50–50.

Joint probabilities really stink, don't they? No wonder technical traders hate to declare a forecast! The more contingencies you admit, the lower the probability of the outcome. You can become very neurotic imagining all the contingencies that can destroy your forecast.

To make life more complicated, markets have hidden contingencies. You may see two securities that have identical charts. You apply an indicator and it works on one security — the price obediently moves the way you forecast. But it fails to work on the seemingly identical security, whose price perversely goes in the other direction. The technique can't be said to be scientific when this is the outcome.

Obviously, there were underlying differences in the two securities, or a hidden contingency — and you may never know what it is. The cause of the divergent behaviour could be something as simple as two different types of traders.

In the first case, the traders who trade that specific security were also using the same technical indicators as you, and obeyed the forecast embodied in the method. In the second case, perhaps the market participants ignored the indicator in favour of a different one.

When you hear a market guru predicting a price change with a 75 per cent probability, chances are he's talking through his hat. He may have failed to incorporate all the reasonable contingencies, or he may have attributed too small a probability to any of them (or to all of them). Read financial history, and you find the ground littered with the corpses of traders who failed to include a key contingency in their calculations.

Sample size

In setting up the Blue Sky Mining example, we attributed a 75 per cent chance of the price rising because three out of the last four times that conditions looked the same, that's what happened. But a sample size of four instances is hardly sufficient. Statisticians say you need a minimum of 30 cases before you can say anything valid about the probability of history repeating itself. Scientists who do really serious science, like missiles and moonshots, demand a minimum of 200 cases.

Your price data seldom presents you with 30 cases, let alone 200. Why should you accept less? The answer is that you're using a technical analysis method that works across a wide range of securities and time frames, even if you don't have enough cases in this specific security. As an example, when you have a support line (described in Chapter 8) and your price breaks it to the downside, that's a sell signal. Over the past 100 years, technical analysts have used the break of a support line hundreds of thousands of times, maybe millions, and it worked. It was the correct trading decision in the majority of a very large number of cases.

Still, it doesn't work every time. A support line break is an example of a technical forecast that has a high probability in the context of many different contingencies and over many sets of conditions. Other techniques are less reliable. You may think it would be wonderful to have a list of techniques with their *reliability quotient,* which is a ranking of how often they're right. Some writers and software suppliers claim that their techniques are 'over 75 per cent correct'. This is hardly ever true. For one thing, they aren't considering new contingencies and conditions. Markets are dynamic. Something that worked 75 per cent of the time in the past may work only 65 per cent of the time in the future, or some other percentage of the time, including zero — which is precisely what happens at the end of manias and panics.

Part II
Observing Market Behaviour

Glenn Lumsden

*'I want you to study this price pattern chart
carefully and tell me what your gut feels.
Apart from seasick.'*

In this part . . .

Security prices move in regular ways that most professional traders (who dominate the market) expect — and therefore create. One of the keys to understanding charting and other forms of technical analysis is to understand the price bar. Everything in technical analysis, even the most sophisticated indicator, arises out of the price bar and its components. When you take the time to look closely at the price bar and at small batches of price bars, you begin to see how the trading crowd responds to the security.

Other key concepts to know are support and resistance and breakout. Even a rough application of these two concepts — which we introduce in this part — will save you a bundle or help you make profits, because they're among the top technical ruling concepts in the market.

Chapter 4

Reading Basic Bars: Showing How Security Prices Move

Charting is a visual art. In the beginning, you may see what looks like a bunch of unrelated dots on a security's price chart. It takes a little practice to see, but inside each dot on the chart lies a world of information. On closer examination, the 'dot' is really a price bar, which graphically represents all the transactions done in the security, revealing supply and demand at each point.

In this chapter, we define each component of the price bar. We demonstrate how to transform the numbers on the price bar from abstract dollar amounts into the market sentiment of the participants in that security, either optimistic or pessimistic. You know the phrase 'Actions speak louder than words'? Reading price bars is the perfect application of that saying. Traders may *say* they feel optimistic about the price of the security going up, but the price bar will tell you what they really think by showing you what action they took. To 'read' price bars is to be a detective examining the hard evidence — and disregarding witness accounts. This visual analysis is the basis of charting.

The price bar is also the basic building block of the mathematical approach to technical analysis. All the mathematics behind the multitude of technical indicators available to you are nothing more than an arithmetic manipulation of one or more of the four price bar components. After you have a grip on the price bar, almost nothing in technical analysis will confuse you. Honest. Resist the temptation to skim over the bar chart material to get to the more glamorous-sounding techniques. You can't grasp the principle of most indicators without first understanding the price bar.

The price bar is also your yardstick for identifying whether trends exist — trendedness — and critical changes in trendedness. Prices change from day to day in numerous ways, but seldom in random or meaningless ways. Every major trend starts with a change in the price bar on a single day or over only a few days, and the earlier you take a position when a new trend develops, the more profit you make. In Chapters 6 and 13, we describe two other ways of displaying price information, but here, focus on getting down pat the components of the standard bar.

Building Basic Bars

We start off here with a brief overview of the price bar and then detail each piece of it at length in the sections that follow.

The *price bar* describes and defines the trading action in a security for a given period. *Trading action* means all the real-money transactions conducted during the period. The price bar measures actual deals done with cold, hard cash, not what somebody wished, imagined or contemplated. For the sake of simplicity, this chapter refers to a daily price bar because most of the time, you're working with daily price information. As we explain later in this chapter, a price bar can encompass different periods — anything from a minute to a month. But the scope of the period doesn't change the price bar dynamics described in this chapter.

Check out the standard price bar in Figure 4-1. Like all bars, it consists of four components:

- ✔ **Open:** The little horizontal line on the left is the opening price.

- ✔ **High:** The top of the vertical line defines the high of the day.

- ✔ **Low:** The bottom of the vertical line defines the low of the day.

- ✔ **Close:** The little horizontal line on the right is the closing price.

This Open-High-Low-Close component set of the price bar is often abbreviated OHLC.

The two little horizontal lines on the price bar are called *tick marks*. In trading parlance, a *tick* represents a single trade at a single price, so the tick mark representing the open or the close refers literally to a single transaction or to a batch of transactions all at the same price and at the same time. The high and the low don't need a tick mark because the end of the bar conveys that information.

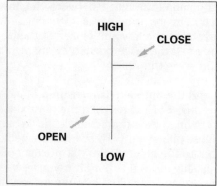

Figure 4-1:
The
standard
price bar.

The daily price bar shows the effects of every factor in the market for that day, including:

- ✔ Events in the general environment (war, elections, natural disasters)
- ✔ The specific security's *fundamentals* — news and perceptions about the security itself
- ✔ The collective intellectual and emotional condition of the traders buying and selling the security

Throughout this chapter we give you examples of each of these factors. Practise looking for these factors as you look at price bars.

Consulting the source

Analysing price bars and bar charts is useful for those times when you're befuddled by the patterns and indicators we detail in Parts II, III and IV. If you're like most people, you'll eventually try to apply so many technical tools to a chart that you'll hardly be able to see the original bars underneath it all. At that point, return to the basics — a clean chart that contains only the price bars — and ask yourself, 'What are these bars saying?' Chances are they're singing quite a tune. Price bars are the raw material of indicators, so when indicators are giving you conflicting or confusing signals, go back to the source. Observing the characteristics of the price bar and interpreting changes correctly can save your hide. In fact, many traders make all their decisions on the price bar alone. For more information, check out setup trading in Chapter 15.

The price bar tells you the outcome of the battle between the buyers (bulls) and the sellers (bears). Hidden in every price bar is a winning group and a losing group. If the price opened at the low and closed at the high, the winners that day were the buyers. If the price opened at the high and closed at the low, the winners that day were the sellers.

This is a very real contest — and the outcome is measured in money. If the bar is very tall, encompassing, say, a $1 range when the normal bar for this security is only 30 cents, the trading was a titanic battle. If the bar is very short, say 10 cents, it was a mere pillow fight. This warlike aspect of trading is why you often see references to the great military strategists of history in books on trading, which seems silly at first — but after you've been trading for a while, you see that a military analogy often hits the nail on the head. In every trade that makes up the price bar, somebody won and the other fellow lost in the context of the next price and the price at the end of the day. Because one party wins and the other party loses on every single trade, trading — like war — is called a 'zero sum game'.

The relationship between prices and volume is also important in gauging the outcome of a trading session. *Volume* is the number of shares or contracts traded during the period. Everything that you infer about the state of mind of the market participants is subject to confirmation by volume. For example, we just said that you can deduce a titanic battle from the price bar being triple the usual size, but in practice, you would also verify that a large number of traders were active that day by looking at volume. It would be wrong to see a 'battle' if only one trade was done at the $1 high. In that case, the $1 price is something of an anomaly. Somebody made a mistake — either the buyer at $1 or the data collection department at the exchange.

Setting the tone: The opening price

The *opening price* is theoretically the very first trade done between a buyer and a seller on the trading day. It reflects the new day's hopes and fears. The meaning of the open, like all the price bar components, comes from its relationship to the other components of the bar as they develop and to the components of the bars that come before.

The opening price's most important relationship is to the close of the day before.

When the open is up

If the open is up from the close of the day before, you imagine that the first trader of the day is expecting favourable news or has some other reason to think the price of that security will improve. If you, too, want to be a buyer today, that higher opening price reinforces your feeling. The first trade sets the tone, in this case a hopeful one.

Sometimes a good opening is due to a practice called *buy on open*. You can't automatically attribute optimism or hopefulness to an opening bounce, because managed fund and other professional managers have preset allocations to specific securities. When fresh money comes in the night before, they're going to distribute a certain percentage of it to all the securities in the fund selected by the new customer. To 'buy on open' is the easiest way to top up a fund, and not necessarily a judgement on that security that day.

Fund managers and other professionals control far larger sums than individuals, and you don't know what proportion of opening trades are due to genuine research-based enthusiasm and what proportion is due to the mechanical buy-on-open effect. The market can take up to an hour to get down to new business. Some technical-trading advisers recommend taking advantage of the first half-hour or hour, while others shun it.

How do you know whether an opening bounce is due to fresh enthusiasm or just the mechanical buy-on-open effect? You have to study each security to see whether it normally displays the effect. Big-name securities (such as BHP Billiton stock) are more susceptible to an opening bounce than specialised securities with a narrower trader base (like SFE Greasy Wool futures).

When the open is down

If the opening price is below the close of the day before, look out! Chances are the tone is sour. Maybe bad news came out after the close last night. The bad news may pertain to a political event, a change in interest rates, a bankruptcy in the same industry or a zillion other factors (see the discussion of events in the section 'The high' later in this chapter).

Some traders may have executed a *sell on open*, but don't count on it unless you study the security and find that the open often falls below yesterday's close. To sell on open isn't a common practice.

It's always possible that the opening price means nothing at all. Market prices are sometimes random because people make decisions about their money that have nothing to do with the price, but rather with their personal needs. Maybe Uncle Bob got up this morning and said to himself, 'I think I'll sell my Blue Sky shares at the open today and go on a cruise'. Randomness can also affect the other parts of the price bar, not just the open, although people commonly make a money decision first thing in the morning or last thing before the market closes.

Should you use the open?

You also need to consider the convention for quoting prices when evaluating the opening price. The open is supposed to be the very first price of the day at which a buyer bought and a seller sold. And this is usually the case in the futures markets. Trading begins and the price of the first trade is entered into the exchange computer.

Because of the importance placed on the opening trade, many exchanges and data analysts report the opening price differently. In the United States, different exchanges use different methods to generate a synthetic opening price. This is why the opening price varies from one data source to another. In Australia, the trading day commences with limit orders being placed for a pre-open auction. A complicated algorithm is then applied to these orders to establish the opening price. In the futures market the opening price is fair dinkum, but because trading has been going on overnight, it's hardly ever a surprise. To use the opening price you see on your charts effectively, you need to understand how it has been derived.

So should you heed the open? Yes. In equities, any particular opening price may not be accurate, but over a series of days, the open adequately represents the sentiment at the beginning of the day. Heed the opening price in futures, too, including equity index futures. The open is your benchmark for evaluating the price action over the course of the day.

Summarising sentiment: The closing price

The *closing price* is literally the last price at which a buyer bought and a seller sold before the closing bell. The close is generally considered the most important part of the price bar. In fact, if you were to draw a chart using only one of the daily components, you'd usually pick the close, and you do sometimes see close-only charts, in which case the 'dot' really is a single-number dot and not a full bar. A set of closes over a small number of days is an indicator in its own right.

The close is the most important part of the price bar because it summarises what traders feel about the security. They've watched this price all day, and by the end of the day, they have a sense of how popular it was near the lows (lots of buying going on) or how unpopular near the highs (lots of selling going on). Remember, they're also looking at volume to confirm these impressions. As the close approaches, traders have to decide whether to hold the security overnight, a course of action they take only if they think it's going up further tomorrow and they won't be able to get it more cheaply than they already have.

After-hours trading creates a problem in evaluating the close. How do you treat the close when your security makes a new high or new low in after-hours trading — only ten minutes after the close? The answer is that you don't adjust the close. In terms of managing your data, the open and close are associated with the trading hours of the primary exchange where the security is listed — the Singapore Exchange, the Tokyo Stock Exchange, the Chicago Mercantile Exchange and so on. If the security trades wildly higher or lower from the 'official' close, even five or ten minutes after the close, the new information is included in the price data for the next day. This can result in some peculiar outcomes, such as the price opening at $5 and closing at $7 on its primary exchange during the exchange's regular hours, but both the high and the low occurring in after-hours trading — and reaching (say) $2 at the low and $150 at the high. For purposes of technical analysis, this is the next day's data even though the trades were recorded within minutes of the official close.

You often hear 'it's up on the day' or 'it's down on the day' or 'it's unchanged on the day', referring to the closing price relative to the close the day before. Here are the distinctions:

- An *up-day* is one where the close is higher than the close the day before. On an up-day, buyers are said to be keener than the sellers and have driven the security higher.

- A *down-day* refers to a day when the close is lower than the close the day before. On a down-day sellers are keener than the buyers and have driven the security lower.

- An *unchanged-day* refers to a day when very little or no change from the day before occurs. On an unchanged-day neither buyers nor sellers are keen.

When the close is up

As with all price bar components, what's important is the relationship of the close to other price bar components, especially the open today and the close yesterday. You may think that you don't care about a single day's worth of information embedded in the price bar because your trading style is for a longer period than one day, but over time, the cumulative relationship of the close to the close the day before gives you a visual impression of directional bias. If today's close is consistently higher than the close yesterday, day after day, buyers are demanding more and more of the security and are willing to pay an ever-higher price to get it. As shown in Figure 4-2, with the exception of Day 4, every close is higher than the close the previous day.

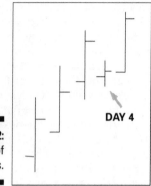

DAY 4

Figure 4-2:
A series of
up-days.

When the close is down

In Figure 4-3, you can see that after the first bar each close is lower than the day before. Here the sellers are willing to take ever-lower prices to get rid of the security. Notice how we impute supply and demand to the price bar. The market assumes that those holding an inventory of the security are willing to sell at lower and lower prices in order to get buyers to demand it. This is the same as your car dealer putting last year's cars on sale just before the new models come in. By lowering the price, they create demand.

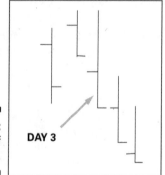

Figure 4-3:
A series of
down-days.

DAY 3

Greed, fear and risk management at the close

On an up-day, you hear that 'today the bulls won' or on a down-day, 'today the bears won'. This talk of bulls and bears acknowledges the emotional aspect of trading — bulls are buyers who are hopeful of higher prices later when they can sell for a profit, and bears are pessimists who foresee prices falling. You can also say that the bulls are motivated by greed and the bears are motivated by fear. Greed and fear aren't the only emotions traders feel, but over the years, market lore has boiled the emotional aspect of trading down to these two. Like a lot of market lore, it's an oversimplification, and you should remember that greed and fear are not the only emotions motivating buyers and sellers. Traders also make buy/sell decisions on hard-headed reason.

Just as *buying on open* is so common that it affects the opening price, keep in mind that another common market practice is to *sell on close*. Traders sell at the close to eliminate the risk of loss if something happens overnight that causes the price to fall. This simple risk management tactic is used by institutions as well as individuals.

Because so many people exit on the close, the close is seldom the high of the day. And when the close *is* at the exact high of the day, that's useful information. It means people who do hold overnight positions are buying right up to the last minute, offsetting the usual end-of-day sales.

An *overnight position* is a purchase or sale that you don't close out the same day you put it on — you hold it overnight. If you're accustomed to the traditional 'buy and hold' strategy of the mainstream investment community, you probably think of holding your securities overnight as nothing special — after all, you're planning to hold it for months or years, so of course you hold it overnight. But if you're an active trader aiming to make small amounts of money quickly and repeatedly, like many professionals, you care a lot about all the things that can occur overnight to drive down the price of your security. Every minute you hold a position, you risk catastrophic loss, especially if you're using leverage (borrowed money). As we describe in Chapter 14, catastrophes happen all the time in financial markets.

The high

The *high* of the price bar is literally the highest point of the bar. It's the highest price at which a buyer and seller made an exchange of cash for the security. The buyer obviously thought he was getting a bargain or good value and thinks that the price will rise some more. The seller holds the opposite view, that the price is going to fall. The high represents the limit of the strength of the bulls for the day.

The high of the day has meaning only in the context of its relationship to other parts of the same bar, especially the close, and to the high the day before.

When the price closes at the high of the day, traders are extremely optimistic of more gains to come (bullish). The bulls had strong control at the close and they were committed. When the high is at the open and it's all downhill for the rest of the day, traders are pessimistic (bearish).

You seldom see the high at the open or the close because

- ✔ Over the course of the day, the market responds to fresh news and fresh perceptions that are caused by any number of factors.
- ✔ Most traders 'buy on open' and 'sell on close' (which we discuss earlier in the chapter).

The low

The *low* of the day is the cheapest price at which the buyer and seller exchange cash for the security. The buyer thinks he's getting a good value and that the price will rise. The seller believes the price is going to fall or is already falling. The low represents the limit of the strength of the bears for the day.

As with the high of the day, the low has meaning only in the context of its relationship to other parts of the price bar and the bars that precede it. When the low is lower than the open, it probably means that some fresh news has come out after the opening bell that offsets any buy-on-open orders or initial sentiment. When the close is at the low, it means that bad news or negative sentiment ruled for the day. The bears had strong control at the close and they were committed.

You can judge the power of fresh negative news by checking whether it inspired traders to close the day at or near the low, but also whether the low for the day is lower than it was the day before.

The range

The difference between the high and the low is called the *range*. The position of the close within the range can tell you whether the buyers or sellers were in control that day, and also how committed they were to pushing the price. The closer the close is to one extremity or the other, the greater the control and commitment that one side (the bears or bulls) had.

Look at the example of Air New Zealand trading in Figure 4-4. On Days 4 and 5 the close was at the highs. This signifies that the buyers were strongly in control and fully committed. But on Day 6 the close was mid-range — neither the buyers nor sellers had control of Air New Zealand when the market closed, and neither side showed any commitment. This serves as a signal to take profits or keep a close eye on this stock.

Traders should also look at how the range expands and contracts as the trend develops. The perfect scenario is to see the range continually getting bigger as the trend develops. This suggests that the side that is pushing the market is becoming increasingly eager. Contracting range is a sign that either the buyers or sellers are becoming less eager and suggests that the trend may be about to fail.

In Figure 4-4, Days 3, 4 and 5 are good examples of *up-days*, where the buyers are becoming increasingly keen and are driving Air New Zealand higher as the chart develops. Almost no-one is selling at close because they expect the price to go higher again the next day.

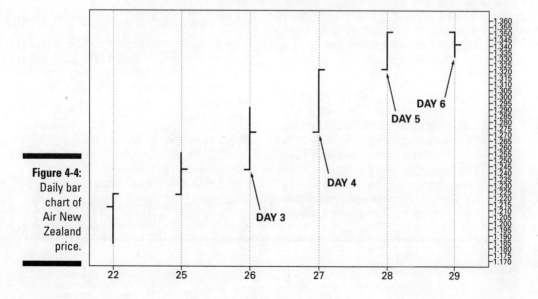

Figure 4-4: Daily bar chart of Air New Zealand price.

Current events: Buy on the rumour, sell on the news

New highs and lows are often the seed of a new trend, and usually arise directly from a specific piece of news. Fresh news that causes a new high or a new low is an *event*. The risk that a new high or low will ensue from the news is *event risk*. It may seem odd, but most events are not surprises, but rather scheduled, such as

- News or a rumour pertaining to the security itself, such as a company's earnings announcement
- Market-related events such as the date when options expire or the end of a calendar or tax period
- Scheduled releases (such as a central bank's interest rate statement or any of a dozen economic reports).

Traders treat forecasts prepared by economists and analysts as though the event had already happened precisely as predicted. In other words, they 'build in' the forecast to the price. This is why you often see a new high *before* the actual event. This practice is named *buy on the rumour*, where *rumour* refers to the forecast. (Sometimes, of course, traders buy on real rumours, which are then either confirmed or denied.)

The rest of the phrase is *sell on the news*. The news is the event itself. You sometimes get the seeming paradox of a price reaching a new high *before* the event and falling to a new low immediately *after* the event, even when the news matches the forecast. The new low comes about because the early birds are taking profit on the upmove that they themselves engineered. The new low is usually short-lived. After all, the forecast was for good news and the good news occurred, so the news was properly built in and the new high is the appropriate price. If the news is hugely better than forecast, though, traders don't take profit because better-than-expected news draws in new players and sends the price higher still. Then the early birds are positioned to make even better profits. Should the news fail to match expectations, traders and investors alike sell, and the dip may turn into a longer-lasting price drop. Either way, to 'buy on the rumour' pays off for the short-term trader who keeps his finger on the trigger. Evaluating forecasts and being mentally ready to buy or sell at the moment of impact of the news is a difficult and risky business. It's no wonder risk-averse traders get out of the market altogether around scheduled event dates.

Event risk also refers to unexpected developments:

- Acts of terrorism and war
- Natural disasters
- Correlation of a stock to the performance of the major indices. Even if your stock is doing well, for example, it can open down from the close the night before as a side-effect of a drop in the index or sector to which it belongs
- Previous technical levels, such as a round number (like 10,000 on the Bombay Stock Exchange SENSEX index) or a historic high or low. We discuss historic levels in Chapter 14.

But look at Day 6. The close is *below* yesterday's close! On Day 6 the characteristics of Air New Zealand changed. The sellers are now keener than buyers and have driven prices lower. Sometimes this may serve as a warning to traders that the previous trend may be about to end and that they should consider taking profits or at least keep a very close eye on this market. (Note that in this case the stock went lower during the day than it closed; there's still some confidence in the general upward trend of the last few days.) Also note that you don't need to look to the news to confirm what the charts are telling you. Without any idea of the fundamentals that may be driving this change in sentiment, a technical trader knows that it's time to keep a close eye on this stock.

Figure 4-4 shows that from Days 2 to 4 the range was expanding. The buyers were becoming increasingly eager — this is a healthy trend. But at Day 5 the range contracted — the buyers were not so eager. Alarm bells started going off in some technical analysts' heads: Is this trend still healthy; are the buyers still eager and committed to pushing this trend to higher levels? Day 6 shows a further large contraction in the range. The technical analysts are now hearing: 'Warning, warning, the trend no longer looks healthy — time to take action'.

Putting It All Together: Using Bars to Identify Trends

In the previous sections, you interpreted market sentiment on a particular day from the relationship of the price bar components to one another largely *within* a single bar. When you look at the components *across* a series of bars, you get even more information. In fact, you get so much information that you risk information overload. Interpretation — figuring out supply and demand from the bars — becomes a lot more complex.

You may feel overwhelmed when you first start looking at bar charts, and say 'No way does this thing make sense!' And some charts or parts of a chart are such a chaotic mess that no regularity or pattern exists at all. But a security whose price jumps around all over the place without rhyme or reason would soon run out of people to trade it. As we discuss in Chapter 2, the law of supply and demand states that for every security, there's some price that persuades suppliers to part with it or buyers to purchase it. After a price is established through the execution of a real cash trade, traders have a baseline from which to track prices. *Any* transaction may occur at a random price, but not *every* transaction can occur randomly, or the market in that security would collapse.

Reading charts is based on the central observation that the price bar embodies all the supply-demand dynamics of the day. You can deduce from there that a series of bars on a chart shows the evolution of the supply-demand dynamics over time. Some percentage of the time, the evolution is visible in the form of a trend. (What percentage of time any particular security spends in trended mode is addressed in Chapter 1.) In the following sections, we describe how to use combinations of bars to help identify a trend.

Identifying an uptrend

The textbook-perfect *uptrend* is a series of up-day price bars (close higher than the close yesterday) that have higher highs *and* higher lows in a majority of the bars.

When the high today is higher than the high yesterday or higher than the high of the past few days, you have a *higher high*. A series of higher highs often signals that the market is feeling enthusiastic about the security. But you usually don't know at the time whether a new high or a small series of new highs is the beginning of a trend.

You need to qualify the higher high as truly indicating that a trend may be forming. What you want is an additional confirming condition — you can specify that you must also have *higher lows*.

Now you have two pieces of evidence that bulls outnumber bears. A series of higher highs together with higher lows hints that a trend is forming. After two days, you aren't yet sure what's happening, but you're starting to get excited. After all, your goal in identifying a trend is to buy near the beginning of the trend. As we describe in Chapter 1, your key assumption is that a trend, after it's formed, will continue. If you have two higher highs with two higher lows, can you assume that Day 3 will also deliver a higher high and a higher low?

Not necessarily. Alas, prices don't move in straight lines. You often see a series of two or three higher highs interrupted by one or two lower highs. This happens for several reasons:

- Traders already in the security are taking an early profit.
- The market is reconsidering whether the new high is really justified.
- The higher highs were just a random accident.

You seldom see an unbroken series of higher highs on every single day. For example, go back to Figure 4-2, which shows a series of days on which the close is higher than the close the day before. At the same time, the price is making a fresh high nearly every day, but not every day without fail. See the bar marked 'Day 4'; on that day, the close was higher than the open and the low was higher than the day before, but the high of the day was not higher than the day before.

What does that mean? Remember, you don't know yet what Day 5 is going to bring at the time you're looking this chart.

Most analysts may tell you not to worry about this particular configuration of bars. It's an uptrend, all right, and you know this because you have an unbroken series of higher *lows*. Day 4 is a disappointment — it doesn't deliver a higher high — but the low is higher than all the previous lows. By considering the additional factor of higher lows, you confirm that the probability of getting a higher high and a higher close on Day 5 is pretty good.

An uptrend is defined as a series of higher highs accompanied by higher lows. *Higher highs* refers to visible peaks, not a higher high every single day.

Identifying a downtrend

The textbook definition of a *downtrend* is a series of down-day bars (close lower than yesterday) characterised by lower lows and lower highs in a preponderance of the bars.

Go back and look at the down-days in Figure 4-3. After the first day, each of these bars has a close lower than the close the day before. Day 3 has the same high as the day before, but a lower low. On Day 3 you're starting to get the idea that this may be the beginning of a downtrend.

When identifying a downtrend, a series of lower highs is a good confirming indicator to the series of lower lows. The same psychology applies as when an uptrend starts, only in reverse. Sellers see that new lows are occurring — somebody must know something negative about the security. Traders aren't willing to hold a falling asset, and they unload it at ever-lower prices. Meanwhile, fans of the security can't give it support at yesterday's low — selling pressure is too great.

But Wait . . . Nothing Is That Simple

A trend has two identifiers — a series of higher highs (or lower lows) and a series of up-days (or down-days). There is no hard-and-fast rule on which identifier is more important. Traditional technical analysis emphasises that you need higher lows to confirm the higher highs in an uptrend, but candlestick analysis, which we cover in Chapter 6, says that the position of the close trumps every other factor, including a new high or low.

In practice, you find that the weight you place on the position of the close is a direct function of how far out in time you want to extend your forecast. Traditional bar chart reading generally has a longer forecasting time frame in mind than candlestick chart reading, and a longer expected holding period over which you plan to own the security. In traditional bar analysis, you may accept two, three or even more days of *countervailing bars* (bars that don't confirm the trend). In candlestick analysis, you may accept only one day or none because the trading style associated with candlestick analysis is very short term.

Bar components influence the next bar

Most of the time, a series of higher highs with higher lows or a series of lower lows with lower highs does mean that a trend is emerging, even if the close is not yet in the right position to confirm it. Higher closes are the logical outcome of new highs if they persist in a series, just as lower closes are the outcome of a series of lower lows. The mind of the market isn't hard to read. Market players start wondering why new highs or lows are occurring. They know a new high or a new low can occur only if other traders decide to buy or sell there — so what do they know that the rest of us don't know? New highs and lows arouse emotions:

- ✔ A new high or low makes market participants nervous. A sufficiently large number of new highs triggers the greed instinct — better buy now so you don't miss out, even if you don't have a reason for new highs to be occurring. The result is a higher close as buyers pile in near the end of the day.
- ✔ New lows scare just enough traders that they sell their positions, even in the absence of any fresh news that would justify the selling. Sellers are unwilling to hold a falling asset and sell near the end of the day, causing a lower close.

But sometimes it's the other way around — you get a series of up-days without getting a series of higher highs. In other words, the close today is higher than the close yesterday, but the high today isn't higher than the high yesterday. Pay attention anyway because new highs may start to appear. These new highs may happen solely because so many people are aware of the meaning of up-days and down-days. In other words, so many people look at technical indicators — and a series of up-days or down-days is a basic indicator — that they *anticipate* higher highs or lower lows. By acting on that expectation — buying or selling ahead of the actual appearance of a higher high or lower low — they make it happen. This is called a 'self-fulfilling prophecy'.

Understanding relativity

The textbook uptrend is a series of up-day price bars (close higher than yesterday) that have higher highs *and* higher lows in a preponderance of the bars. A downtrend is a series of down-day bars characterised by lower lows and lower highs in most of the bars. But markets are not neat and tidy, and not every bar is going to qualify on all three criteria.

The chart shown in Figure 4-5 depicts an uptrend — even though not every bar qualifies as belonging to an uptrend. You see lower lows as well as several days on which the bar is a down-day. Down-days are coloured black, and up-days are grey. This figure demonstrates two points where textbook definitions of trends are relative.

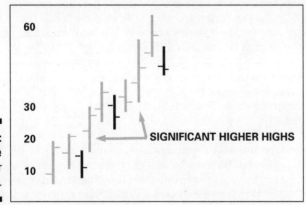

Figure 4-5:
Relative
higher
highs.

SIGNIFICANT HIGHER HIGHS

✔ **Significance:** In Figure 4-5, not every high is higher than the day before, but every significant high is higher than the highs that came before.

What is a 'significant' high? Simply put, you determine the answer to that question. You can judge significance by eyeing the chart, or you can specify rules, such as 'a significant high is one that is x per cent higher than the average of the past y highs'. You can use software to develop a 'filter' that defines criteria like a 'significant high'. In Figure 4-5, two significant higher highs stand out. They each represent a 50 per cent gain from the previous up-day high.

If you use charting software to look at charts, turn on the feature that lets you visually differentiate between up-days and down-days. Some traders make up-days green and down-days red. It takes no practice to see where a trend is interrupted by bars that don't qualify.

✔ **Preponderance:** In addition to revealing that some bars in an uptrend can be net down-days, Figure 4-5 illustrates that not every high in an uptrend has to be higher than the one before. You just need to identify a preponderance of higher highs and a preponderance of higher lows. What is a preponderance? Again, that's your call. You can eyeball it, or use software to develop a precise definition and back-test it on historical data. For example, a preponderance of higher highs may mean a simple majority, say six of ten bars, accompanied by six of ten higher lows.

Your eyes can deceive you

A series of price bars isn't always trended, of course, but sometimes you can misinterpret what you're seeing if you aren't careful. You may see a series of higher highs but forget to make sure that each bar has a higher low and is an up-day, or you see a series of lower lows but forget to check that the high is lower or that the bars are all down-days.

You may see a price series where every day brings a new high but every day also brings a close lower than the day before and a low that is lower than the lows on preceding days. This situation is shown in Figure 4-6. What does such a chart mean?

Figure 4-6 reminds you that it's not enough to have a series of higher highs in an uptrend — you also have to have higher lows. This set of bars is a series of down-days (the close is lower than the close the day before). It's hard to swallow, but this figure displays a downtrend emerging at the third bar. Your eye may want to see an uptrend, but when you look more closely and analyse the bars for all three conditions, you have only one uptrend condition (higher highs) that is more than offset by the two downtrend conditions (down-days and lower lows). Appearances can be deceiving.

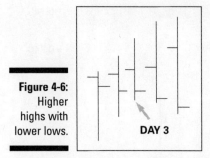

Figure 4-6:
Higher
highs with
lower lows.

DAY 3

You may never know for sure why such a strange series of bars develops.

✔ Some traders are going to exit at the end of the day no matter what (we describe the exit on close strategy earlier in the chapter). This is a risk management decision, not a commentary on the price.

✔ Some group in the market wants to see this security make higher highs, and so they buy near the highs, hoping that a new high will 'create demand', as in an auction. Such buyers may be insiders or option traders trying to trigger a specific price level.

✔ A trader may be trying to test or support a resistance line (which we describe in Chapter 8).

Bar-reading doesn't always work

Some price series are unreadable. You can't figure out what the market is thinking because the market is changing its mind just about every other day. Figure 4-7 is such a chart (the Swiss franc). The series of grey up-days is a minor uptrend and the following series of black down-days is a minor downtrend — but then things fall apart. You see higher highs followed by lower lows and no consistency in the placement of the close (up-day or down-day).

What do you do in a case like this? Nothing — at least not anything based on interpretation of the bars. When bars are in a chaotic mess like this, the probability of picking the right direction (up or down) is very low. You'd just be guessing. And although you have to accept imperfection and a certain amount of ambiguity in bar chart analysis, the whole purpose of charting and the mathematical approaches to technical analysis is to obtain a higher probability of making the right decision. Guessing defeats the purpose.

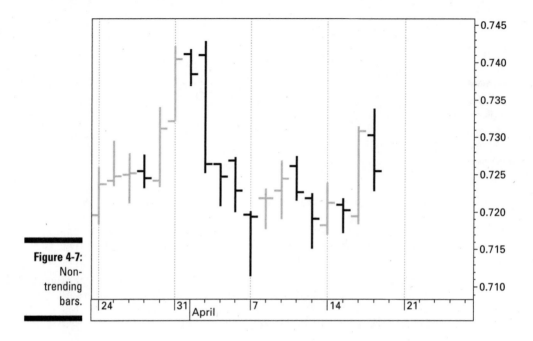

Figure 4-7:
Non-
trending
bars.

Zooming Out and Zooming In

Throughout this book, we refer to the price bar and to bar charts as generally containing daily data. In practice, you find that looking at data in a different time frame is often useful when you're facing a trading decision. You can zoom out to a higher time frame (such as weekly) or zoom in to a shorter time frame (hourly).

You can't tell by looking at a chart what time frame the bars represent because the bar components and trends work the same way no matter what time frame you select, whether it's a series of weekly bars or of 15-minutes bars. If a chart isn't labelled, you can usually assume that the bars are daily bars. No matter what time frame you select, everything we've written about the price bar and its components is valid.

Using daily data

If you're a novice at charting, start with the daily price bar. Daily data is widely available and free or cheap. A surprising number of highly computer-literate people choose to get their raw data from the public domain (like a free Web site or the newspaper) and type it into their database themselves. Doing so gives them a 'feel' for the information, even though an automatic download from a data service would take a lot less time at little cost. That some traders like to work with raw data is a tidbit of market lore that should remind you of the importance of the components of the price bar. You become very familiar with the data when you're typing it into your database by hand or drawing it by hand on a chart with mouse or pencil. You're less likely to miss the relationship of today's open to yesterday's close, for example. Daily data is preferable also because

- ✔ Most of the commentary in newspapers, magazines and Web sites refers to daily bars. It's the 'base case'.
- ✔ Embracing daily price bars puts you on the same page with the majority of people in the market.
- ✔ Even people who use intra-day data (such as hourly bars) also look at the daily price bars.

Zooming out

You can display prices in a weekly or monthly format. Quarterly and annual charts are seen less often. The universality of standard bar notation isn't hard to understand — after all, a week has an opening price (the first trade on Monday morning) and a closing price (the last trade on Friday afternoon), with a high and a low somewhere in between. And the weekly close is a summary of the sentiment of the majority of market participants for the week, just as the daily closing price summarises sentiment for the day.

You can often see trends and patterns over longer time frames that are hard to see on a daily chart. If you're using charting software, make a habit of toggling the chart from a daily time frame to the weekly and monthly time frames, and see whether anything pops out at you. In addition, you can use, say, a weekly chart to confirm a new trend that you discover on a daily chart.

Zooming in

Many traders today also track smaller time intervals. With the advent of inexpensive data delivered online, the number of people using intra-day data has positively exploded.

Getting the data

Live real-time data used to be too expensive for the little guy and only big firms could afford to buy it for their professional traders. Now anyone can buy it for a few hundred dollars a month. If you don't mind 10 or 15 minutes of delay, you can get intra-day price bars for free on many Web sites. If you type **equity price data** into a search engine, you'll get over 700,000 entries, including brokers who can give you free live data in return for your opening an account. By comparison, typing **commodity price data** yields over 300,000 entries. The quality of the data and the reliability of transmission vary, so choose carefully.

When you subscribe to a data service, you can organise intra-day data in any interval you like — 5-minute bars, 15-minute bars, 60-minute bars and so on. You could have 7-minute bars or 73-minute bars if you really wanted to. The notation is the same as in daily bars, though. The opening price is the price of the first trade during the period, the closing price is the last trade done during the period and so on.

Technical analysis writers are sensitive to the increased use of intra-day data and today usually speak of *periods* rather than *days*. Changing the vocabulary has the unfortunate effect of making some technical analysis writing sound formal or pompous — but it's more accurate.

Choosing an interval

If you start using intra-day price bars, how do you select the interval? It's hard to find anyone willing to give you advice on this point. Leading data suppliers, such as MarketCast or eSignal, offer standard intervals of 1, 3, 5, 10, 13, 15, 30 and 60 minutes, as well as daily, weekly, monthly or custom intervals of your choice. (You have to wonder why users told eSignal they wanted the 13-minute interval, though.)

The only logical way to select an interval is to try them all on your favourite security and see how they look. Remember, bar reading is a visual art. You want an interval that accurately represents activity in the security and suits your needs at the same time. If you're trading an equity that has trading volume of only 1000 shares during the day and all of that is done in five trades, spacing your bars at 3-minute or 15-minute intervals is silly. You'll get a chart that is mostly blank, and every trade will look like it gapped from the one before. For an explanation of gaps, see Chapter 5.

If you're watching heavily traded Telstra, though, you'll get a complete bar for every 1-minute interval, and each bar will contain the open, high, low and close of that minute. This chart will have few gaps. Gaps are important. Be careful not to sabotage your analysis by selecting a time frame that's out of sync with the normal flow of trading in the selected security.

The key to selecting the right interval is the liquidity of the security you're trading. *Liquidity* refers to potential volume in this context — kind of like a group of buyers waiting around for their chance to bat, meaning a price that pleases them, with an opposing group of sellers willing to bowl cricket balls until somebody plays a shot. A liquid security has lots of buyers and sellers, with some of them active at all times. Liquidity results in real trades that are measured as 'volume'. A security with only one or two interested parties is not liquid, as you may have discovered if you ever tried to sell a thinly traded penny stock.

Select intra-day bar intervals that are proportional to the minimum volume of the security being charted.

How do you judge what is proportional? You match the interval to your purpose. If you're trading on a daily time frame in which you make two decisions per day, one to buy and one to sell, you want to see bars that have enough substance to convey real information. If a 1-minute or 3-minute bar chart produces just a dot, you need to increase the interval. If 15-minute bars are big enough to read, perhaps you can stop there. But try the 30-minute and 60-minute bars while you're at it. You may like them better.

Selecting the interval to use in displaying bars is subjective. If you can't make up your mind which one you like, do some research. If you type **intra-day trading** into a search engine, you'll get over 170,000 hits. You can quickly discover which time frame is popular for each class and type of security. You want to look at what others are looking at, anyway, because part of the art of technical analysis is reading the mind of the market.

Chapter 5

Reading Special Bar Combinations: Small Patterns

The price bar is the basic building block of technical analysis, and a series of price bars on a chart is your basic workspace. (For the basics of the price bar, see Chapter 4.) Charts contain endless combinations of bar configurations, and you can't possibly memorise all the combinations and permutations. Being able to identify a few special cases, however, is useful because you see these cases often enough that they serve as signposts to guide your interpretation of what the price is going to do next.

'Special bars' are a small series of two to five bars — called *combinations* or *configurations* — that stand out on a chart. You can see them immediately, and so can everyone else. Over the years, traders have interpreted these special bar combinations in particular ways. Knowing how other market participants feel towards specific bar configurations helps you make your own trading decisions. As a general rule, you want to go with the flow — trade with the conventional wisdom about the meaning of the configurations. If you're a very short-term trader (3 to 5 days), a good time frame to trade when you're new to technical analysis, the special-case configurations literally tell you how to trade. If you're a longer-term trend trader, the earlier you use these configurations to identify a new trend, continuation of the trend or the end of an existing trend, the more profit you make.

Finding Clues to Trader Sentiment

You use price bar combinations to determine whether your security is starting a trend, staying on a trend or losing its grip on the trend. The start of a new trend is sometimes the end of an old one, called a *reversal*.

Tick and bar placement

In Chapter 4, we define an *uptrend* as a series of bars featuring higher highs together with higher lows, and a *downtrend* as a series of lower lows together with lower highs. An uptrend also features bars that have a close higher than the day before — up-days. A downtrend contains mostly down-days (close lower than the day before). A fourth factor is whether the close is above the open (or below the open in the case of a downtrend).

You hardly ever see a series of bars where every single one of these factors confirms the trend. Because prices never move entirely in a straight line, you have to accept that some bars in a trend don't fall into line with all the trend criteria. You may have one or two bars in an uptrend that don't have higher highs or a few bars where the close is lower than the day before. Such variations in *tick placement* (the small horizontal dash marking the open and close) and *bar placement* (position of a price bar relative to the bars that precede it) are normal in even the best-behaved trend.

Some bars are just a little out of line, but sometimes you see bars that really stand out. It takes almost no practice at all to differentiate ordinary out-of-line bars from special configurations that technical traders consider to be associated with specific interpretations.

In a series of three bars, each having four components, you can get any one of 2,463 permutations of configuration. When you specify joint conditions, such as higher high together with higher low, the number of combinations reaches into the millions, and that's just with three bars! So, when you see the special cases, you know you've got a valuable clue to upcoming price behaviour.

The interpretation guidelines aren't 100 per cent right at all times. In fact, nobody can tell you even roughly what percentage of the time the standard interpretation is correct, because it may be correct all the time in one security but only 10 per cent of the time in another, or correct 75 per cent of the time in one year but never correct in another. The lack of statistically verified and perfectly reliable guidelines is frustrating and annoying to all technical traders and especially beginners, but remember, you're seeking meaningful information about crowd psychology from an excess of evidence.

A bar component or even the placement of the entire bar can be random. Random highs and lows, and even a few random bars, are caused by a 'greater fool' making a trade at a sucker price or a whole batch of traders mistakenly believing a false rumour. Often you never know the reason for some weird bar configuration. Some securities have a high number of known configurations, and some have a high number of out-of-whack (meaningless) configurations. The regularity (or lack of regularity) is a function of the crowd that trades each security, and should be a consideration when you're choosing what securities to trade.

Types of configurations

When you spot a special configuration in a small series of bars, you're looking for one of two things — the pattern either confirms the trend or signals that the trend is at risk of ending. Watch for the following:

- **Continuation patterns:** The trend is continuing. The direction and pace of the trend are about the same as they were before. Relax. The more confirmation you can get, the safer you feel. You see hard evidence of the trend continuing, such as a preponderance of higher highs and higher lows marking bullish sentiment on the part of the trading crowd, even though perhaps some other qualifying factor isn't present.

- **Reversal patterns:** The trend is switching direction. When the trend shifts from down to up or up to down, the configuration of the bar components and their placement across a series of price bars often shouts 'The trend is changing' from the rooftop. Listen up. If you have a position in the security, a reversal pattern tells you to exit. If you hold on to the position anyway, your risk of loss is much higher.

  A reversal pattern is not only a warning to exit when you're invested in the security, it's also advance notice that a good entry place may be coming up. For example, when a downtrend ends, you may see one of the very specific reversal patterns that is a reliable precursor to a buy signal. You can get ready to enter the upcoming uptrend.

All the special bars and configurations we discuss in this chapter are either confirmation or reversal patterns.

Trading range

The *daily trading range* is the difference between the high and the low of the day. It measures the maximum distance that the price travelled for that period. You can also say that the range defines the emotional extremes of the day:

- If you have a bar with a small range in a sea of larger bars, the market is indecisive and not very eager. Indecisiveness isn't the same thing as indifference. Indecisiveness can be dangerous — nobody wanted to buy at a higher high, so perhaps buyers are getting tired of that security at current prices. A change in sentiment may be brewing, such as deceleration in a price rise that precedes the end of the trend.

- When it's one very large bar in a sea of smaller ones, pay close attention. Something did happen. Traders are willing to pay a *lot* more for a rising security, or they want to dump a falling one so badly that they'll accept an abnormally low price.

In every instance of special bars in this chapter, the size of the daily high-low range is a key factor. (For more information on how ranges work, refer to Chapter 4.)

Concerning Common Special Bars

Use logic and common sense when you're looking at special bars. Keep it simple. The simplest explanation, like the explanations of what buyers and sellers might be thinking that we give in Chapter 4 and in this chapter, are the likeliest ones. In other words, don't find a zebra when you're looking at a horse.

Closing on a high note

It's wildly bullish when the price closes at the high over several days. A series of *closes at the high* — and its downtrending counterpart, *closes at the low* — indicate that a new trend may be starting or the existing trend is likely to continue. In Figure 5-1, configuration A illustrates close at the high. The price has closed at the high of the day for three days running, and the third bar is much longer than the others, which means the high-low range is wider than the previous two days. So, what's happening?

The first two bars show the close at the high at about the same level. On the second bar, the low of the day was lower than the low the day before, meaning that sellers came out of the woodwork. But the bulls fought back, buying more and more, so that the close was at a fresh high on that second day. The close at the high for a second day trumps the lower low, and Day 3 delivers a whopping gain — and a third close at the high. By now you may be ready to bet the house on this configuration. But beware! Anyone who got in early on Day 1 or Day 2 may be tempted to cash out after seeing the huge gain on Day 3.

A big gain is often followed by *profit-taking* by active traders who get in a move early. Three days isn't long enough to call this configuration a *trend,* so we call it a *move.* It doesn't matter whether the closes at the high are occurring at the start of a trend or while the trend is in progress — a fat gain always inspires short-term traders to take profit. Profit-taking doesn't change a trend, but can put a dent in the performance of the bar the next day. You may see a lower high or a lower close, which can be very discouraging when you're trying to identify a new trend. It's also annoying to put on a new position in a promising move — three higher highs and three closes at the high — only to take a paper loss on your first day. It's Day 4 of the move, but Day 1 for your position. If you're using bar-reading alone to make trading decisions, stick with the trade (while cursing short-term traders), but also reconsider where you placed your stop-loss order.

You can use your imagination (or turn the book upside down) to envision the parallel configuration — closes at the low. As you may expect, a series of closes at the low implies that a downtrend is forming or worsening.

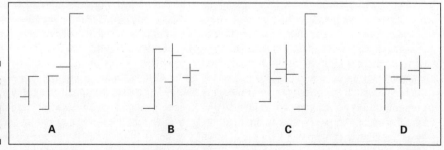

Figure 5-1:
Common special bars.

A   B   C   D

Spending the day inside

Configuration B in Figure 5-1 shows the inside day. An *inside day* refers to a price bar that meets two criteria:

- ✔ The high is lower than the previous day's high.
- ✔ The low is higher than the previous day's low.

An inside day is a bar 'inside' the previous day's high-low range and usually the average high-low range of the past few days. It reflects indecision. Buyers didn't feel strongly enough about this security to buy more. Sellers weren't particularly inspired to sell, either. The inside day doesn't suggest what's going to happen the following day. But it does warn that the market is starting to reconsider what it feels about this security.

Testing folklore

An inside day signals that the market is having second thoughts about a security. Some analysts think that an inside day generally implies a continuation of the existing trend. Others, notably folks who use candlestick charting (see Chapter 6), see an inside day (named a *harami*) as a warning of a possible trend reversal. Which interpretation is correct?

No-one can give you a definitive answer. The Trading Systems Analysis Group (or TSAGroup, online at www.tsagroup.com) examined the data of 60 equities over four years — over 60,000 price bars — and found 2,000 instances of inside days. About half the time in an existing uptrend, the bar after an inside day delivered a higher high (a continuation) and about half the time it didn't. For existing downtrends, the percentage was the same — about half the time the inside day was followed the next day by a lower low (a continuation). (Actually, there was a tendency to continue the existing trend on the day after the inside day — a higher high in an uptrend and a lower low in a downtrend — but it was so small as to be right on the edge of the margin of error.)

So, is the inside day a useless indicator? No. It signals that sentiment may be ready to change. Also, keep in mind that the TSAGroup study is limited to the exact question asked — what happened the next day? This leaves the door open to consider what happened two days later, or three days. Or you can test the inside day over a long period of time, like 20 years — what percentage of inside days correctly predicted a continuation? Third, you can rephrase the test to cover a class of securities, say equities in the ASX 200 index or interest rate futures. You may find that in the specific security or class of securities that you're following, traders tend to believe that the inside day means continuation rather than reversal. If you can discover what they think, you have a clue to their behaviour.

Getting outside for the day

Configuration C in Figure 5-1 is the outside day. On an *outside day,* the high-low range of the bar is outside the range of the preceding bar (the current bar engulfs the previous bar). The open and close ticks can appear anywhere on the outside day bar, but two variations stand out:

- **The open is at the low and the close is at the high.** This configuration suggests that something new has happened to inspire bullish buying right up to the end of the day.

- **The open is at the high and the close is at the low.** You can deduce the opposite supply-demand setup here. Sentiment turned bearish and sellers overwhelmed buyers, right to the end of the day.

Although the size of an outside day bar gets your attention, its appearance alone doesn't tell you much. After considering where the open and close are located on the bar, take a look at what else is going on in the market, especially the configuration of the preceding bars:

- **No trend exists:** The outside day alerts you to a possible trend beginning.

- **A trend is in place:** The outside day may suggest a reversal or a continuation, depending on where the open and close are and which direction the security is trending. The outside day has a higher high by definition, but a higher close as well implies continuation in an uptrend and reversal in a downtrend, especially if the close is exactly at the high. This signifies control and commitment from the buyers. Similarly, the outside day has a lower low by definition, so it confirms continuation in a downtrend, especially if the close is at the low, signifying control and commitment from the sellers.

Finding the close at the open

Configuration D in Figure 5-1 shows a series of bars where the close is at or near the open. *Close-at-open* ordinarily occurs near the centre of the daily price range, not at the high or the low. As you can guess, a close at or near the open reflects indecision among market participants. Trader opinion is divided as to whether this bar generally signifies a continuation or reversal pattern. Consider it a clue to look at what else is going on, such as trading volume.

In specific instances, the interpretive process gets a bit more definite: When the open and close are at (or almost at) the same price, *and* they're at the high or low of the day, you have a greater chance of determining whether the trend will continue or reverse. Which way the cookie crumbles depends on what was happening before:

- ✔ **In an uptrend:** If the open and close are near the high, look for the uptrend to accelerate (continuation with gusto). If they are near the low, look for a reversal.

- ✔ **In a downtrend:** If the open and close are near the low, expect more of the same. If they are near the high, think about a reversal.

Understanding Spikes

If the inside day and the outside day are a little unusual, they probably don't look particularly odd. Their high-low ranges vary enough for you to detect a size change but they don't make your hair stand on end. Sometimes, though, the market delivers a price bar that looks like the market went crazy that day — the high or the low is very far away from the general trend of things and the bar itself is abnormally large (wide high-low range). Figure 5-2 shows two of these uncommon price bars, called spikes.

A *spike* is a bar that encompasses a much bigger high-low range than the bars immediately preceding it. Right about now, you're probably asking yourself, 'Is a spike meaningful to me?' The earth-shattering answer is . . . maybe.

In some cases, a spike turns out to be an anomaly. The top example in Figure 5-2 shows just such a case. The spike low suggests that some people panicked and were selling at such a high quantity and at such a frantic pace that the few buyers still around were able to buy at abnormally low prices. On this chart, the sellers panicked unnecessarily. The next day, the price resumed its uptrend and its same 'normal' high-low range. The spike was just an oddity — a random move. Maybe the sellers believed a rumour that other traders knew was false. (Or perhaps they were deliberately trying to break a support line, as we describe in Chapter 8.) You may never know why they panicked.

Even though price spikes *can* be an anomaly, you can't afford to ignore them. The spike may be a reaction to fresh news or perspective that has the potential to create a new trend. Or it may be a message that sentiment has changed dramatically.

The bottom spike example in Figure 5-2 is a key reversal because on the next few days, the price proceeded to make lower highs and lower lows.

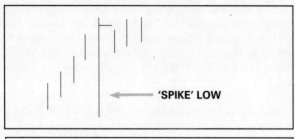

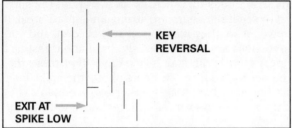

Figure 5-2:
Uncommon
special
bars.

This spike in the size of the daily high-low range was a warning of a reversal. *Key reversals* can be ordinary bars and aren't always spikes, but when you see a spike, always ask yourself whether it may mark a reversal.

You may have noticed that the discussion on spikes, to this point, has focused on the price bars that *follow* the spike. The reason? You seldom know whether a spike is random or meaningful on the day that it happens. Only hindsight can tell you that.

Though hindsight has the final say on the meaning of a spike, you can still use spikes for immediate analytical purposes:

✔ **Investigate the environment:** Sometimes you *do* know when a spike is a key reversal because you can determine what shock caused it and your judgment in interpreting the news or event is sound.

✔ **Trust the close:** As a general rule, you're safe assuming that the close is the most important part of the bar because it sums up the sentiment for the day. To see the usefulness of the close, take a look at the two examples in Figure 5-2:

• **Continuation spike:** The close is near the high. The wider high-low range and the lower low are a worry, to be sure, but the position of the close near the high trumps those worries.

• **Key reversal day:** The close is near the low. Now you have three worries — a lower low, an abnormally big bar and a close near the low.

A key reversal bar is also called a swing bar, although not all swing bars are spikes. A *swing bar* is any bar that is the final and lowest low in a series of lower lows or the final and highest high in a series of higher highs, as in the bottom chart in Figure 5-2. You can see a spike bar at the end of the day after the close, but you can't identify it as a swing bar until after two additional closes.

A conservative trading tactic is to order your broker to sell the security if the price falls below the low of the spike day over the next two or three days. Everybody who trades this security knows about the spike low and will be watching to see if the bears are strong enough to break the level and take the price lower. If so, they plan to sell at that level, and you should, too. In an upmove, bulls are often curiously timid about testing a spike high. The bar following a spike is often an inside day. Other times the following bar has a new higher high only a few cents above the spike high and a close lower than the spike bar close. Neither bar is helpful. They're simply inconclusive and you have to wait for additional evidence to get guidance on how to trade.

Grasping Gaps

A gap is one of the most important of the special bar configurations. A *gap* is a major, visible discontinuity between two price bars on a chart. Because every bar encompasses all the transactions made during a specific period, a gap marks the absence of any transactions at the prices covered by the gap. Check out the gap in Figure 5-3.

The gap is a void — no demand if there was supply and no supply if there was demand, at least not at those prices. Prices had to shift considerably in order for supply and demand to meet again and for both buyers and sellers to be satisfied. On daily charts, a gap is initially seen when the opening price today diverges dramatically from yesterday's high or low, although you can also see gaps between bars on intraday charts.

You can *identify* a gap at the open but you can't *measure* a gap until the day's trading is over. Then you measure it from yesterday's high to today's low (for an upside gap) or from yesterday's low to today's high (for a downside gap). The gap is between the bars, not between the opens and closes. If the security opens on a gap but then the gap is filled during the day, the gap doesn't show up on a daily chart. The same thing is true if a security gaps during the day on an hourly chart — the daily bar doesn't show it.

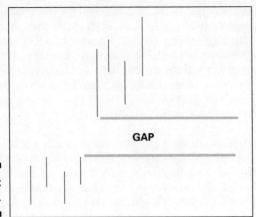

GAP

Figure 5-3:
Price gap.

Gaps are often the result of positive or negative news, like earnings or some other event, whether true or invented (rumours). Events are the source of most key price moves, including trends, whether starting or stopping. Prices don't, on the whole, move randomly — traders have reasons, right or wrong, to buy and sell. Even the strongest trend can be broken by a piece of fresh news contrary to the trend direction. Authentically big news trumps the chart (nearly) every time.

The reason to read bars and to use technical analysis is to get an accurate assessment of whether news is big or merely ordinary. Some news is easy to interpret. News will start a new uptrend if it's wildly favourable or halt an uptrend dead in its tracks if it's wildly unfavourable. But much of the time, you don't know how to interpret news — and there's so much news! — until you see how the market treats it in the form of the bar on the chart. Traders often get the bit between their teeth and shrug off favourable or unfavourable news, until the 'balance of the news' starts to affect overall sentiment. That's why gaps are such a valuable pattern — you know instantly how the market is interpreting the news.

Consider how a gap develops. Blue Sky Mining stock closed on Monday at $5 per share. After the closing bell, it announces bad news — the bookkeeper embezzled several million dollars and ran off to Rio. Companies tend to wait, if they can, until after the market closes to deliver bad news. Presumably they hope that what looks just awful at 5 pm won't look so bad the next morning. However, in this case, the market is unforgiving and the next day, Blue Sky Mining opens 'gap down' at $3. Most people deduce that the opening gap down implies further price drops, and they proceed to sell — in droves.

The total gap for the day may not be $2, though. During the course of the day, Blue Sky Mining may trade as high as $4, making the net gap a $1 gap. If the price of Blue Sky Mining normally trades in a 65 cent range, meaning the average difference between the high and low of a given day is usually 65 cents, $1 is still a significant number — roughly 50 per cent higher than the normal trading range. Gaps are significant when they're proportionally large compared to the trading range (see the 'Kicking things off: Breakaway gaps' section later in this chapter).

Gaps occur on good news, too. If Blue Sky Mining announces a fabulous new copper strike, the opening price on the following day may be a gap up, like the one in Figure 5-3. You may deduce from this gap that some traders (including well-paid professional mining analysts) had a whole night to evaluate the news, and *they* bought the stock at the open, so you should buy it, too. The gap implies buyers anticipate the stock rising throughout the day from the opening price, and this is a bandwagon you want to jump on.

Gaps are, indeed, a wonderful trading opportunity if you can differentiate between a common gap and uncommon gaps. In the next sections, we describe the main types of gaps and how to use them.

Lacking opportunity: Common gaps

A *common gap* is one that appears out of nowhere for no particular reason (no fresh news). Common gaps can occur in trending and non-trending prices. If the price is trending, it fails to change the trend. If the price isn't trending, it fails to initiate a trend. Common gaps are generally insignificant.

What causes a common gap? Simple error. Common gaps often occur when liquidity is low, meaning few players are in the market. Some trader sees a price offered that's a gap away from the last price posted and decides to buy. The offer may have been a mistake, too, or the offering trader could be trying to break a trendline or have some other hidden agenda. But because the market doesn't have many participants and the fresh news is minor, if there's any at all, the effort fizzles.

Figure 5-4 shows a bar chart of Rio Tinto stock. You can see a common gap within a trading range at A. The power of the bears was not sufficient to break out of the trading range.

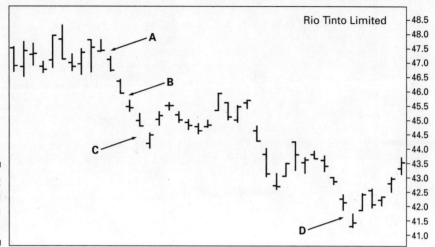

Rio Tinto Limited

Figure 5-4:
Identifying
common
gaps.

A common gap tends to have low volume on the gap day. If you see an opening gap, one way to evaluate whether to take it seriously is to consult volume. To consult volume, you need access to live data. If volume is low or normal, traders aren't jumping on the bandwagon and it's probably a common gap. If volume is abnormally high, traders are jumping on the bandwagon and the gap will probably lead to a big rise or fall in the coming days.

A security that normally has low volume tends to have more gaps than heavily traded securities. A low-volume security is described as *thinly traded,* meaning few market participants. Don't try to interpret gaps in thinly traded securities. These gaps are usually just common gaps and mean nothing at all.

Kicking things off: Breakaway gaps

A *breakaway gap* is an important event because it almost always marks the start of a new trend. Not only do you get the gap and a new trend, but you also get a major change in the appearance of the chart, such as a widening of the normal high-low daily trading range, an increase in day-to-day volatility, and much higher volume. All these changes occur because the breakaway gaps draw in new traders. A breakaway gap is event-driven, usually on some news about the security itself. Figure 5-5 illustrates a breakaway gap.

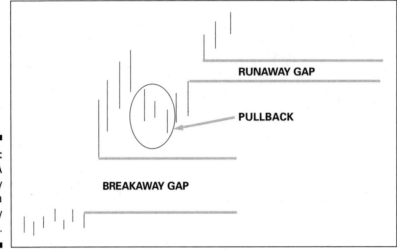

Figure 5-5:
A
breakaway
gap and a
runaway
gap.

To qualify as a breakaway gap, the gap has to

- ✔ **Be proportionately big to the usual trading range:** If the security normally trades in a 30 cent range between the daily high and low, and the gap is $1.50 between the preceding day's high and the gap-day open, you can instantly recognise that 'something big happened'.

- ✔ **Occur when a price is either slightly trending or moving sideways:** Nothing much is going on in the chart, and then wham! Fresh news creates new supply and demand conditions and ignites a trend.

You interpret a breakaway gap depending on whether it's upward or downward. Here's the bottom line:

- ✔ **Upside breakaway gap:** Good news creates demand. New buyers want to own the security and are willing to pay ever-higher prices to get it. Volume is noticeably higher than usual.

- ✔ **Downside breakaway gap:** Traders can't wait to get rid of their holdings and accept ever-lower prices to achieve that goal. Volume may or may not be abnormally high.

Continuing the push: Runaway gaps

A *runaway gap* occurs after a security is already moving in a trended way and fresh news comes out that promotes the existing trend. See the second gap in Figure 5-5. What's the difference between a breakaway gap and a runaway gap? A breakaway gap starts a trend. A runaway gap continues a trend. In both cases, buyers become enthusiastic and offer higher and higher prices. Sometimes there's fresh good news, sometimes traders make up fresh good news, and sometimes the buying frenzy is just feeding on itself in the absence of any news at all.

Notice that after making new highs following the breakaway gap, the price fell a little. A falling price after a dramatic move up is called a *pullback*. The security stops making new higher highs and actually makes some new lower lows, but doesn't go as far as the low on the breakaway day. A pullback after a dramatic price move represents profit-taking by the early birds and is very common. In fact, professionals count on the pullback to 'buy on the dip'. If they get really enthusiastic, re-entering professional traders often supply the energy for a runaway gap that follows a breakaway gap.

You can also see a runaway gap at B in Figure 5-4, the chart of Rio Tinto stock. The gap is produced by enthusiastic bears offering lower and lower prices and continues the downtrend.

Calling it quits: Exhaustion gaps

Exhaustion gaps occur at the end of a trend, signalling the party's over. Volume is usually low. What's exhausted is the news that propelled the security up in the first place and the energy of the early buyers. An exhaustion gap is usually followed by a reversal.

Here's how it works. Our example is an exhaustion gap at the end of an uptrend, but the mechanics are similar for a downtrend exhaustion gap as well. When you see that a gap up after an uptrend has been in place for a while *and* volume is low on that day, you have to wonder why the gap appeared. Volume tells you that buyers aren't pounding on the sellers' doors to get the security.

Presumably some greedy seller is out there, along with one last fool who's willing to pay a gap-worth more than the last trade. The buying frenzy is over, but the buyer doesn't realise it. He fails to see that there are a lot of offers and few bids. In short, everybody who wanted to buy has already done so. But somebody has to be the last buyer, and this particular one got taken to the cleaners — in the form of the gap. When he turns around and tries to unload his recent purchase, he finds no buyers, at least no buyers at a profit to him, and has to dump the security at a loss. The advent of online trading, where players can see and evaluate the tide of supply and demand, may put an end to exhaustion gaps.

You can distinguish an exhaustion gap from a runaway gap by looking at volume, which is usually low at an exhaustion gap. Anytime you see wild new highs (or lows) that aren't accompanied by wild new high volume, be suspicious of the staying power of the move. You can exit altogether or move up your stop-loss order.

Scoring big: Island reversals

Sometimes an exhaustion gap is followed immediately by a breakaway gap going in the other direction. This is how an island reversal forms. An *island reversal* is a single isolated price bar with a gap up on one side and a gap down on the other. It looks like an island in a sea of price bars and is almost always an unusually long bar — a wide high-low range.

Take a look at Figure 5-6. You can see a series of higher highs, including a minor gap up, but then the last buyers realise they're all alone on top of the mountain. They start to sell in a panic and are willing to accept a much lower price. Now the price takes off in the opposite direction on a breakaway gap. Remember, a breakaway gap tends to have high volume. It gets a little tricky watching volume. The island reversal bar has a higher high but is accompanied by low volume. This combination is the warning. The next day, as the breakaway gap develops, it has unusually high volume. You need live data to evaluate the new breakaway gap as it emerges at the open. High volume in combination with the downward gap is an indication that early selling is strong and prices later in the day aren't going to go back and fill that gap.

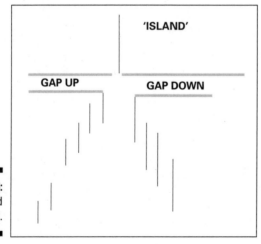

Figure 5-6:
Island
reversal.

Now consider this case in reverse order. Every man and his dog has been dumping the security and it's been gapping downward as it trends downward. This time the frenzy is a selling frenzy. At some point, one trader — let's call him Bruce — realises that the selling has gone on long enough and maybe the price is now too low, a bargain. Somebody out there will buy it from Bruce at this price. So he buys a little and offers it in the market at a gapping price — and wins. Turn Figure 5-6 upside down and that's how an island reversal at the bottom looks.

The chart tracking Rio Tinto stock in Figure 5-4, shows two island reversals at C and D. You can see how each bar looks like an island, all alone by itself. In this case the island reversals provided excellent opportunities to take profits on short trades for a short-term swing trader.

Examine price bars, and you'll see a lot of gaps. Seldom, though, will you see an island reversal. But when you do see it, you know what to do:

✔ An island reversal at the bottom: Buy.

✔ An island reversal at the top: Sell.

Despite its rarity, chances are good that a large number of other people will identify the makings of an island, too, and cause the expected reaction — the self-fulfilling prophecy aspect of technical analysis.

Although you can't know for a day or two after the second gap that you have an island reversal, many commentators speculate that an island is forming when they see the *first* gap. Close your ears when you hear market chatter like this. Form your own judgement. 'Is an island reversal forming?' is the second most-asked question that market technicians hear and one that can't be answered on a technical basis until a day or two *after* the second gap. ('Is it a head-and-shoulders pattern?' is the most often asked. See Chapter 7 for a discussion of head-and-shoulders patterns.)

Will the Gap Be Filled?

Filling the gap means that prices are returning to the level they occupied before the gap. Figure 5-7 illustrates filling the gap.

You will hear that a gap *must* be filled. This emphasis on filling the gap is usually nonsense uttered by people who are trying to sound worldly and wise, but really don't know what type of gap they're dealing with.

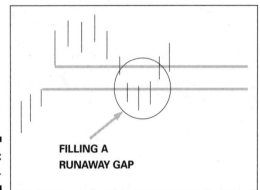

Figure 5-7:
Filling a gap.

FILLING A
RUNAWAY GAP

If a security takes off on a breakaway gap, sometimes the price doesn't return to fill the gap for many months or even years — if ever. Stop and think about it — when the fundamentals of a security change dramatically, why would market participants sell it back down to the level it was before the big event? Conditions have changed permanently and so has the price of the security. If a company has invented some new must-have product, the new higher stock prices may not be the right price, but the old prices based on the old conditions aren't right either.

A runaway gap or a common gap is another matter. Demand for the stock is more a function of buyers egging each other on than changing conditions, so the gap may be filled quickly. Sometimes a gap gets filled just because all the chatter about 'filling the gap' in the market makes it a self-fulfilling prophecy.

How do you know whether a gap will be filled? If it's a breakaway gap, it probably won't be filled, at least not in the near future. If it's a common or runaway gap, it might get filled or it might not. You need to look at other indicators to confirm whether a price move is at risk of going backward to fill a gap.

Using the Trading Range to Deal with Change Effectively

The length of the price bar, the *trading range,* plays a role in the special bar configurations, spikes and gaps we discuss in this chapter. But the trading range has meaning in its own right. As we define in the 'Trading range' section earlier in this chapter, the trading range is the difference between the high and the low. It measures the maximum distance that the price travelled that period. If you see a security that has been averaging a 30 cent high-low range and suddenly it starts trading consistently in a 50 cent range, something happened — no matter where the opens and closes are.

Paying attention to a changing range

Market prices are seldom boring. Events unfold, information leaks and stories break. When conditions change, the average trading range is sometimes the first aspect of price behaviour to change.

A change in the high-low range, which you can see in Figure 5-8, usually precedes or accompanies a change in the direction or slope of a trend. Take note — it's often a leading indicator.

- ✔ *Range expansion* is a lengthening of the price bars over time — the high-low range is getting wider (as seen in chart A in Figure 5-8) — and it usually suggests a continuation pattern.

- ✔ *Range contraction* is a shortening of the price bars — the high-low range is getting narrower (as seen in chart B in Figure 5-8) — and suggests that a trend reversal is coming soon.

A change in the size of the bars — range expansion or contraction — doesn't tell you anything about the *existing* direction of the price move. The range can expand or contract in both uptrends or downtrends.

Figure 5-8:
Range
expansion
and
contraction.

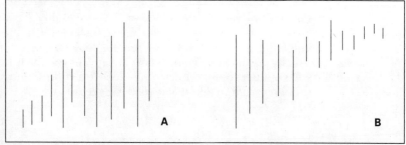

Determining the meaning of a range change

As a general rule, an expanding range is a continuation pattern and a contracting range suggests that a trend reversal is impending. Sometimes your only clue to a shift in market sentiment about your security is a change in the high-low range, but check for these confirming conditions as well:

- **Volume:** Look to see whether the volume is rising or shrinking.

  - **Rising volume:** More people are trading the security, or existing traders are taking bigger positions. This usually accompanies range expansion and is an excellent indication of an accelerating trend. The acceleration can be in either direction, up or down. (If you see an expansion of the range and it fails to have an accompanying rise in volume, you have a mystery and need to look at some other indicators.)

  - **Shrinking volume:** Fewer people are in the market for this security. This usually accompanies range contraction.

- **Open-close position:** Here's an outline of the four possible open-close combos and what they likely mean.

  - **Expanding range, higher closes:** Buyers are excited about the prospect of the price going higher still.

  - **Expanding range, lower closes:** Sellers are ever more anxious to unload the security.

  - **Contracting range, higher closes:** In all range contractions, traders are starting to feel uneasy about the direction that the security has been trending. But a higher close can offset some of the negative sentiment inherent in a contracting range.

  - **Contracting range, lower closes:** This is a doubly negative indicator. Traders may not be causing lower lows, but they're unloading near or at the close, forcing it lower. Range contraction usually means that activity is drying up and volume is low — so if you see high volume and a lower close in a contracting range, you probably want to take a hike (exit the security).

Looking at the average trading range

The trading range is a valuable analytical tool. But you want to capture a change in the range in some more efficient way than eyeballing a bunch of bars and trying to figure out whether they're getting bigger or smaller. You can calculate the average high-low range on a piece of paper, in a spreadsheet or by using charting software.

The *average trading range* is the average distance between the high and the low over a specified period of time. You know what an average is — you measure ten of something, add up the measurements, and divide by ten. If you have ten days' worth of high-low ranges that add up to 32, you know that the average daily trading range for the ten-day period was $3.20.

The average trading range is one of the best tools you have for keeping your sanity and perspective. If you know that the average daily trading range is $3.20, the most you can expect to make on this security in a single day is $3.20, and that's assuming that you could buy at the exact low and sell at the exact high — and assuming that it's an average day.

When your broker, a taxi driver, or an email solicitation says you can make $500 in the next month in this specific security, you know that it's hardly likely. If the security moved up by its average range every day with no pullbacks for the 22 days in a trading month, your most likely gain would be $70.40. Unless your informant has certain knowledge of some news or event that's going to change things, his forecast is silly. Under normal, average conditions, you can expect the normal, average trading range to persist.

Introducing a gap

What do you do about a gap? If you're merrily averaging your daily high-low ranges and suddenly you have a gap, you need to take it into account. Remember, a gap is measured from the high one day to the low the next day, or vice versa, depending on whether it's a gap up or down (refer to the section 'Grasping Gaps' earlier in this chapter). If you don't account for the gap, you're literally missing something.

Figure 5-9 displays the problem. On Day 1, the high-low range is $2. The next day, the price opens gap up, but the daily range is the same $2. Therefore, the average range for the two days is also $2. Looking at the average range alone, without inspecting every bar and every space on the chart, you wouldn't know that the gap occurred. Well, so what? Maybe the gap is just a common old gap that doesn't mean anything (refer to the 'Lacking opportunity: Common gaps' section earlier in the chapter). If it were an important gap, like a breakaway gap (check out the section 'Kicking things off: Breakaway gaps' also earlier in the chapter), you'd see the range expanding (plus a rise in volume), and the whole issue would be moot, right?

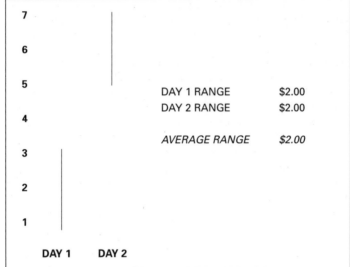

DAY 1 RANGE	$2.00	
DAY 2 RANGE	$2.00	
AVERAGE RANGE	*$2.00*	

Figure 5-9:
The
averaging
problem.

DAY 1   DAY 2

The reason you need to account for the gap is that it often precedes a longer-term change in the range, which is what you're looking for. If you measure each day separately and average those numbers, the range looks the same from day to day. For the first two days in Figure 5-9, though, the range is actually from the low on Day 1 at $1 to the high on Day 2 at $7, or a $6 range. In short, the range doubled but the averaging process doesn't capture this change. In fact, if the range on Day 2 had been smaller, say $1.50, the average would be less than $2. Just looking at the average range on a numerical basis, you would think that the range had contracted — exactly the opposite of what really happened.

Accounting for gaps: The average 'true' range

If you want to make a trading decision based on a change in the average trading range, you need to adjust the averaging process to account for possible gaps. You do this by starting at the most important component of the price bar, the close. To calculate Day 2's true range, you start at Day 1's close and end at Day 2's high. You're substituting Day 1's close for Day 2's open in order to incorporate the gap.

Day 1's range was ordinary. The gap happened afterward. Why not use Day 1's high instead of the close? Aren't you double-counting by including the space between the high and the close from Day 1? Well, maybe, but it's a minor drawback that you can live with because you acknowledge that the close is more important than the high.

Figure 5-10 shows this new measurement. Pretend that the close on Day 1 was $3. Subtracting that close from the high on Day 2, we get a true range of $4. Averaging that with the original Day 1 range, we get $3, the average true range.

Why the word *true?* Because the inventor of the idea, Welles Wilder, selected this word. The average true range is sometimes called *Wilder's average true range,* or simply ATR. If Day 2's price bar gaps downward, you incorporate the gap by measuring from the close on Day 1 to the low on Day 2.

The bigger the shift in the size of the range, the bigger the trading opportunity (or warning to exit).

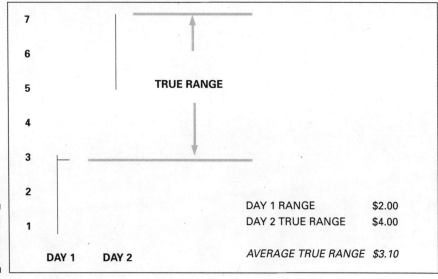

Figure 5-10: The average true range.

TRUE RANGE

DAY 1 RANGE	$2.00
DAY 2 TRUE RANGE	$4.00
AVERAGE TRUE RANGE	*$3.10*

DAY 1   DAY 2

Chapter 6

Redrawing the Price Bar: Japanese Candlesticks

Candlestick charting displays the price bar in a graphically different way from the standard bars described in Chapters 4 and 5. Candlestick charting was developed in Japan at least 150 years ago, where traders applied it to prices in the rice market. All charts in Japan today display the candlestick notation form as a matter of course.

A trader named Steve Nison brought candlesticks to the attention of western traders in 1990. Candlesticks became instantly popular. Today you can buy dozens of software packages that identify candlesticks by name and give guidance on interpreting them.

In this chapter, we explain why candlesticks are so useful and break down the components of a candlestick. Note that in some instances, a stand-alone candlestick is a 'pattern' in its own right, and such candlesticks always have a name. Named candlesticks and small series of candlestick patterns number in the dozens, and we can't cover all of them in this chapter. We select a few candlesticks and combinations that stand out.

Candlesticks in the Spotlight

Candlesticks are visually compelling: Specific patterns pop out at you. They aren't just a notation method — they do many other things, as well:

- ✔ Many candlesticks are simple to interpret and are thus a splendid place for a beginner to start figuring out bar analysis — as well as for old hands to achieve new insights.

- ✔ Candlesticks are easy to use. Your eye adapts almost immediately to the information in the bar notation.

- ✔ Candlesticks and candlestick patterns have delightfully descriptive and memorable names — charming and sometimes alarming — that contain the seeds of interpretation. The names help you to remember what the pattern means.

- ✔ Naming candlestick bar patterns not only helps you to remember how to interpret bar behaviour, it helps others, too. Candlestick bar interpretations are widely known, so you can expect other participants in the market to respond in a specific way to a specific pattern.

- ✔ You can use candlesticks on any chart, with any other indicators, just like standard bars.

- ✔ Candlestick shapes can be dramatic, and so they can often bring your attention to a trend change sooner than standard bars do. As we describe in Chapter 5, some exceptional bar patterns embody a forecast that's usually correct, such as the breakaway gap and the island reversal. Standard bar analysis offers very few such patterns, though. Candlestick analysis offers dozens.

- ✔ Candlestick patterns excel in identifying strategic market turning points — reversals from an uptrend to a downtrend or a downtrend to an uptrend.

Anatomy of a Candlestick

The candlestick form emphasises the open and the close. See Figure 6-1. The open and the close mark the top and bottom of a box, named the *real body*. A thin vertical line at the top and bottom of the real body, named the *shadow*, show the high and the low. (Refer to Chapter 4 for a discussion of the basic bar components — open, close, high and low.)

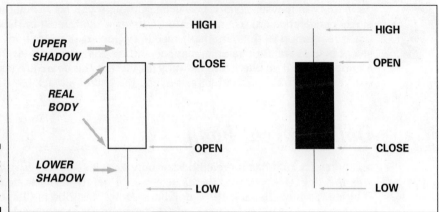

Figure 6-1:
Candlestick
bar notation.

Drawing the real body

The real body encompasses the range between the open and the close. The colour of the real body in Figure 6-1 tells you how the daily struggle between the bulls and the bears played out:

✔ **White real body:** The close is higher than the open. A white body is bullish, and the longer the body, the more bullish it is. A long candlestick indicates that the close was far above the open, implying aggressive buying. In the daily battle of bulls and bears, the bulls won.

✔ **Black real body:** The close is lower than the open. A black body is bearish, and the longer the body, the more bearish it is. A long black candlestick indicates a preponderance of sellers throughout the session. In the daily battle of bulls and bears, the bears won.

The two candlestick bars in Figure 6-1 show the identical open and close, but colouring one of them black creates the optical illusion that it's bigger. That black bar demands your attention, which is one reason candlestick charting is appealing — and effective.

In standard bar notation, described in Chapter 4, a bar is coloured to denote an up-day if the close is higher than the close the day before. A down-day is when the close is lower than the day before. In candlestick notation, the colour of the bar is determined only by today's open and today's close, without reference to yesterday's prices.

As in all bar analysis, *context* is crucial. Although you may sometimes use a single candlestick bar as an indicator in its own right, most of the time you use it in relation to the bars that precede it. One small white-body bar in a sea of black bars, for example, may mean the bulls won that day, but it was a minor event. The one white bar may signal that the bears are losing power, but you wouldn't use it all by itself to call the end of a black-bar downtrend.

Doji: No real body

A candlestick that has no real body or only a very small one is called a *doji.* In a doji, the open and the close are at or nearly at the same level. See Figure 6-2, which displays three doji bars. As we describe in Chapter 9, when the close is at or near the open, market participants are indecisive. Bulls and bears are at a standoff.

On its own, a doji doesn't tell you much about market sentiment. You interpret a doji bar in the context of the pattern of the preceding bars, (although the length of the shadow lines, denoting the high and low, which we cover in the next section, is also important). A doji implies that sentiment is in a transitional phase. It's a neutral bar, neither bullish nor bearish, that gains meaning from its placement within a set of bars. If the price series has been in an uptrend, for example, the doji may reflect that the buyers are coming to the end of their bullish enthusiasm. A doji coming immediately after a very long white bar shows that the market is tired.

Figure 6-2: Doji candlestick patterns.

PLAIN DOJI   DRAGONFLY DOJI   GRAVESTONE DOJI

The shadow

The high and the low are shown in the *shadows,* which you can think of as a candlewick (on the top) or a tail (on the bottom). Although the shadow is secondary to the real body in importance, shadows contribute useful information about market psychology, too, and modify your interpretation of the body. Shadows offer special interpretive clues in three instances:

- The real body is a doji.
- The shadow is missing.
- The shadow is extremely long.

Shadows in the doji bar

In many instances, the doji is just a plain one, as shown in Figure 6-2. The two most useful types of doji bars, also seen in Figure 6-2, are:

- **Dragonfly doji:** Long lower shadow. A very long lower shadow tells you that the open, high and close were all the same or nearly the same, meaning sellers were trying to push the price down and succeeded in making a low — but they didn't succeed is getting it to close there. Because the close was back up at or near the open, buyers must have emerged before the end of trading and fought back, getting the price to close at or near what was both the open and the high. How you interpret the dragonfly depends on what bar patterns precede it:

  - If the price move is a downtrend, the dragonfly may mean that buyers are emerging and the downtrend may be ending.

  - If the dragonfly appears after a series of uptrending bars, buyers failed to push the price over the open to a new high while sellers succeeded in getting a low, so the uptrend may be in trouble.

- **Gravestone doji:** Long upper shadow. This bar, the exact opposite of the dragonfly, is formed when the open, low and close are the same or nearly the same, but a high creates a long upper shadow. Although buyers succeeded in pushing the price to a high over the open, by the end of the day the bears were fighting back and pushed the price back to close near the open and the low. This is a failed effort at a rally, but you can interpret the bar only in the context of the other bars that precede it:

  - If the gravestone bar appears after a series of uptrending bars, buyers failed to get the close at the high. Sellers dominated and the uptrend is at risk of ending.

  - If the price move is a downtrend, the gravestone doji may mean that buyers are emerging and the downtrend may be ending.

Missing shadows

The absence of a shadow at one end is called a *shaven top* or a *shaven bottom*. To get a shaven top or bottom, the open or close must be exactly at the high or the low, as you can see in Figure 6-3, and you interpret the events exactly the same way as in analysing standard bars.

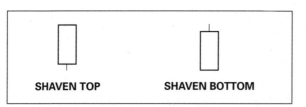

Figure 6-3:
Missing
shadows.

SHAVEN TOP   SHAVEN BOTTOM

✔ **Shaven top:** No upper shadow exists when the open or close is at the high. A shaven top can be black or white, and comes about in two ways:

- If the open is at the high, the day's trading was all downhill from there. Not only is it a black candlestick, bearish to begin with, but it's doubly bearish that no net new buying occurred after the open.

- If the close is at the high, the net of the day's trading was at higher prices, which is bullish. The candlestick is also (by definition) white, a bullish sign.

✔ **Shaven bottom:** No lower shadow exists when the open or the close is at the low of the day. A shaven bottom can come about in two ways:

- If the open is at the low, all the day's trading was euphoric. This is bullish, adding to the bullishness of the white candlestick.

- If the close is at the low, all the day's trading points to developing negative sentiment (depending on what bars precede it, of course). This is a black bar, with bells on.

Really long shadows

When the shadow is as long as the real body, or longer (see Figure 6-4), traders are expressing an extreme of sentiment. They may or may not follow through the next day by pushing the *close* to the high or low extreme. It can be tricky, therefore, to evaluate a long shadow. As a general rule, you judge a long shadow by its placement on the chart (relative to preceding bars).

Figure 6-4:
Very long
shadows.

LONG UPPER SHADOW   LONG LOWER SHADOW

✔ **Long upper shadow:** The high of the day came well above both the open and the close, whether the real body is black or white.

- If the price series is in an uptrend, the long upper shadow is a failure to close near the high. If the uptrend is nearing a resistance level (see Chapters 7 and 8), the long upper shadow may signal a weakening of the uptrend. If a long upper shadow follows a doji bar indicating indecisiveness, you should worry that the uptrend may be over.

- If the price series is on a downtrend, the long upper shadow suggests that some market participants are buying at higher levels. Especially if a long upper shadow follows a doji bar, you should wonder if the downtrend might be ending.

✔ **Long lower shadow:** A long lower shadow means that the low of the day came well under both the open and the close, whether the real body is black or white.

- If the price series is in a downtrend, the long lower shadow is a failure to close near the low. If the downtrend is nearing a support level (see Chapters 7 and 8), the long lower shadow may signal a weakening or an end of the downtrend.

- If the price series is on an uptrend, the long lower shadow suggests that traders were not willing to keep buying at the high levels right up to the close. They were exiting under the high, and therefore think that new highs are not warranted. This can be a warning sign of the trend decelerating or ending.

Sizing Up Emotions

We mention at the beginning of the 'Anatomy of a Candlestick' section that the longer the bar, the more bullish or bearish it is. If you're looking at a series of medium-sized bars and suddenly see one relatively long bar (as you can see in Figure 6-5), it may be telling you that support or resistance has been reached. Support marks an extreme level where buyers perceive that the price is relatively cheap, and resistance marks an extreme level where sellers perceive the price is relatively high, inspiring profit-taking or least an end to accumulation. (See Chapter 8 for all the details.)

Identifying when traders are reaching the end of their emotional tether is one of the primary goals of candlestick charting. And a change in the size of the bar is one of the best indicators of this. The candlestick technique sensitises you to spot extremes of emotion, which is why it is a valuable tool for marking possible support and resistance at overbought or oversold levels.

Check out Chapter 2 for a discussion of overbought/oversold levels. You can also easily spot range expansion or contraction (refer to Chapter 5).

In the top illustration in Figure 6-5, you see a series of three white bars making higher opens and higher closes, followed by a doji and an exceptionally long white bar. If you were looking at this in standard bar notation, as seen in the bottom illustration, you might say to yourself, 'Higher high, higher lows, higher closes, trend okay'. But the unusually tall bar stands out more prominently in candlestick mode — especially following the transitional doji — and it alerts you to the possibility that all the buyers who were going to buy have just done so in one last burst, and the price may have formed a resistance level at the top of the bar (the close, in this case).

If the long bar were a black bar, denoting that the close was lower than the open, you would find it easy to deduce that the upmove might be ending. A long black bar implies panic selling. But to interpret the *white* bar as an ending burst in an uptrend is more subtle. In fact, an expert in reading standard bars would see the same thing. Candlesticks just make it easier, especially for a beginner.

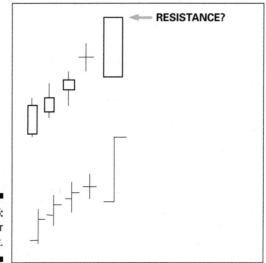

Figure 6-5:
Bar
placement.

Identifying Emotional Extremes

Dozens of possible bar placement combinations and permutations are possible. This section introduces two of the more popular general patterns, while the next two sections look at reversal patterns and continuation patterns.

Two similar candlesticks or candlestick patterns often have the exact opposite interpretation, depending on where they fall in a series. You have to memorise the exact patterns to avoid getting confused. We select two of the many candlestick patterns to illustrate.

Hammer and hanging man

Both of these candlesticks have a small real body and only one shadow — a long lower shadow. The long shadow of the hammer extends to the downside off a white body, while the long shadow of the hanging man extends to the downside off a black body, as shown in Figure 6-6.

You'd think that the white-body version would automatically be a bullish indicator and the black-body version a bearish one, but interpreting this candlestick depends on its placement on the chart, regardless of the real-body colour. If the candlestick appears in a downtrend, for example, it marks the likely end of the trend even if the real body is white.

You may see a hammer in many other contexts, but when it has a white body and it comes after a series of black downtrending bars, you identify it as implying a reversal. Note that the close is higher than the previous close, too. In this context, the long lower shadow means the sellers were able to achieve a new low, but buyers emerged at some point during the day and the close was higher than the open, indicating last-minute buying.

The hanging man looks the same except it has a black body coming after a series of white uptrending bars. The long lower shadow marks the bulls' failure to prevent the bears making a new low and also from keeping the close below the open. You may see this bar in other places within a series of bars, but when you see it at the top of an uptrending series, you should consider that the trend is probably over. The wise course is to take your profit and run.

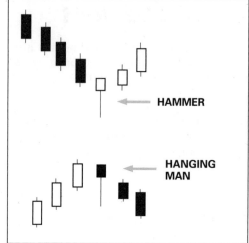

Figure 6-6:
Hammer
and hanging
man.

Harami

A small real-body candlestick that comes after a bigger one is called a *harami,* which means *pregnant* in Japanese. A harami (see Figure 6-7) implies that a change in sentiment is impending. Technically, the harami pattern requires two bars, so it doesn't stand alone. On this chart, we show the shadows of the harami bar as also inside the scope of the first big bar, although this isn't essential to identifying the pattern.

A harami can be white or black, and in fact, it can even be a doji (inside day). The smaller the real body is, the more powerful the implication that a reversal is impending. In Figure 6-7, we see white bars that are seemingly downtrending — already a confusing combination. Then we see a large white bar. As we discuss in the section 'Sizing Up Emotions' earlier in the chapter, the size of the bar is important. It reflects a high level of emotion. Seeing just the big white bar after a series of smaller ones that are downtrending, you might think that the bulls finally got the upper hand, and this is the start of an uptrend — especially because you have an indecision doji just ahead of it. The black harami following the big white bar should disillusion you. If an uptrend was forming, the harami just put the kybosh on it.

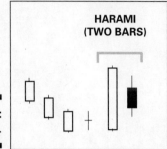

HARAMI
(TWO BARS)

Figure 6-7:
Harami.

Turning to Reversal Patterns

Reversal patterns number at least 40, and identifying reversals is the main application of candlesticks. The following are some of the most popular and easily identified candlesticks.

Bearish engulfing candlestick

An *engulfing pattern* signals the reversal of a trend. The word *engulfing* refers to the open and close of the bar encompassing a wider range than the open and close of the day before. In Figure 6-8, the engulfing nature is the dominant characteristic, so that the lower close pops out at you even though the bar also has a higher open. When a bar starts out at a higher open but then closes at a lower level, the bears won that day. Not shown is a *bullish engulfing candlestick,* which is white. The higher close is visually compelling because the real body is so big.

Shooting star

The *shooting star* is characterised by a small real body and a long upper shadow, as you can see in Figure 6-8. As we discuss in 'Really long shadows' earlier in this chapter, the shadow in an uptrend implies a failure of the trend — a failure to close near the high. Notice the indecisive doji bar just before the shooting star.

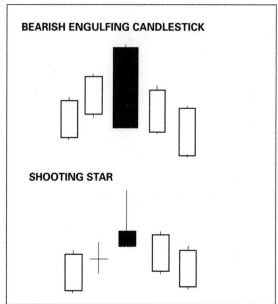

BEARISH ENGULFING CANDLESTICK

SHOOTING STAR

Figure 6-8:
Reversal
patterns.

Continuation Patterns

Candlestick patterns are most often used to identify reversals, but continuation patterns do exist. As the name suggests, a continuation pattern gives you confirmation that the trend in place will likely continue.

Rising window

Rising window is the term for a gap, in this case, an upward gap. You can review gaps in Chapter 5. (A downward gap is a *falling window*.)

In Figure 6-9, the gap separates two white candlesticks, which are themselves bullish. The next bar doesn't 'fill the gap'. (In Japan, they call this 'closing the window'.) Refer to Chapter 5 for the lowdown on filling the gap. The gap between the two price bars is confirmation of the existing trend, and the market's refusal the following day to go back and fill the gap is further confirmation that the trend is okay.

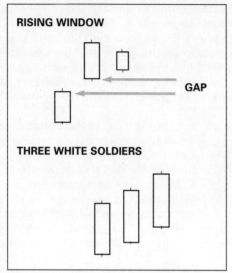

Figure 6-9:
Continuation
patterns.

Three white soldiers

The second exhibit in Figure 6-9 is of *three white soldiers*. In this pattern, what's important are three large white candlesticks in a row. Seeing the close consistently over the open for three days confirms that the price series is in an uptrend, and the size of the bars indicates its robustness.

Combining Candlesticks with Other Indicators

You can combine candlesticks with other indicators to get a more powerful description of what's going on in the hearts and minds of the people who trade the security.

Many traders who don't act directly on the information contained in the candlestick patterns still use the notation on every chart because of its visual appeal, and because often a candlestick bar or pattern confirms some other indicator to which they give priority.

Figure 6-10 shows a set of parallel support and resistance lines called a channel (we cover channels in Chapter 9). A channel is used to outline the probable limit of future prices moves, either up or down. You should recognise each of the candlesticks on this chart from the descriptions in this chapter. The harami is followed by a rising window (upward gap) and a big white candle. These three candlesticks together are bullish and alert you to go back and start the channel at the lowest low, the bar before the harami.

The real bodies proceed to push against the top of the channel resistance line, but the doji, which suggests that traders are having second thoughts, is followed by two higher white candles. The two white candles indicate that the reconsideration of the move on the doji day culminated in traders' decision to keep taking the price up. This was an occasion when the doji wasn't a reversal indicator, at least not for the next day. After the two white candles comes a bearish engulfing candle, a reversal warning that this upmove may be ending. The engulfing candle alerts you to watch the next day's activity, especially the open, with an eagle eye.

To evaluate support and resistance, use the real body and ignore the shadow. Because most bars do have shadows, to use only the real body has the effect of narrowing the channel and thus delivering earlier breakouts than standard bars. This can be helpful or not helpful, depending on how jumpy your security is and how prone it is to false breakouts.

Candlesticks can also be used to confirm relative strength, momentum and many other indicators. Relative strength and momentum are covered in Chapter 11. Note that in Japan, a favourite indicator to use with candlesticks is the moving average, covered in Chapter 10.

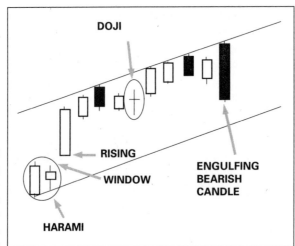

Figure 6-10:
Candlesticks as confirmation.

Trading on Candlesticks Alone

Many traders use candlesticks alone to guide their trading decisions. Reading candlesticks is like reading standard bars — endlessly fascinating, even addictive. But be aware that all bar reading takes practice.

Some specific bars and patterns of bars are well known — and thus likely to get the expected response from market participants — but other combinations are not so well known and the interpretation can vary from person to person.

You can study candlestick patterns for a long time and still only scratch the surface of the art. In addition to specific named patterns, you have to learn the context of specific bars and patterns. To do a good job interpreting candlesticks, you need to understand the dynamic and complex relationships of many patterns all at once, like juggling six oranges instead of three.

As with standard bar interpretation, the predictive power of a particular bar or pattern of bars may be limited to the next day or next few days. Some bars and patterns are particularly powerful and nearly always have a more lasting effect, but many are of fleeting use. If you're a swing trader (check out Chapter 14 for definitions of trading types), candlesticks are going to be of more interest to you than if you're a position trader with a very long holding period (weeks and months), although key candlesticks can alert you to an impending pause in a long-term trend, or even a reversal.

No matter how compelling a particular bar may seem, you still need confirmation of the interpretation, which comes only after you see the next day's bar. Sometimes you get a strong reversal pattern that is invalidated the very next day, for example. As with all technical indicators, candlesticks don't always work.

Candlestick analysis may offer a forecast of the general direction of the price move over the next day or few days, but it doesn't suggest the extent of the move — a price target.

Chapter 7

Seeing Barriers and Patterns

· ·

In This Chapter

▶ Identifying support and resistance levels

▶ Explaining common patterns

▶ Figuring out continuation patterns

▶ Going over reversal patterns

▶ Moving on to the measured move

· ·

*P*atterns, support lines and resistance lines sound like sewing terms, but they're very important concepts for technical traders. A *pattern* is a type of indicator traditionally applied to a chart by hand drawing, although software packages are now available to remove some of the subjective element. Technical traders have been recognising and naming patterns from the earliest days of technical analysis. Chart patterns are powerful indicators, and having some basic knowledge of patterns is a good idea for the most sophisticated indicator trader and the beginner alike.

Support and resistance lines, or zones, serve as excellent indicators to either enter or exit a trade and also as places to put protective stop-loss orders. They form barriers to the price movement and are carefully observed by most traders.

In this chapter, we discuss lines of support and resistance and show how they work, then we describe a few of the 50 or so most common patterns you're likely to encounter in indicators.

Pinpointing Barriers: Support and Resistance Lines

The idea behind *support and resistance* is that barriers control the flow of price action. When a trend is obvious, the lines of support and resistance fundamentally define the trend. They create a range in which traders feel the price should remain. Traders are reluctant to cross support and resistance lines, so they form barriers to price movement. Defining this range and noting how the price reacts when it gets close to the borders of that range gives you an indication of the current market psychology.

Defining support and resistance

A *support line* is a price level that defines the bottom of a price range in which the market is trading. The support line identifies the point where bulls have enough power to end any downward price move created by the bears. Because the bulls are following the trend and keen to keep the price high, they remember the support level, and come back in whenever the line is approached, and push prices back up. In effect, the support line defines the point considered by the bulls to be good value for going long. Figure 7-1 shows a horizontal support line, but it can also be used to define an upward trend.

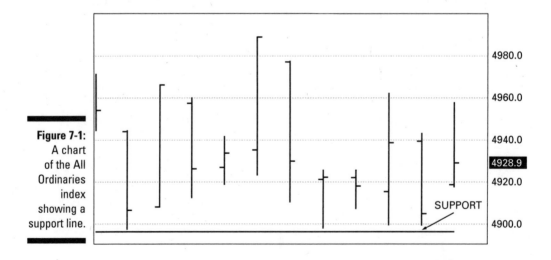

Figure 7-1:
A chart
of the All
Ordinaries
index
showing a
support line.

A line of resistance, on the other hand, defines the edge of a range where bears call the shots. When a price reaches or breaks a line of resistance, the bears sell strongly in sufficient numbers to push prices back down. The resistance line, such as the one shown in Figure 7-2, defines the zone considered by the bears to be good value for going short.

The significance of a line of support or resistance depends on how many times the level has been approached, how much volume is traded at the level, how old the level is and whether the level is a major high or low or a round number.

Sometimes support and resistance lines are precise. Most times, however, they're not. Support and resistance tends to work within zones. Often you'll find that the bulls or bears will anticipate that the level will hold and so may take their positions early. Sometimes the level can be slightly exceeded by the enthusiasm of the market.

The lines of support and resistance shown in Figures 7-1 and 7-2 are horizontal, representing a particular price that the market feels is a barrier. (The concept of a support or resistance line can also define a trend, as we discuss in Chapter 8.)

In Figure 7-3, a chart of the All Ordinaries index shows an example of support and resistance zones. You can see the support level acting within a zone between 4890 and the round number 4900, and the resistance level acting within a zone between 4978 and 4996.

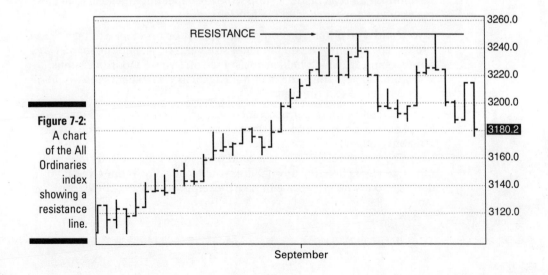

Figure 7-2: A chart of the All Ordinaries index showing a resistance line.

Reversing the roles

Quite frequently, after a level has been broken, support may become resistance and resistance may become support. This may be due to traders getting out at breakeven after being in a losing trade. For example, if you went long at a support area of $5 and the market subsequently traded down to $4, you would be happy to have a chance to sell your holding at $5 when prices got back up to that level. In the chart of the All Ordinaries index in Figure 7-4, note how a previous support line, after it's been broken, becomes a resistance line (see Chapter 8).

Using the strengths of support and resistance

You can use support and resistance in many different ways in your trading.

✔ If you're bullish about a stock, you could use support as a low-risk entry level, expecting the level to hold if it's approached in the future. Alternatively, if you're bearish on a stock, you could use resistance as a low-risk level to go short, expecting the level to not be breached if approached in the future.

✔ If you're bullish about a stock, you could buy an upside break of a resistance level, expecting the level to hold as support, if approached in the future. Alternatively, if you are bearish about a stock, you could go short on a break below a support level, expecting the level to act as resistance if approached in the future.

✔ If you hold a position, you could use support or resistance to take profits. For example, if you bought a stock at say $4, and the market was approaching $5, which held as resistance on two previous occasions, you would expect the $5 level to hold again as resistance. This would be a good place to exit the trade.

✔ You could use support or resistance as a price to place a stop-loss order. For example, if you went long (buying a security when the price breaks out above a resistance area), then a support level not too far below the price you purchased at, is a good place to get out of that trade — if the price starts heading down. Sure, you'll lose some money, but if you don't get out when the price breaks the support line you could lose a lot more.

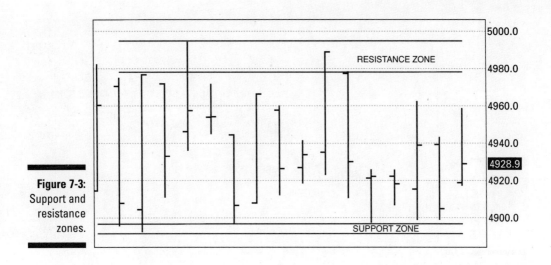

Figure 7-3:
Support and
resistance
zones.

Figure 7-4:
Switching
from
support to
resistance.

Support and resistance zones help when trading trends. Figure 7-5 shows a chart of Telstra stock illustrating how support levels can be used to identify stop losses to protect your gains. If the price drops below a support line, you get early warning that the trend may have reversed. (We show you how to draw these trendlines in more detail in Chapter 8.)

Figure 7-5: Raising stops to lock in profits.

Understanding Patterns

Chart patterns are indicators consisting of geometric shapes drawn on the chart, such as a triangle. As with most indicators, a price forecast is embedded in the pattern identification. In other chapters, we cover some classic patterns, such as the inside day (Chapter 5) and support and resistance lines (covered earlier in this chapter and in Chapter 8). Other bar patterns are also covered in Chapter 5 (island reversal), and all the candlestick formations are considered patterns, too (Chapter 6). Here's a quick pattern roundup:

- ✔ Most patterns employ straight lines (such as triangles), although a few use semi-circles or semi-ellipses (such as head-and-shoulders).

- ✔ Pattern lines generally follow either the highs or the lows.

- ✔ Pattern types are usually organised according to whether they forecast a continuation or a reversal of the current price move, although many patterns can be applied either way, such as triangles.

Laughing at squiggles

The lingo of pattern analysis — double bottom and dead-cat bounce, for example — makes some people laugh. Some of the names do seem a little silly until you realise that they are apt — they describe the price action efficiently — and the names are at least easy to remember.

As with most aspects of technical analysis, a pattern is a work in progress. You may think you see a pattern developing, only to have the price action change course and fail to complete the expected formation. You may have to erase your work and start over a number of times on any single set of bars.

In short, pattern identification can be frustrating and time-consuming. Resign yourself to making a lot of mistakes, and then, even valid patterns fail some of the time, like all indicators. The reason to tolerate the pattern recognition process is that when you get it right, you have a powerful forecasting tool that can deliver 20 to 40 per cent returns in a short period of time. In the sections that follow, we cite performance data from Tom Bulkowski's path-breaking *Encyclopedia of Chart Patterns* (published by Wiley Publishing, Inc.).

Got imagination?

Not everyone can see patterns right away. Pattern identification takes practice — and a lot of drawing and redrawing of lines and shapes until you get the hang of it. For example, consider Figure 7-6. Do you see the pattern?

The pattern in Figure 7-6 is a symmetrical triangle, as you can see more clearly in Figure 7-7. The triangle is characterised by a series of lower highs along which you can draw one boundary line, and a series of higher lows along which you can draw another boundary line. The two boundary lines eventually come together at an apex. Before that point is reached, the price must pierce one of the boundary lines simply in the course of trading in its normal range. Which one? Because most of the bars are trending downward, you imagine the odds favour a break to the downside.

Figure 7-6:
Find the
pattern.

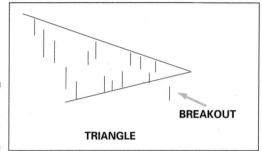

Figure 7-7:
Pattern
revealed.

And you're right. In a major study of this pattern by Tom Bulkowski, which covered 500 stocks from 1991 to 1996, the symmetrical triangle pattern appeared 146 times. On 83 occasions, or 57 per cent of the time, it was a downside breakout. The average decline was 19 per cent, and the average decline lasted 74 days. In these cases, the triangle was a continuation pattern.

But sometimes the breakout is to the upside. In the same study, the price delivered an upside breakout 63 times out of 146, or 43 per cent of the cases. The average rise was 41 per cent and lasted an average of 163 days. In this instance, the pattern forecast a reversal, not a continuation.

Figure 7-8 is a chart of QBE stock, showing a symmetrical triangle. You need to wait for a breakout above or below the drawn boundary lines before trading the pattern.

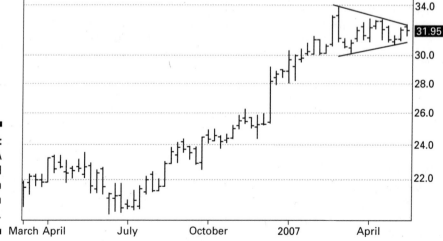

Figure 7-8:
A
symmetrical
triangle in
real life on
QBE data.

You usually see a burst of higher volume when a pattern reaches completion. This makes sense — other chartists in the crowd are seeing the same pattern. For triangles, low volume often *precedes* the breakout, and serves as a bonus warning of an impending move.

Most patterns don't deliver a gift-wrapped buy/sell signal until near the end of the formation. As the symmetrical triangle pattern develops, the forecast is only that a breakout will occur, not the direction of the breakout.

Colouring inside the lines

Pattern identification doesn't require that each single price in a series line up perfectly. Not every price high hits an overhead resistance line, for example. It suffices that several hit the line. All triangles — symmetrical, ascending and descending — incorporate support (top) and resistance (bottom) lines, as do flags and pennants, described in the 'Pennants and flags' section later in this chapter, and other patterns. Opinion differs on whether the top and bottom lines must enclose every part of every price bar, or if it's okay for the bar to break the line by a tiny amount as a triangle pattern is developing.

Generally, when a pattern includes a form of support and resistance, 'colour within the lines' so to speak. Plenty of valid patterns break the boundary lines, but discarding the pattern when a bar breaks support or resistance is safer.

In many patterns, such as double tops and head-and-shoulders, drawing a rough outline that breaks some price bars is good enough to identify the pattern. How do you know when you may break a bar and when you shouldn't? Fortunately, technical traders and software designers are rapidly qualifying the conditions that define each pattern. The real key is practice.

Continuation Patterns

A *continuation pattern* tells you that buying or selling pressure is pausing. If a big-picture trend is well-established, the pattern suggests it will accelerate after the pause. A continuation pattern, therefore, is a good place to add to a position, because you expect an additional move in the same direction. Continuation patterns tend to be fairly short-term, sometimes only a few days, and are often neglected as a consequence.

Continuation patterns serve as reassurance that you've identified the trend correctly. They also often point you to the ideal level at which to place a stop-loss order, such as the ascending line in the ascending triangle described in the following section, 'Ascending and descending triangles'. (See Chapter 17 for a discussion of stops.)

Ascending and descending triangles

To draw ascending and descending triangles, you draw a boundary line along the highs of a price series and another one along the lows (see Figure 7-9) — just like you do with symmetrical triangles.

In the ascending triangle, the price isn't making new highs, and the topmost (resistance) boundary line is horizontal. You may worry that the failure to make new highs means the upmove is over. But the price isn't making new lows, either — it's making higher lows. The higher lows represents the bulls becoming increasingly eager to accept higher prices, creating an expectation that the bulls are becoming stronger. You expect a breakout of the top boundary line to the upside.

When you can draw a horizontal boundary line along a series of highs, remember to look for a rising boundary line along the lows at the same time. Not only does the ascending line confirm the trend continuation, but it also provides you with a ready-made stop-loss level at the ascending support line. The ascending triangle pattern delivers the expected rise about two-thirds of the time, but according to Tom Bulkowski's study, it fails about 32 per cent of the time. If you wait for prices to close above the top boundary line, then the failure rate drops to a mere 2 per cent. The *expected rise*, by the way, is equal to the height of the triangle pattern. See the section 'The Measured Move' later in this chapter.

A descending triangle is the mirror image of the ascending triangle. The important point is that in this case, the price is failing to make new lows in the prevailing downtrend, and is making lower highs. You wonder if the trend is failing. But if you can still draw a boundary line along the series of lower highs, it would be a mistake to buy at this point — the probability is high that the downtrend is going to continue.

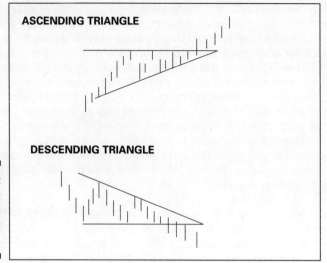

ASCENDING TRIANGLE

DESCENDING TRIANGLE

Figure 7-9:
Ascending
and
descending
triangles.

Pennants and flags

A *pennant* is shaped like a triangle — converging boundary lines —
but the price swing between the top and bottom lines is smaller (see
Figure 7-10). Usually a pennant lasts only a few days and hardly ever
longer than three weeks (whereas full triangles can last months). A
pennant is a form of retracement accompanied by a drop in volume.
A *flag* is another retracement, but its support and resistance lines are
parallel (see Figure 7-11).

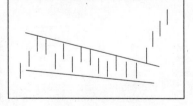

Figure 7-10:
Pennant.

As described in Chapter 2, a trend is usually punctuated by minor retracement moves in the opposite direction when traders take profit and set off a small cascade of profit-taking by others. With pennants and flags, the pattern lasts an average of 10 to 11 days and is accompanied by falling volume. In Figure 7-11, note the grey line that roughly describes the overall uptrend. Whenever you get a retracement like a pennant or a flag, and often with ascending or descending triangles, too, you have to broaden your vision of the price move because the pattern causes the longer-term high-low range of the entire period to widen. Technically, a series of lower lows in an uptrend breaks and ends the trend, and a series of higher highs breaks and ends a downtrend. But if the retracement is minor and the pattern qualifies as a continuation pattern, the trend is still in place — it just has to be seen in a wider perspective.

If you have confidence in the trend, you can tolerate a minor and short-lived break when it's a pennant or flag doing the breaking. In fact, pennants and flags are what pattern chartists call *half-mast patterns*. That is, they form midway in a trend and you can project the distance already travelled from the start of the trend from the pattern to estimate the end of the trend. See the section 'The Measured Move' later in the chapter.

If you don't see a drop in volume with flags and pennants, you may be looking at a reversal rather than a continuation pattern, and indeed, the pennant pattern fails in its continuation prediction 19 per cent of the time in an uptrend and 34 per cent in a downtrend, so it pays to watch volume. In the Bulkowski study, 90 per cent of the pennants show falling volume. Flags fail 13 per cent of the time in an uptrend and only 12 per cent in a downtrend.

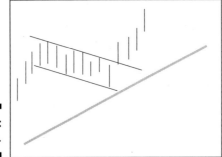

Figure 7-11:
Flag.

Dead-cat bounce — phoney reversal

A dead-cat bounce is a peculiar continuation pattern that looks like
a reversal at the beginning, with a sizeable upward retracement of a
downmove, but then moves back to the same downward direction. Note
that a dead-cat bounce occurs only in downmoves and no equivalent named
pattern exists for a parallel sequence of events in an upmove.

The dead-cat pattern starts off with a negative fundamental event that
triggers a massive downmove. The average size of the downmove is
25 per cent — but the price can shoot down by 70 per cent or more in the
space of a few days. The *bounce* is an upward retracement that may make
you think the drop is over. The pattern includes a breakaway downside
gap about 80 per cent of the time, and sometimes the bounce upward fills
part of the gap. (Refer to Chapter 5 for a discussion of gaps.) Many traders
mistakenly think that if a gap is filled, even partly, the preceding move has
ended. The dead-cat bounce is one of the patterns that disproves that idea
— by the end of six months after the gap, only 54 per cent of price moves
had fully closed the gap in the Bulkowski study, which found 244 versions
of the dead-cat bounce pattern in 500 stocks between 1991 and 1996.
See Figure 7-12.

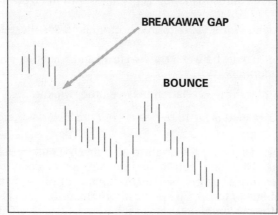

Figure 7-12:
Dead-cat
bounce.

Bulkowski's statistics on the dead-cat bounce are extensive. A few of the points that stand out:

- The bounce upward averages 19 per cent from the lowest low.
- The average decline from the top of the retracement bounce is 15 per cent and lasts an average of three months.
- The pattern fails to deliver an additional decline only 10 per cent of the time, making the success rate 90 per cent.

Classic Reversal Patterns

Patterns come into their own when used to identify a trend reversal. No matter what way a trend comes to an end, chances are good that a pattern exists to identify it.

Double bottom

A double bottom looks like a W. The double bottom predicts a price breakout to the upside and substantial gains, as shown in Figure 7-13.

The identification guide for a valid double bottom includes these factors:

- A minimum of 10 days between the two lows and sometimes as long as two or three months.
- A 4 per cent or less price variation between the two lows.
- A centre upmove of at least 10 per cent from the lower of the two bottoms.
- The price must rise above the confirmation line to confirm that the pattern is indeed a double bottom and the forecast of a continued rise is correct. The *confirmation line* is a horizontal line drawn from the highest high in the middle of the W. The point where the price rises above the line is called the *confirmation point*.

Reaching the confirmation line drawn horizontally from the confirmation point, as shown on Figure 7-13, is the most important identification key of the double bottom. This is where you buy.

Notice that some of the price bars break the lines you draw to form the double bottom pattern. Breaking some of the bars is allowed in a formation where the line is not a support or resistance line.

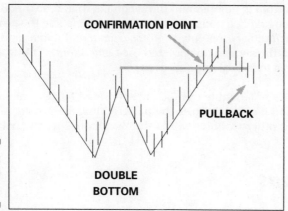

Figure 7-13:
Double
bottom.

Not every twin bottom is a true double bottom. Only about one-third of all the patterns that look like a double bottom end up meeting the confirmation criterion. In short, the pattern fails about two-thirds of the time.

This sounds terrible, but wait — on the occasions when you do get confirmation, the double bottom is tremendously reliable. If you wait for the price to break above the confirmation line, the pattern delivers a profit an astonishing 97 per cent of the time — and the average gain is 40 per cent.

Other characteristics of a double bottom are

- A large increase in volume on the price crossing above the confirmation line, demonstrating increased interest by the crowd and perhaps implying widespread recognition of the pattern.

- Frequent retracements to the downside right after the price breaks the confirmation line. Bulkowski prefers the term *throwback* for the retracement after an upside breakout, as in the double bottom, and *pullback* for the retracement after a downward breakout, as in a double top, but these words aren't engraved in stone and you can use the words *retracement, correction, throwback* and *pullback* more or less interchangeably.

A throwback occurs 68 per cent of the time in confirmed double bottoms, and can make it hard, psychologically, to hang on to the trade that you just put on only a few days before when the price crossed the confirmation line.

The version of the double bottom illustrated in Figure 7-13 is clear and obvious, but not every pattern is so easy to detect. For example, one or both of the two lows of the double bottom could be rounded instead of pointed.

When the first bottom is pointed and the second is rounded, Tom Bulkowski names it the *Adam and Eve* double bottom. You can imagine the other combinations, including two pointy bottoms (*Adam and Adam*) and the first one rounded with the second one pointed (*Eve and Adam*). This is, by the way, as raunchy as technical analysis ever gets.

Often the two lows of a double bottom are separated by several months or even a year, and it's easy to miss the pattern altogether. Also, minor retracements and other wobbles within the W can obscure the pattern.

Double tops

A double top is the mirror image of the double bottom — it looks like the letter M. The price makes a high, pulls back on profit-taking (as usual), and then bullish traders try but fail to surpass the first high. The failure to rally a second time through the first high means the bulls were beaten and the bears are now in charge. A true double top is usually accompanied by falling volume as the second top is being formed.

As with the double bottom, you need to see the price surpass the confirmation level (the lowest point in the centre bar of the M) for the pattern to be valid. When that condition is not met, twin tops fail to deliver a sustained downmove 65 per cent of the time. When the condition is met, however, the pattern delivers a downmove 83 per cent of the time, which is less reliable than the double bottom (97 per cent), but still impressive. The average drop after a confirmed double top is 20 per cent and lasts three months.

Again, as with double bottoms, the price pulls back after the confirmation 69 per cent of the time, leaving you to doubt the pattern. Fortunately, the pullback period averages only ten days before the downtrend resumes.

Topping reversal patterns like the double top are usually more short-term than bottoming reversal patterns like double bottoms. Tops take less time to form (57 days on average) than bottoms (70 days), because traders are more fearful of taking losses after a big gain than they are trusting of early signs of a bottom. Topping reversals are often more volatile, too, although they occur with equal frequency. According to Bulkowski, nearly all bottom chart patterns — of any type — perform better than tops. Bottoming patterns have average gains of 38 per cent, but tops show losses of just 21 per cent.

The ultimate triple top: Head-and-shoulders

A triple top or bottom is somewhat rarer than the double version, but the meaning is the same — the price fails to surpass the previous low or high, signalling a trend reversal.

The head-and-shoulders pattern is a triple top that's easy to see; one bump forms the left shoulder, a higher bump forms a head, and a third bump forms the right shoulder. (See Figure 7-14 for two examples.) The head-and-shoulders pattern is the most widely recognised of all the patterns, and deserves its popularity because when the price surpasses the pattern's confirmation line, it delivers the expected move a whopping 93 per cent of the time.

The confirmation line connects the low point of each shoulder and is named the *neckline*. The price breaking the neckline predicts a price decline, whether the neckline is sloping upward or downward. Seldom do you see the neckline perfectly horizontal. A downward-sloping neckline tends to deliver the biggest price move.

If you stop and think about it, a head-and-shoulders pattern is a logical development of crowd behaviour. A head-and-shoulders usually forms after a long uptrend. The dip from the first shoulder represents the normal retracement after a new high. The head then represents the triumph of bullish sentiment and sets a new higher high. The dip after the higher-high head represents more profit-taking, whereupon the bulls buy again. When the bulls are making their third try at a rally, their price target is the last highest high, which is the top of the head. The failure of the second shoulder to surpass the head is the end of the rally and signifies a loss of momentum by the bulls. Buying demand diminishes and selling pressure takes hold, forcing prices down, completing the pattern.

According to the Bulkowski study, which examined 500 stocks over the period 1991 to 1996, the head-and-shoulders pattern appeared 431 times, and resulted in 406 reversals. A confirmed head-and-shoulders delivers an average decline of 23 per cent from the neckline, and the most often seen decline is 15 per cent. The average length of the pattern is 62 days.

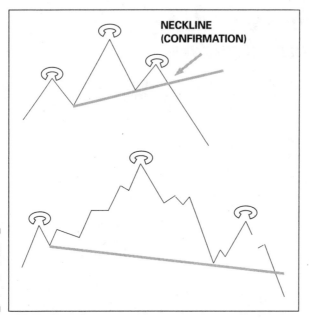

Figure 7-14:
Head-and-
shoulders
patterns.

Figure 7-15 is a chart of Woodside Petroleum stock showing a recent head and shoulders pattern. As you can see, the left shoulder, head, right shoulder and neckline have been marked on the chart. The signal to go short is on the marked breakout below the neckline. The target for this pattern is the distance from the top of the head to the neckline projected down from the breakout below the neckline.

As with double tops and bottoms, however, some traders refuse to accept the pattern, and they cause a pullback to the confirmation line 45 per cent of the time. Pullbacks average only eleven days before the stock resumes its decline. This is your last chance to jump off before the price hits the wall. Don't listen to that little voice that says, 'See, it's coming back'. That little voice is wishful thinking. The pullback is the only free lunch in technical analysis.

As with every trend that is losing steam, volume falls after the head, although about half the time the highest volume is at the left shoulder and about half the time at the head. Volume is low at the second shoulder. Volume on the breakout day and the next few days after the breakout day, however, tends to be very large. This is not surprising, because by now a great number of chart-oriented traders have identified the pattern and its neckline.

Figure 7-15:
A real
head-and-
shoulders.

2004 April   July October 2005 April   July October 2008 April   July October

The head-and-shoulders patterns shown in Figure 7-14 are easy enough to see, but many head-and-shoulders patterns are more complex and contain other patterns within them. The second head-and-shoulders pattern in Figure 7-14, for example, contains a little double top and a gap (refer to Chapter 5). The right shoulder in Figure 7-15 contains a small upswing, which could give you hope that the pattern won't be confirmed at the neckline. You may also see what appears to be two heads or two shoulders, although one is always higher, which makes it the head.

The Measured Move

The term *measured move* is used in a number of contexts in technical analysis, so it can become confusing. In essence, a *measured move* is a forecast of the upcoming price move after a chart event, including completion of a pattern. Unfortunately, these forecasts are seldom correct, or rather, they vary by too much from actual outcomes to serve as reliable trading guides. In the following sections, we outline three types of measured moves. (Point-and-figure charting also features its own version of the measured move — see Chapter 13.)

Taking dictation from the pattern

One definition of *measured move* is the price change expected to result from a particular pattern. For example, in the ascending triangle pictured at the top of Figure 7-16, the grey lines denote the height of the pattern. For example, suppose the distance between the high and low within the pattern is $5. After the price breaks out above the top of the triangle, you expect the subsequent rise to be the same amount, $5.

One useful (if general) observation is that the size of a move after a pattern is proportional to the size of the pattern. When a pattern takes a long time to form (three months or more) and when it is very deep (30 to 50 per cent of the annual high-low range), the eventual reaction to the pattern will be bigger.

As we mention in Chapter 9, you often get a sideways movement that results in a horizontal channel (a *Darvas box*), also called a rectangle. You project the height of the existing box into the future to gauge the extent of the breakout move. A measured move of this type has a certain amount of logic. The traders in a particular security may become accustomed to rises or falls of a certain amount before pausing or retracing.

Tom Bulkowski, in his books and articles, provides measurement guidelines for the range, average and *mode* (most often seen) price change upon the completion of a pattern. Seldom are they exactly 100 per cent of the height of a pattern. Every pattern is measured in its own way. The expected move after a head-and-shoulders, for example, is measured from the top of the head to the neckline. You then subtract that number from the neckline at the breakout point to derive the expected stopping point of the downmove. This target is met only 63 per cent of the time in Bulkowski's study, which falls short of a convincing forecasting technique.

That the downmove on confirmation of a head-and-shoulders is equal to the expected move only 63 per cent of the time doesn't mean you shouldn't heed a head-and-shoulders pattern when you see it. It's still a valid reversal pattern and if you own the security, you should exit at the pattern confirmation neckline, if only because so many other traders are going to identify the pattern and do precisely that, causing a self-fulfilling prophecy.

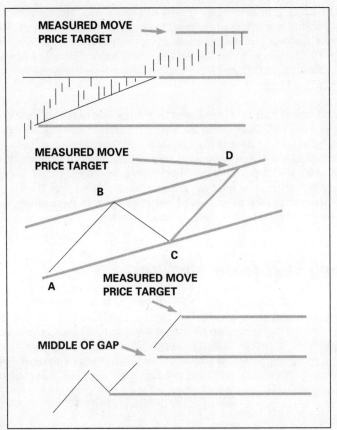

Resuming the trend after retracement

Another type of *measured move* is when a price repeats the extent of a first
move after a retracement. The retracement takes back 30 per cent of the
gain from the low to the high, or some other percentage. The point is that
after the retracement, you often see the price resume the trend at the same
slope and to the same extent as in the first move.

This is illustrated in the second chart in Figure 7-16. Here you see an already established channel consisting of support and resistance lines. (For more information on channels created by support and resistance lines, see Chapter 9.) The price is oscillating between the two channel lines. After you see the price stop at C, you simply copy and paste the A-to-B move to C to arrive at price target D.

Bulkowski found that in a measured move up, the first A-B leg averages 43 per cent over 87 days while the second leg, C-D, averages 37 per cent in 65 days. You have to decide for yourself whether these numbers confirm or repudiate the idea of the measured move. In a measured move down, the first leg averages 25 per cent and the second leg averages 27 per cent, and that seems to affirm the idea of proportionality. Note that the retracement in measured moves up averages 14 per cent over 45 days while in measured moves down, the corrective retracement averages 16 per cent over 39 days.

Measuring from the gap

A third type of *measured move* is when you have a gap. (Refer to Chapter 5 for a discussion of gaps.) A *gap* is a price bar whose high or low is separated from the preceding bar by open space, meaning no trades took place at those intervening prices. A gap is important because it shows, graphically, that something happened in the world of fundamentals to alter perception of the security. In Figure 7-16, you measure the distance from the lowest low in the upmove to the middle of the gap, and then project that height from the middle of the gap to the upside (in an uptrend). You do the opposite in a downtrend.

Part III
Trading on Trends

Glenn Lumsden

'Darling, I've discovered a new method to forecast market trends. I'm predicting a crash.'

In this part . . .

In this part, we show you how to detect and measure
trends and then use that knowledge to your advantage.
Whether you're following the visual cues provided by
the charts or using technical indicators, the information
given by the trends tells you enough to start making
predictions. Forecasting what the market will do and
watching for confirmation of your forecast gives you the
advantage that allows you to trade profitably.

Chapter 8

Drawing Trendlines

*O*ften you can see a trend with the naked eye, but to impose order on your visual impression, you can connect the dots, so to speak, by actually drawing a line along the price bars. A *trendline* is a straight line that starts at the beginning of the trend and stops at the end of the trend. You can do this the low-tech way by using a piece of paper and a pencil, or go high-tech with software like Excel or special charting software. Figuring out where trends start and stop can be complicated, but in this chapter, we explain how to spot them, plot them and figure out what they're telling you.

Looking Closely at a Price Chart

When you look at a chart of a securities price, sometimes the trendline pops out at you. The price is moving in a consistent fashion, either up or down. On some occasions, a line isn't instantly obvious and you have to look at the chart for a few minutes and even draw a few experimental lines before a trendline is visible. To see what we mean, take a look at Figure 8-1. The alternative lines are experimental trendlines. Which one is correct?

Figure 8-1:
Experi-
menting
with
trendlines.

NEW LOW

Well, none of them — and all of them. The first two lines on the left connect a series of lows but then the price breaks each of the lines to the downside, so you're forced to abandon them.

Suddenly you get a shock by the appearance of a new low (at about the middle of the chart), and you don't know how to evaluate it. The heavy line through the centre is another kind of statistical trendline, the linear regression, which may be of little technical use to beginners new to charting or trading (check out Chapter 9 for more on linear regressions). Note that it does a pretty good job of cutting off the high-low extremes and representing the essence of the total move. Finally, the longest trendline connects the three major lows. How do you know if this is the right trendline or another new low will come along?

You don't know. You know only afterwards that new highs are going to reappear and keep the trendline alive.

The time frame of the chart you're looking at influences what you see. A trader with a long-term time frame in mind sees one trend on this chart, whereas a swing trader with a shorter time frame in mind sees three trends, two upmoves punctuated by a downmove. In order to see the single long-term trendline, you have to accept that charting, like price action, is a dynamic process. Your work is never done and prices never stop changing. Every day (or hour, or week) provides new data. You need to be ready, willing and able to discard a trendline when it stops representing the trend — or to restore an old trendline with some minor modifications if your original drawing turns out to be right, after all. In this case, the move is a big-picture uptrend, but you don't know it for sure until late in the move.

You may not be able to see or place a trendline on certain charts. No security is in a trending mode all the time. On other occasions, you draw one trendline only to realise later that you can draw a better one. Some trends are orderly, making it easy to spot them, while other trends are disorderly and hard to see (if they exist at all).

In the transition from a downtrend to an uptrend, you can't draw a single line that captures the trend, because no single trend exists that captures both moves. In other instances, all you can see is a meandering line that's practically horizontal. This may be a pause, and the same trend resumes later, or it may mark the transition period from an uptrend to a downtrend or vice versa.

Be realistic about whether a trendline is drawable. Often, you can't draw a trendline on the chart you have in front of you, but if you generate another chart with a longer time frame (for example, a weekly chart), drawing a trendline becomes possible.

Try it yourself: Figure 8-2 shows a security that has at least six possible trendlines, or more. Get out your pencil. Don't be afraid to erase. Even the top experts erase.

Figure 8-3 gives one solution to the question of how many trendlines could be put on the chart in Figure 8-2. You can draw other equally valid trendlines on this chart. 'Valid' trendlines are the trendlines that work for you to identify the direction of the price move. Note here we connect the low of the trend with a high to create an impressionistic trendline.

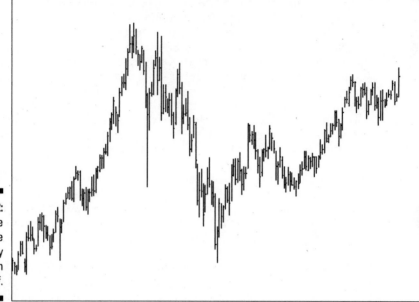

Figure 8-2:
Where
are the
trends? Try
finding them
yourself.

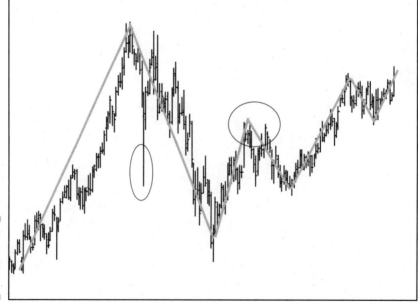

Figure 8-3:
Take a
look at the
trends.

Forming an Impression of Trends

Impressionistic trendlines are useful to confirm or deny that a security is on a trend — and to identify which direction the trend is going. It's common sense that you don't want to buy a security when it's on a downtrend. You may want to think twice about selling a security when it's still on an uptrend, too — you're probably passing up an opportunity to make a bigger profit.

The first thing to do when your friend (or broker) recommends a hot stock is to draw a trendline on the chart. If it's not going up, it's not hot.

You can visually identify trends in many different and equally valid ways. Usually, though, you're aiming to start and stop your trendlines at obvious highs and lows. Here's how:

- **Uptrend:** Spot an obvious low and carry your eye along higher highs (*tops*) and higher lows to an obvious higher high. Take another look at Figure 8-3 and the freehand trendlines we drew there. The first line, starting from the left, starts at a low and ends at a high.

- **Downtrend:** The next trendline in Figure 8-3 is a downtrend. It starts at that high and goes to the low. In the case of a downtrend, your eye starts at an obvious high and follows successively lower highs and lower lows (*bottoms*) to an obvious low. Of course, you know it's the lowest low only after the fact.

The third line is an uptrend, and it stops at a high. That high is duplicated a little later by another high at nearly the same level — see the area in the circle in Figure 8-3. But wait a minute — shouldn't that second uptrend go to the second high and not the first?

Congratulations! You've just deduced a technical analysis rule. Intuitively you know that the trendline should end at the highest high, and if you see a higher one, you shouldn't end the trendline yet. In this case, the second high is near the first high, but not actually higher. That's why the trendline stops at the first high. In fact, the second high forms a pattern named a double top (refer to Chapter 7).

For purposes of drawing trendlines, use the highs and lows, but don't totally ignore the close — you may want to use the highest and lowest closes, rather than the highest high and lowest low. It's possible to get a wild random move that creates a spike high or a spike low that isn't consistent with the overall trend. In fact, Figure 8-3 shows a doozy of a spike.

See the price bar in the ellipse. The relationship of the high (or the low) to the close is covered in Chapter 4, and spikes are also covered in Chapter 5. What should you think about this spike? Well, its sheer size confirms negative sentiment towards the security, even if the sharp upmove afterwards gives you cause for doubt. But the high after the downward spike doesn't match or surpass the highest high, confirming that the bulls are losing this battle and the bears are about to triumph.

So far you have been looking at charts without labels and considering trendlines in a general way. Figure 8-4 illustrates a trendline drawn freehand on a real security, which happens to be IBM stock.

The trendline is drawn from an obvious low to the end of the price data. The trendline gives a satisfactory impression of the trend. If you had used this trendline to buy and sell the security, you would have made a 35 per cent profit in less than three months. The maths is pretty simple:

27/09/01	Buy	$90.00
14/12/01	Sell	$121.10
	Profit	**$31.10**

The example is unrealistic, however, because you don't know until afterwards that the price on 27/9/01 (labelled 'Buy') was the low and therefore the best place to buy. Besides, how would you have known to hang on during that flat spot marked by the horizontal lines? The price wasn't consistently making higher highs and higher lows, and on one day, even made a lower low than the low a month before (marked 'Lower Low' in Figure 8-4). On that date, you had no reasonable expectation that the trend was going to continue upward, at least not from looking at the chart alone. Finally, the 'Sell' mark is located at a suspiciously convenient location — the end of the chart!

We provide solutions for most of these objections in the section 'Creating Rule-Based Trendlines' later in the chapter, where we show you how to devise rules for identifying where to start and end the line. But don't rush to complicate your understanding just yet. The point of this chart is that a 35 per cent profit in one quarter of a year isn't impossible, and you can achieve it just by drawing a single line on a chart with your pencil. No computer or fancy software necessary. The trick, though, is to identify as early possible the start of a trend, and then be as quick to identify when the same trend ends.

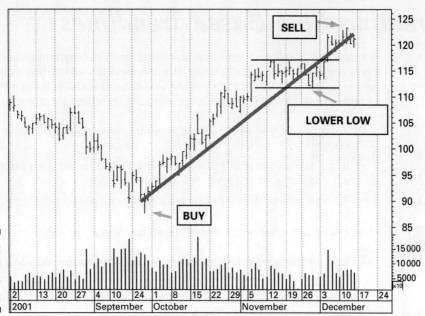

Figure 8-4:
Freehand
trendline,
IBM stock.

We've already pointed out some challenges to the freehand trendline drawing, and you've probably come up with some of the others at this point:

- ✔ The freehand trendline illustrates that hindsight is a wonderful thing.

- ✔ Drawing a line doesn't provide specific guidance on exactly where to enter and exit.

- ✔ If you believe that an uptrend is in place, you may be able to fool your eye and hand into drawing one that by any objective standard doesn't belong there.

- ✔ Not every trendline is obvious and easy to draw.

You never know in advance when a trendline should start or stop. You know only after the fact. So a trendline is a work-in-progress that needs constant re-evaluation. Yes, this means you need to check the price after the close to see where it stands in relation to the trendline. To help in the process, you may extend a trendline artificially out into the future in the hope and expectation that new prices will be near it, but remember that the extended line is only a hope and expectation, and may not become the reality.

Creating Rule-Based Trendlines

A *rule-based trendline* is one that starts and stops according to well-defined conditions, such as a line starting at the lowest low of the last three days and ending at the highest high of the last three days. A rule-based trendline is better than an impressionistic or freehand trendline for three reasons:

- ✔ It doesn't let you impose your personal view of what the trend should be.

- ✔ It improves your ability (and self-confidence) to buy a security when its price is rising or sell it when the price is falling.

- ✔ It helps prevent loss by showing you the exit at the right time.

Here's how you draw a rule-based trendline for an uptrend:

1. **Start at the lowest low and connect the line to the next low that precedes a new high.**

2. **As long as new highs are being made, redraw the line to connect to the lowest low before the last high.**

3. **When prices stop making new highs, stop drawing. Extend the line out into the future at the same slope.**

Here's how you draw a rule-based trendline for a downtrend:

1. **Start at the highest high and connect the line to the next high that precedes a new low.**

2. **As long as new lows are being made, redraw the line to connect to the highest high before the last low.**

3. **When prices stop making new lows, stop drawing. Extend the line out into the future at the same slope.**

Notice that this is a dynamic process. You often have to erase one line and draw another one as conditions change.

Using the support line to enter and exit

In Figure 8-5, the trendline illustrates the rule-based trendline named a *support line*. It's named *support* because you expect the line to support the price — traders won't let the price fall below it (for more information about barriers, refer to Chapter 7). You start at the lowest low and draw a line to the next low that follows a higher high (in this case around 97). This generates a tentative trendline that can be extended at the same slope, but it becomes a trendline only when another daily price low touches the line. The third touch is confirmation that the line is more than just a line and is a valid trendline. When you use the support trendline as a trading guide, you initiate a new position on the confirmation, or the bounce from the third touch.

The support line entry rule says: Buy on the third touch of the support line by the low of a price bar.

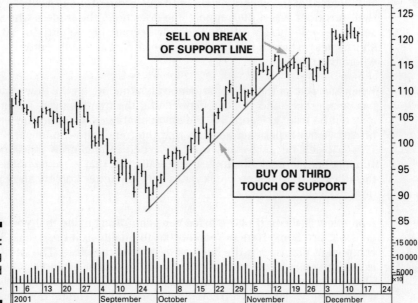

Figure 8-5: Drawing a trend support line.

You use the support line to identify it as an uptrend. The price is rising, and rising consistently. This provides comfort that the purchase of this security will return a profit. Notice that on many days, the low price touched the line but didn't cross it.

The more times that a low-of-the-day touches the support line without crossing it, the more confidence you should have that it is a valid description of the trend. This is called a *test of support* and encourages buyers of the security to buy more after the price passes the test. Fresh buying constitutes demand for the security and is called *accumulation*. Those who already own the security are reluctant to sell it after support has passed the test, and now require a higher price to put their inventory of the security on offer.

Sometimes traders engineer a test of support by selling the security down to the support line to see if support will hold. If you put on a new long position above the support line, you're sweating bullets when traders test support. Will holders of the security rush in to buy more of the security to defend their position? When the support line does hold, the traders who were selling reverse their positions and now become big buyers (to exit their short sales). They've just been given proof that the bulls put their money where their mouth is.

When any part of the price bar penetrates the line on the downside, support has been broken and you can deduce that the trend is over. This may or may not be true. In Figure 8-5, the move continues after the line was broken — but experience teaches that the trendline is no longer reliable. This is logical because every market participant can draw the same support line. A break of support is literally just that — some holders of the stock were willing to break ranks with the other holders and to sell at progressively lower prices.

A *breakout* is the part of the price bar penetrating a line that you drew on the chart. Some traders require that to qualify as a breakout, the bar component that breaks the line has to include the close. The word *breakout* is used in a many contexts in technical analysis (for example, refer to Chapter 5 for the discussion on breakaway gaps), but it always refers to a significant violation of a trend. Sometimes the offending breakout is quickly roped back by the herd, but usually a breakout means that the trend has 'broken' and is now changing direction, either right away or sometime soon.

Sometimes the low extends beyond the support line for just one day, and then prices rise back into line. Subsequent prices respect the support function of the line. A one-day break of the line is called a *false breakout*. The word false is misleading because the price really does break the line; what's false is the conclusion you draw from it. To estimate whether a breakout might be false, master trader Larry Williams recommends you consider the position of the close on the day before to confirm a breakout. In an uptrend, if the close is at or near the high, chances are good that it's a false breakout. The breakout could have been due to profit-taking that got carried away; maybe it was triggered by a false rumour or maybe it was a random move. If the close on the day before is at or near the low, though, chances are the breakout is real.

The support line exit rule says: Sell when the low of the price bar falls below the support line.

A trader who follows the entry and exit rules that we explain in this section has this trade profile:

19/10/01	Buy	$102.65
14/12/01	Sell	$114.50
	Profit	**$11.85**

Discard the support line as a trading tool after it has been broken. However, you may want to leave it on the chart for a while because sometimes old supports become new resistances (and vice versa; see the section on resistance later in the chapter). In Figure 8-5, for example, if you extend the now defunct support line out into the future, you may see that the new higher prices of the resumed uptrend never do surpass the line.

You often get only two touches of a trendline. Some technical traders say that to require a third touch is to be overly cautious and to miss out on some perfectly good trends that fail to meet the third-touch rule. This is true — many valid trends do have only two touches before they end. If you're waiting for the third touch, you may miss the entire move. You may even say that two touches is better than three or more because that means this security doesn't have a crowd of trend followers already onboard the trend. But, experience shows that your trust is better placed in a trendline with three or more touches. You're taking more risk if you accept only two touches to confirm your trendline.

The other side of the coin: Using resistance to enter and exit

Resistance is the mirror image of support: It's a line drawn along a series of highs that marks out where buyers resist buying more — they're saying the price is too high for them. (For more information about how to spot resistance lines, refer to Chapter 7.) Traders expect sellers to emerge at the resistance line (taking profit or selling short). You may be wondering why you should care about resistance lines if all you ever do is buy securities. As a buyer, the only trendline you care about is the support line. But you should care about identifying a downtrend using the resistance line for two reasons:

- ✔ When a downtrend ends, the next move may be an uptrend. You want to get in on the action as early as possible, so you want to know when a downtrend is broken to the upside. The break of a resistance line is an important clue that an uptrend may be starting and you should start paying attention.

- ✔ You may someday do the unimaginable — sell short. If you have been trading exclusively in the stock market, chances are you're not familiar with *initiating a short position,* or selling a security first and buying it back later after its price has fallen (refer to Chapter 1 for more information about trading in different markets). Commodity and futures traders, on the other hand, are familiar with the practice. After all, we're striving to be emotionally neutral about whether prices are rising or falling. Why not profit symmetrically? To make a profit only when a price is rising is to lose 50 per cent of the opportunity presented by following trends.

Figure 8-6 shows multiple trend resistance lines drawn according to the rule. They each start at the January high and end at different places where the price breaks the trendline.

Looking at the first (shortest) line, start at the January high and connect the line to the first high on January 17. The third touch comes on February 6. The price tests resistance for the next two days and breaks above the line on February 11. The trend may be over. You should buy it back, or cover the short position, the first time the price closes above the line. The break of a resistance line is effectively a signal to buy.

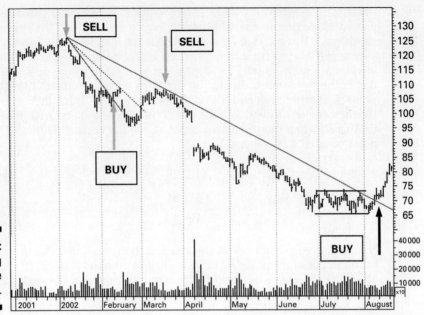

Figure 8-6:
Drawing
resistance
lines.

The logic is the same as for the support line, but in reverse. The more times the high-of-the-day touches the resistance line and doesn't cross it, the more confidence you have that it is a valid description of the trend. This is called a *test of resistance* and encourages sellers of the security to sell more after the price passes the test. Those who own the security are reluctant to hold it after resistance was proved successful in resisting efforts to break above it. They're then willing to sell their inventory at increasingly lower prices, just to get rid of the stock they fear will now fall further.

05/01/02	Sell	$125.41
06/02/02	Buy	$106.63
	Profit	**($18.78)**

Drawing rule-based trendlines is a dynamic process. After the buy-back exit specified on the chart, the price moved up a bit and then resumed its downtrend. You could start a new resistance line, but — following the rules — you can also go back to the highest high on the chart. You draw another line, but it connects only two highs and is violated to the upside on the very day of the third touch. Finally, on the third try, you connect the starting point to another high and it's confirmed by a third touch in March — several touches, in fact. You initiate the short trade position and hold it all the way to August, when the price breaks out above the resistance line, at which point you see a buy signal.

25/03/02	Sell	$103.56
08/08/02	Buy	$71.61
	Profit	**$31.95**

Notice that you didn't sell at the absolute bottom of this downtrend. The absolute bottom was $66.47 on July 26. The amount you left on the table is $5.14, the difference between the absolute bottom and the exit. (Don't be too disappointed, however. Remember, you only know the absolute bottom after it has occurred.)

This is the ruling characteristic of trend-following trading: In trend-following trading, you never enter at the absolute high and never exit at the absolute low. The goal is to capture most of the trend. Traders hardly ever capture all of the trend.

Fine-tuning support and resistance

You need patience and persistence to work with trendlines because you need to adjust the lines often, sometimes daily.

- ✓ **Trend reversal:** The uptrend that you identified by drawing the support line (Figure 8-5) turned into a downtrend a few weeks later. This is often — but not always — the case. As the resistance case demonstrates (Figure 8-6), breaking a trendline doesn't necessarily lead immediately to the formation of a trend in the opposite direction. In the resistance case, it only led to resumption of the same trend (downward). The move upward that occurred after the first breakout above the resistance line is called a retracement, *correction* or a *pullback*. When it's occurring, you don't know whether it's a full trend reversal or just a retracement. Drawing trendlines is especially frustrating and difficult during retracement periods, and you'll take a lot of losses if you use trendlines alone to make trading decisions. So note them, but don't necessarily act on them.

✔ **Sideways movements:** In both the support and resistance trendline cases, the price entered a period of sideways price movements just before the breakout of the line that triggered the exit rule (refer to the 'Sell' point in Figure 8-5). Such sideways periods are quite common during trends as well as when a trend is ending. They're named *congestion* areas or simply *ranges,* aptly describing the market participants milling around like people on a crowded sidewalk trying to dodge one another and progress in both directions being impeded as a result. Another term for a sideways price movement is *consolidation*. This refers to market participants consolidating their ideas about the security being traded. Consolidation often — but not always — precedes a breakout of the trendline (as a reversal).

Understanding how support and resistance lines can be manipulated

Support and resistance lines occur so often on charts, and nowadays so many people are aware of them, that to some extent they become self-fulfilling prophecies. This is reason enough to identify them, so you have a better idea of what or where the trading orders are likely to be. A large number of people draw and respect the same lines. Some people want to defend the price because they own the security and want to see it survive a test of support so that more buyers will be encouraged and it can rise some more.

Others want it to fall so they can buy it more cheaply, or to cover a short position. In some instances, the big players in a market know where the small players have placed their buy or sell orders, because as amateurs, they select the obvious support or resistance levels. Then the professionals can pick off the amateurs for a quick buck. You end up going through a tricky and complicated train of thought whereby you don't place your order at an obvious level because that's exactly where the big guys expect you to — and then you miss an entry or exit at the best level.

Drawing good and valid trendlines isn't enough. You also want to study how often the crowd that trades your specific security abandons their selling at a resistance level, or breaks support by a hair only to take the price up afterwards. It's not the line that counts — what counts is the crowd psychology that created the line. Don't fall in love with your trendline analysis; include it in your trading toolkit, but don't rely on it solely.

The chief issue with support and resistance is that the line itself becomes the focus of attention, rather than the *trend*. People make decisions about buying and selling because of what happens to the line — without anything real actually happening within the underlying trend.

Support and resistance lines are valuable tools. Be aware, though, that sometimes lines get broken without the trend actually changing.

Chapter 9

Transforming Channels into Forecasts

Drawing a straight-line trendline and extending it out into the future suggests what the price may be in days to come. Actually, a trendline suggests only the general neighbourhood of future prices. If the trendline is a support line, you expect the price not to fall below it, but that doesn't tell you anything about how high it may go. With a linear regression line, you expect future prices to cluster around the line, but some outliers are always possible. In short, common sense tells you that you can't forecast future prices to the penny.

Although nobody can create a pinpoint forecast, we can forecast the range of probable future prices. *Range* refers to the same high-low range of the price bar described in Chapters 4 through 6, only encompassing a larger number of price bars in a series — weeks and months rather than only a few days.

In this chapter, we describe the straight-line channel and its forecasting capabilities. (We cover dynamic line channels in Chapter 11.) We show you two ways to build a straight-line channel forecast and outline how to interpret the information you see on the chart. We also talk about using pivot-point analysis to draw horizontal support and resistance, for use either in non-directional situations or with trend channels.

Channel-Drawing Basics

A *channel* is a pair of straight-line trendlines (refer to Chapter 8) encasing a price series. It consists of one line drawn along the top of a price series and another line, parallel to the first, along the bottom of the price series.

The purpose of the channel is to train your eye to accept prices within its borders as *on the trend* and to detect prices outside its borders as *off the trend* (and perhaps ending the trend). In other words, the channel is a wider measure of trending behaviour than a single line. As long as prices remain within the channel, you deduce that the trend is still in place.

Depending on the raw material of your price bars, you can

- Start with a top line connecting at least two highs, and draw the bottom line parallel to it.
- Start with the bottom line connecting at least two lows, and draw the top line parallel to that.
- Draw a linear regression line and draw the top and bottom of the channel at equal distances on either side of it.

How do you know when a high or low is obvious and the right place to start a trendline? An obvious high or low is named a *swing point,* because it's the last highest high or lowest low in a series of higher highs or lower lows. The trend may seem to continue for a few more bars after the highest high or lowest low. You don't always get a sharp, clear-cut reversal exactly at the swing bar. But a few days after a swing bar, the reversal or swing point becomes visually obvious. Can you mistakenly identify a swing point? You bet. When drawing trendlines, you have to resign yourself to erasing a lot.

You can draw channels to enclose every part of every price bar in the series, or you can draw the channels to allow some minor breaking of the lines. (In the section 'Neatness counts' later in the chapter, we describe the pros and cons of allowing minor breakage.) Whatever your starting point (top, bottom or linear regression) and whether you encase some or all the price series, consider the top line of the channel to be resistance and the bottom line of the channel to be support (refer to Chapters 7 and 8 for definitions of these terms).

Constructing a channel by drawing parallel support and resistance lines organises your vision. You expect future price highs not to exceed the top of the channel (resistance) and upcoming price lows not to exceed the bottom of the channel (support). The parallel lines tell you the maximum probable future price range. Note that word *probable*. Channels are visually compelling and can seduce you into thinking that the forecast range *must* occur. It's all too easy to start drawing channels and forget that they're only a forecast. A zillion factors can come out of the blue and knock your trend off the rails.

Channels, whether hand-drawn or software-drawn, aren't always as neat and tidy as the examples we use in the following sections. Some securities never offer the opportunity to draw a tidy channel, and some securities offer a tidy channel only some of the time. But the longer a tidy channel lasts, the more confident you can feel that you have correctly identified a trend.

Drawing channels by hand

Figure 9-1 is a model perfect channel, but you'll be astonished at how often you can draw a channel like this on a real security. Here's how you do it:

1. **Start by connecting the two lows at the lower left.**

   This is the support line. Notice that they're the two relative lows because a bar with a higher low comes in-between.

2. **With your ruler or through the magic of software, extend that line into the future.**

3. **Work out the starting point to begin drawing the top of the channel.**

   To form the top of the channel, you have to wait for the next relative high. A relative high can be seen only after you get an intervening lower high (got that?). On the chart, the highest high is the last of three higher highs. You go back to the highest high and start a line parallel to the support line from it. This is the resistance line.

4. **Extend the resistance line into the future.**

Note that sometimes you later get a higher high and have to shift the entire resistance line up, keeping it parallel. Oddly, a high proportion of new highs stop at the old resistance line, even though some stop at the new resistance line, too. It's like having two equally valid resistance lines. To be on the safe side, consider the farther-away channel line as the more important one. The same thing is true of a second, farther-away support line.

On the chart in Figure 9-1, the extension lines are grey. At the time they're first drawn, the extended lines are hypothetical support and hypothetical resistance. *Hypothetical* means not proven.

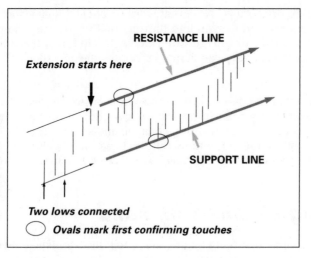

RESISTANCE LINE

Extension starts here

SUPPORT LINE

Two lows connected

Ovals mark first confirming touches

Figure 9-1:
A model channel. Ovals mark first confirming touches.

The lines stop being hypothetical and become actual support and resistance when the next high or low touches the extended line but doesn't break it, validating the extension process. The circles in Figure 9-1 mark where the next high and low occur in this price series — and they occur at the hypothetical support and resistance lines. You know that you've drawn your channel line correctly when a third relative high or low makes a touch of the line but doesn't cross it, making that touch a confirmation point.

Letting your software do the drawing

Another way to capture the collective habit of market participants is to draw the linear regression line, as described in Chapter 8, and then to build a channel on either side of it. Instead of drawing the support and resistance lines by hand and extending them out, you let the software do the drawing.

See 'Riding the Regression Range' later in this chapter for information on how the channel is calculated mathematically.

Whichever way you draw the channel, you apply the same expectations about the collective behaviour of the market participants, and assume that future relative highs and relative lows are going to fall within the same range. The principle of extending support and resistance lines is the same whether you draw them by hand or use the linear regression as an anchor.

Why are the lines parallel?

When you draw a support line connecting a series of lows, you often see a parallel resistance line that mysteriously connects the highest highs. This is so common that most charting software programs have a standard command — 'create parallel line'. No-one knows why support and resistance lines are so often parallel. Here are a few explanations:

✔ This kind of orderliness appears when the high-low trading range is stable. Volume is steady, too. It's an orderly crowd trading the security, so the channel is orderly. Market participants know where the price is relatively high — at the top of the channel. They expect no more gains at this point and are prepared to sell at the top to put their money to better use in some other security. Die-hard buyers, in turn, see when the price is relatively cheap — down around the support line. They add to their position, propelling the price upward.

✔ Many technical analysts perceive a cyclical quality to the ebb and flow of prices within a channel. They rely on the security alternating between support and resistance, and the perceived cycle is the basis of their trading plan..

✔ Humans have an innate need to impose order on a chaotic universe — or market. Parallel lines don't always appear, of course, but they appear often enough that observers speak of trading ranges with a certain air of authority.

Benefits of straight-line channels

When you use straight lines to represent a range, you get a chart that's easy to read. Your eye fills in the blanks. Benefits are:

✔ Straight-line channels imply absolute limits that give you comfort and the sense that you know where you stand.

✔ When a new price touches the channel top or bottom, but then retreats, you believe that the channel limits are correctly drawn and valid — and are likely work next time, too. As we explain in Chapter 8, the more often a price touches a support or resistance line but doesn't cross it, the more reliable you can consider the line to be.

✔ If a channel line is broken, you feel certain that something significant has happened to the perception of the security by its market participants. Violation of the channel alerts you to changing conditions and the need to consider making a trading decision.

A sense of certainty can be illusory and therefore dangerous. Like all technical indicators, channels only indicate, they don't dictate.

Drawbacks of straight-line channels

If your price series is orderly and doesn't vary much day-to-day from the average, the straight-line channel is fairly narrow. But if your chart contains a disorderly price move, one on which each price seems unrelated to the one before and prices jump around all over the place, your channel lines have to be so far apart that you can't judge what is usual or normal.

To some extent, a channel is valid because many others can see the same thing. One of the reasons that technical analysis works is because it creates a self-fulfilling prophecy. When everyone can see the same lines, a consensus builds as to what constitutes breaking the lines.. To forecast a price range is really to forecast the probable collective behaviour of the people who trade the security.

Using Channels to Make Profit and Avoid Loss

When you have confidence that the channel broadly describes the trend:

✔ You can buy near the channel bottom and sell near the channel top — over and over again, as long as the channel lasts.

✔ You can estimate your future gain. If the width of the channel is $5 and you bought near a support line, your maximum probable gain over the next few days is about $5 — as long as the channel remains in place and you're able to sell near the resistance line. This is more useful than you may think at first.

   • **It's a sanity check:** You can't reasonably expect a gain that would call for a price far outside the channel.

   • **It's a reality check:** You can use the channel to evaluate a forecast made by someone else. If the forecaster is calling for a price far outside the channel, you have grounds to question the forecast.

✔ You can calculate your maximum loss. Regardless of where you bought the security, you know that when a price bar breaks the bottom support line of the channel, the channel is no longer valid. The trend is likely over. This is the point at which you want to sell. And you don't have to wait for the actual breakout. You can place a stop-loss order with your broker at the breakout level (see Chapter 17 for information on stop-loss orders).

Dealing with Breakouts

The *breakout* is one of the most important concepts in technical analysis. It's a direct, graphic representation that something happened to change the market's sentiment towards the security. In the simplest terms, a breakout implies that a trend is over, at least in its present form. After a breakout, the price can go up, down or sideways, but it seldom resumes at exactly the same level and rate of change you had before the breakout.

A breakout must always be respected, but you want to be sure it's authentic. As we mention in Chapter 8 and elsewhere, because so many traders draw support and resistance lines, there's always some wise guy in the market who tries to push the price through the lines. In an uptrend that's retracing downward, he tries to break the support line and panic holders into selling. He may believe in the uptrend; he's just trying to get a lower price for himself. In a downtrend, he's the joker who buys so much that the price puts in a new high and a close higher than on previous days, which scares the pants off sellers, who then cover their shorts and propel the price higher. In addition, a breakout can be just a random aberration.

Distinguishing between false breakouts and the real thing

You often see a tiny breakout and don't know how to evaluate it. Say your support line is at precisely $10 and the low of the price bar is $9.75. Is that a legitimate breakout or just an accident? As we note in many places in this book, sometimes you have to accept imperfection and live with ambiguity. The channel lines are an estimate, not a certainty.

Or sometimes you get a minor break of a channel line that lasts one or two days but then the price returns back inside its channel and performs just as before. The breakout was a *false breakout,* which is a breach of a trendline that then fails to deliver the expected additional moves in the same direction (see Figure 9-2). As we note in Chapter 8, to call it false is misleading, because the price bar unmistakably breaks the trendline. What's false is the conclusion you draw from it — that the trend is over.

False breakouts are especially damaging because you may automatically assume that the breakout means a reversal. This isn't necessarily so, but it's tempting to jump on a breakout because the first few periods (usually days) after a breakout are often the best time to get in on the action. As much as one-quarter to one-third of a post-breakout move occurs in the first few days.

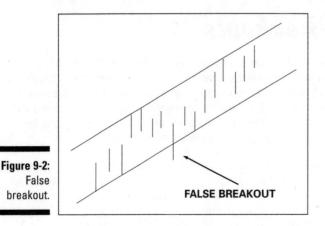

Figure 9-2:
False
breakout.

FALSE BREAKOUT

It takes courage to jump on a security that just had a breakout, especially if you can't discover why it broke out. If you look for fresh news to justify the price pop but can't find any, you need to be suspicious. The breakout may be false.

In Figure 9-2, the channel does define the high-low trading range, after all. Sometimes you have to accept one or two violations of your lines. The challenge, of course, is that you don't know right away whether a breakout is meaningful or just a random outcome. We provide some answers to this question in the following section.

The first line of defence

Your first line of defence is the configuration of the breakout bar. A simple judgement is to see whether the breakout is a violation of the channel line by the *close,* and not just the high or low. As we explain in Chapter 4, the close is the bar component that best summarises sentiment. A high or a low can be a random aberration. The close is less likely to be random.

A special version of the close rule is to evaluate whether the bar that breaks the line is a *key reversal bar,* which is a form of outside day (refer to Chapter 5 for more on the outside day). When you're in an uptrend, the key reversal bar has a promising open — above yesterday's close. The price even makes a new high over yesterday's high, but then the price crashes and delivers a close at or near the low and below yesterday's low. The market psychology isn't hard to read — the day started out well but then something happened to make negative sentiment rule the day, right into the close.

In a downtrend, the key reversal bar initially confirms the trend — the open is below yesterday's close and the price even makes a lower low. But then the price reverses direction and rallies strongly into the close, so that the close is above yesterday's high. Good news must have come out.

Opinion differs on whether the key reversal bar is definitive. Some traders swear by it while others say that you wouldn't want to make trading decisions on the key reversal bar alone — you should have additional confirming factors or at least be able to verify the 'news' that caused the abrupt change of sentiment during the day.

Does volume verify?

Breakouts are often accompanied by a change in volume, usually an easily-noticed higher level. This is in keeping with interpreting events on the chart in terms of supply and demand, as described in Chapter 4. You can verify that the breakout isn't random by seeing an equivalent change in volume:

- ✔ **Increase in volume:** Extraordinarily high volume on one or two days is named a *volume spike* and often accompanies the end of a strong trend, either a rally or a crash. Buying and selling interest is frenzied.

- ✔ **Decrease in volume:** If volume declines steeply after holding steady at about the same level over the life of your trend, demand is falling off but so is selling interest. You don't necessarily know what falling volume means, but it may foreshadow a breakout. All the people who wanted to sell have done so, and the people still holding an inventory aren't willing to sell at the current price. It's like a traffic jam. It will be broken up when either the bull camp or the bear camp takes the initiative and causes a new high or new low, with accompanying higher volume.

Size matters — and so does duration

You can use a filter to estimate whether a breakout is meaningful or can be ignored. A *filter* is a formula or a procedure used to modify an indicator. In this instance, the indicator is the break of the channel line. A filter can modify the amount or duration of the breakout.

- ✔ To modify the size of the indicator, you add some percentage of the total range to the channel line. You stipulate that to constitute a real break of the channel line, the new high or low must surpass this extra amount.

- ✔ To modify the duration, you can specify that you're willing to accept one price bar violating the channel line, but not two. Or perhaps two days of violation, but not three. Again, you have to experiment with each security to see what its habits are. Also, you can combine the duration rule with the close rule and specify that the close beyond the line for *x* number of days is the sign of a true breakout.

Experienced technical analysts warn against making size and duration filters too complex and fancy, for a number of reasons:

- ✔ **Rules count:** The breakout principle is a powerful and well-known concept. A lot of other traders in your security are likely to heed a breakout in a black-and-white way. They *always* exit on a downside breakout of a support line, for example. They feel that a breakout is a breakout, and traders shouldn't try to second-guess it.

- ✔ **One size doesn't fit all:** You can only know that 10 per cent is the right amount to put into your filter if 10 per cent was the amount that worked in the past on this security. Each security has its own habits; or rather, the people who trade it have their collective habits. In one security, the best filter may consistently be 10 per cent and in another, it may consistently be 40 per cent. No single correct filter exists for every security under all circumstances. You only know whether a filter is usable by testing different filters on the price history of each security, one by one.

Putting breakouts into context

A genuine breakout means that your trend channel is now defunct. You need to discard it. To verify that the breakout truly ended the trend, you need to evaluate it in the *context* of the general volatility characteristics of the security itself. By examining conditions at the time of the breakout, you may gather clues as to what the price is likely to do next.

Neatness counts

As a general rule, a breakout that occurs in the course of an *orderly* (low volatility) trend is more meaningful than a breakout that occurs in a *disorderly* (high volatility) trend. See Chapter 12 on volatility.

Figure 9-3 illustrates this point. In the first chart, the security is orderly — prices line up neatly within the channel. The breakout is obvious. In the second channel, the security isn't so tidy — prices jump around a lot. The breakout bar is exactly the same size as the first breakout bar, but in the disorderly price series, you can't be sure it's authentic. The people who trade this security are accustomed to big bars and big jumps. You can see that it broke the support line, but perhaps others won't find it meaningful.

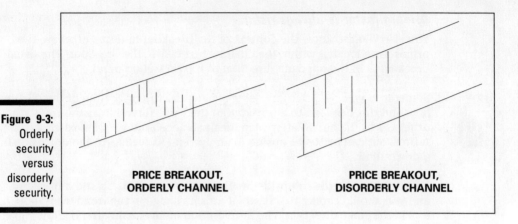

PRICE BREAKOUT,
ORDERLY CHANNEL

PRICE BREAKOUT,
DISORDERLY CHANNEL

Figure 9-3:
Orderly
security
versus
disorderly
security.

Orderliness isn't a word you find in the technical analysis literature. Instead, you find volatility. *Volatility* refers to the extent of variation away from a central reference point (like an average). You should consider that low volatility constitutes orderliness and high volatility implies disorder.

The more orderly your price bars, the more reliable your channels are. A breakout of an orderly channel is more likely to be the real thing than a breakout of a high-volatility (disorderly) channel. If you chose to trade a disorderly security, you must be able to tolerate a high number of false breakouts — and modify your filters accordingly.

If your security generates a lot of false breakouts and you find that intolerable because it makes you nervous, find another security. A number of suppliers offer software you can use to scan a collection of securities for those which are low-volatility and therefore less likely to generate a lot of false breakouts.

Transition from orderly to disorderly (and back)

When a price series morphs from an orderly to a disorderly mode, the transformation is almost always accompanied by a breakout and a change in volume. Weirdly, a shift the other way also foreshadows a breakout. When prices shift from disorderly to orderly, the sharp decrease in volatility warns you that a breakout is impending; buyers and sellers alike don't know what to do, so they do nothing. On the day of the breakout and in the day or two following, you see a big increase in volume.

Driving faster is always risky

You also want to know the context of the breakout in terms of where the prices were located within the channel just before the breakout. The usual breakout is in the opposite direction of the prevailing trend.

Sometimes you see prices pressing against the top or bottom of the channel line, and this can lead to a breakout in the same direction as the trend. In other words, higher volatility can mean an acceleration of an existing trend. A breakout can be to the upside in an uptrend as well as to the downside in a downtrend.

Figure 9-4 illustrates an upside breakout in an uptrend. It's still a breakout, and you should expect that it still marks a change in the trend even though it is in the same direction. The acceleration of an existing trend should make you sit up and take notice. While it may simply signal a steepening of the trend as the crowd develops enthusiasm for the security, it can also occur near the end of a trend. It is sometimes called a *blowout* (or *blowoff*) *top* or a blowout bottom. In other words, an upside breakout in an uptrend is often a warning of an impending *downside* breakout, counterintuitive as that seems at first.

How can such a pattern come about? Easy. The crowd becomes overheated with greed to buy a security that is rising with tremendous force, or overwhelmed by fear to dump a security that is declining with great momentum. At some point, everyone who was going to buy has bought. Because these are traders who bought only to get a fast profit, when the rise slows down and a lower high or a lower low appears, these buyers exit in a horde. For a discussion of a lower high together with a lower low in an uptrend, refer to Chapter 4. By selling a lot of the security in a very short period of time, the market has an oversupply, and just like the price of tomatoes falling to 10 cents in late February, buyers can command a low price.

The same thing happens when a downmove exhausts itself. Everybody who was going to sell has sold. Supply is now limited. Anyone who wants to buy has to start bidding the price up until he induces a longer-term holder of the security to part with it.

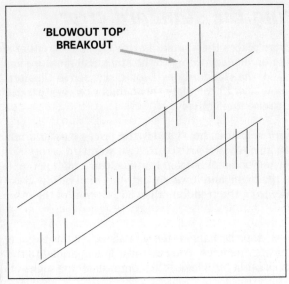

'BLOWOUT TOP'
BREAKOUT

Figure 9-4:
Upside
breakout in
an uptrend.

Riding the Regression Range

You can construct a more 'scientific' set of parallel lines by drawing channel
lines around the linear regression line. As described in Chapter 8, the *linear
regression* is the line that minimises the distance from itself and every point
of the chart. It's the true, pure trendline, and thus the channel built on it,
named the *standard error channel* (also called the *linear regression channel*)
should be the true trend channel. You can calculate the standard error by
hand, but it's laborious. Software is less error-prone and a lot faster.

With hand-drawn support and resistance channels, the channel is defined
by the outer limits (the series of higher highs with higher lows represent
an uptrend, while lower lows with lower highs represent a downtrend). No
centreline exists. In the linear regression channel, you build the channel
from the inside out, so to speak. You start with a centre linear line and draw
the outer lines from that.

Introducing the standard error

Computer software places the standard error channel on either side of the linear regression line according to the statistical measure named the standard error. Like the standard deviation discussed in Chapter 2, you don't need to know how to calculate this number or even precisely what it means in order to use it effectively.

The *standard error* measures how closely the prices cluster around your linear regression line. Most chartists use two standard errors, which results in a channel top and channel bottom that enclose a high percentage (95 per cent) of the highs and lows. An extreme high or low constitutes a bigger error away from the trendline than 95 per cent of the other highs and lows.

If you don't like to draw a channel that you already know is going to have some prices breaking the lines, you can draw lines parallel to the standard error channel lines but a bit wider, to encompass *all* the highs and lows.

The closer prices are to the linear regression line, the stronger the trend. Here are a couple points to keep in mind:

- ✔ If you have an orderly trend, the prices don't stray very far from one another or from the linear regression, and therefore the channel is a narrow one on either side of the linear regression. A price that doesn't vary at all from the linear regression is literally 'on the trend' and has a zero standard error.

- ✔ If you draw a channel and see that it's very wide, your price series has a lot of variation away from the linear regression. Prices far from the norm, the linear regression, are called *outliers* and when you have a lot of them, they're collectively called *noise*. The more noise, the less reliable your channel. Wherever possible, find and trade those stocks that don't have excessive noise.

Drawing a linear regression channel

How 'true' the linear regression and its channel turn out to be depends on where you start drawing. See Chapter 8 for a discussion of starting the linear regression in a reasonable place.

You start a linear regression channel at an obvious low or high, draw a channel line from there to a second relative low or high, and then extend it out. The parallel line comes along for the ride, which often helps you adjust the slope of the line by discovering relative highs or lows that you didn't see at first. As with the hand-drawn support and resistance channel lines, you know that you've drawn your channel line correctly when a third relative high or low makes a touch of the line but doesn't cross it. Sometimes the 'obvious' swing high or low occurs within a previous channel that has been broken and discarded: Go back to the swing bar and use it as the starting point for the new channel.

Figure 9-5 shows a nicely uptrending security with two channels. Look at the shorter one first. We started it at the lowest low, and let the software do the drawing to the bar after the next relative low. Then we stopped drawing and extended the lines by hand, using dotted lines to mark them as hypothetical.

It isn't until three months later that prices break out of the channel — to the upside. Oh, boy. A breakout always means something. When it's a breakout in the same direction as the trend, you start worrying that it may be a blowout breakout, as we describe earlier in the chapter in the section 'Driving faster is always risky'. Whatever it turns out to be, you still need to discard the old channel. It has been broken. In this case, we left it on the chart.

Now we draw a new linear regression and its channel (the darker lines on the chart) from the same lowest low starting point, and keep drawing until just after a new relative high appears. We know it's a relative high because it's breaking the top of the channel and followed by a lower high. We stop drawing at that relative high and extend the channel lines out, as before. Notice that the price does it again! It breaks out of the top of the channel a second time.

As a practical matter, every time a price breaks a channel line, you have a change of state and therefore face a higher risk. The channel defines what is normal and any foray outside the channel is not normal. What does this breakout mean?

- The latest price move could mark a shift to a new high that leads to a new channel extension being formed.
- It may be a blowout breakout forming.
- The price series may subside back into the channel.

You have no way to know which of these three outcomes is the most likely from the information on the chart. You may choose to exit on every channel line breakout, or you can add another indicator to guide your decision.

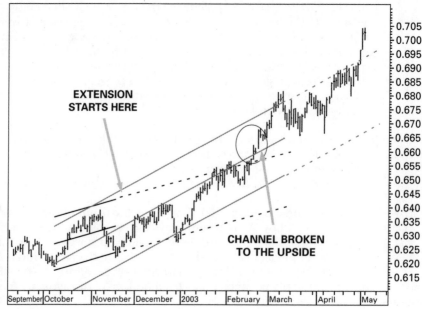

Figure 9-5:
Two
standard
error
channels.

Confirming hand-drawn channels

You can validate a hand-drawn support-and-resistance channel by
superimposing a standard error channel on top of it. Starting at the same
low (or high) point that you used to draw by hand, you draw the standard
error channel and see how closely it tracks your hand-drawn lines.
Sometimes the standard error channel falls exactly on top of your hand-
drawn lines, which is 'scientific' validation that you drew them right and
they accurately represent the trend. More often, the standard error channel
has a slightly different slope.

The chart in Figure 9-6 shows a hand-drawn resistance line between the two
highs, as marked. Notice that it's only in hindsight that we see the first high
as a swing point. We extended the line after the second relative high, and
at that point, drew the support line parallel to it starting at the first low. At
the same time, we drew a standard error channel starting at the first high
and stopping it at the second high. Every line after the second high is an
extension line. And look at how well both the hand-drawn and the linear
regression channel forecast the future course of the security!

Trading a security that moves neatly within its channel, especially a
validated double channel (hand-drawn *and* standard error), reduces the
stress of trading.

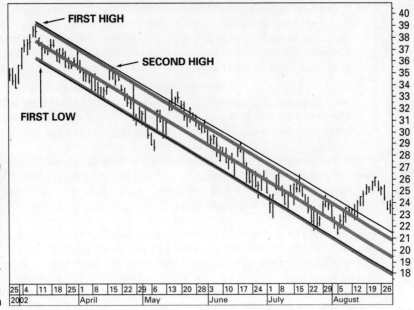

FIRST HIGH

SECOND HIGH

FIRST LOW

Figure 9-6:
Confirming
a straight-
line channel
with a
standard-
error
channel.

Special features of the linear regression channel

You use the linear regression channel the same way you use a hand-drawn channel — to estimate the future range and to determine when a trend has ended by observing a breakout of one of the channel lines. The linear regression has a few special characteristics, though. For example

✔ The linear regression doesn't encompass every price extreme in a series. It encompasses a very high percentage of them. Therefore, some price bars will always break the channel lines without invalidating the channel, unlike the situation in a hand-drawn channel.

✔ To make it more unlikely that you'll mistake a normal breaking of the channel line with a breakout, you can widen the channel lines to encompass the first two or three highest highs and lowest lows, and then extend it out.

✔ You can adjust the width of the channel lines by instructing your software to use three errors instead of the usual two. A three-error channel encloses 99 per cent of the prices. This is handy for a just-emerging channel where you don't have many prices yet.

✔ The linear regression is self-adjusting. Every time you update the channel, your software includes the new day's data and modifies both the linear regression line and the slope and width of the channel accordingly. It's therefore a bit of an odd duck — a set of straight lines that isn't fixed, at least until you fix it by halting the updating process.

✔ In order to see a breakout to confirm a trend change, you have to stop drawing at some point. Otherwise the channel simply adjusts to the new data and gets wider and wider. Don't forget, it automatically incorporates all the price data you put into it. Garbage in, garbage out.

A useful technique to differentiate between the actual linear regression channel and your extension of it is to make the extension a dotted line. This is an important issue — it's all too easy to trick your eye and see regularity or orderliness where it doesn't exist.

You can draw new channels on top of your existing forecast channel. You begin at the same starting point but continue the true channel to the current day. If the width and the slope of the fresh true channel are about the same as your forecast channel, you deem the forecast channel to be stable. A *stable* channel implies that the forecast embedded in the farther-out lines is probably pretty good. If you notice that the new true channel that incorporates the latest prices is starting to widen or to change slope, examine the price bars themselves to see if they indicate a trend change. Check out Chapters 4 and 5 for information on the price bars.

Drawbacks of linear regression channels

Linear regression channels are more difficult to work with than hand-drawn support and resistance — you have to exercise more judgement, and it's more of an art. Linear regression channels can be complicated because they're

✔ **Not a majority process:** A large number of people draw support and resistance lines and channels, but not everyone draws linear regression channels. A big part of why technical analysis works is that many people are observing the same thing and acting on it, like breakouts. The same can't be said of linear regression channels.

✔ **May not stand alone:** You can draw a very large number of channels on the same chart, and each of them is 'right'. Often you draw one channel from an obvious starting point but after fixing it and extending it out into the future, you find that you can draw another channel from a nearby starting point that points to a different outcome.

✔ **Not really 'scientific':** The linear regression channel is scientific in the sense that the software calculates it to enclose a preponderance of prices, but that doesn't mean that you started it or stopped it at the ideal spot, or that the channel extension is correct. The mathematical principle isn't subjective, but your application is always subjective.

Pivot Point Support and Resistance Channel

What do you do when you stop getting higher highs (in an uptrend) or lower lows (in a downtrend)? In other words, the price is still within its channel but moving sideways.

The pause in movement may be temporary, but the sideways action can also be a warning that forward momentum is gone. From this you may deduce that if you're going to take profit, now is the time. The sideways action may also imply that a breakout in either direction is impending.

One technique for dealing with sideways moves within a channel is to draw horizontal support and resistance lines off pivot points. The term *pivot point* is used in many different ways. One standard definition is that the pivot point is the centre bar of three where the centre bar is the highest high or lowest low. Another definition of pivot is the median price (the numerical average of the high, low and close).

Calculating the first zone of support and resistance

The logic of the pivot point is that after a trend pauses, you need a breakout that's a significant distance from the median price to decide whether the old trend will resume or a reversal is really at hand. So you start with the median price and to that you add a factor to get upside resistance and you subtract a factor to get downside support.

On the chart in Figure 9-7, the lightest horizontal line extends off the pivot point calculated on the day of the highest high in the series. You're worried about this bar because it had a close lower than the open, despite the higher high. It's a weak higher high. The next day is an inside day, which may imply a reversal (refer to Chapter 5 for a discussion of the inside day). You're starting to get suspicious that the uptrend is stalling.

To calculate the first (inner) line of resistance, multiply the pivot point value by two and, from that number, subtract the low of the pivot day. To calculate the first (inner) line of support, multiply the pivot value by two and, from that number, subtract the high of the pivot day. This sounds like a lot of arithmetic but it's easy enough to do in a spreadsheet or by hand. It's also a sensible procedure — you're using a multiple of the median price to estimate a range going forward that subtracts the high and the low to yield a 'norm'. Any price higher or lower would be an 'extreme'. If the upcoming price breaks the horizontal support and resistance lines calculated this way, the direction of the breakout is your clue that the trend is truly over.

And that's exactly what happens in Figure 9-7. The day after the inside day, the price makes a new low below the first support line. It closes within the zone and also closes a hair under the linear regression channel, but the low is well below both the directional channel and the horizontal channel. This is a double breakout — it's a break of your linear regression channel and of the first pivot channel as well.

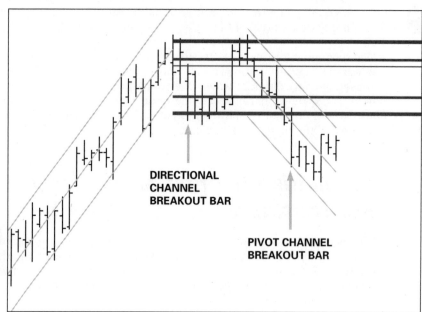

DIRECTIONAL
CHANNEL
BREAKOUT BAR

PIVOT CHANNEL
BREAKOUT BAR

Figure 9-7:
Pivot point
support and
resistance.

Calculating the second zone of support and resistance

The first inner zone is fairly narrow. In fact, it contains only about half of the breakout bar. To get a wider horizontal support and resistance channel, you can add the first zone to the pivot level to get a second resistance level and subtract the first zone from the pivot level to get a second support level.

When you see R1, R2, R3 and S1, S2, S3 noted on a chart or in a table, these abbreviations refer to the first resistance level, second resistance level, and so on, calculated from a pivot point. The pivot point may or may not be the median price. Many technical analysts take the liberty of choosing their own pivot point definition.

Using pivot support and resistance

You can use pivot support and resistance all by itself and many daytraders do. In the case presented in Figure 9-7, upon seeing the inside day, you would set your stop-loss order at the first pivot support level. Anticipating a bounce, you can also place a buy order at the second support level with an accompanying sell order at either of the two resistance levels.

If you're using the standard error channel for directional guidance, the breakout of the channel means you're at a loose end. You can't construct a new channel based on the linear regression because you simply don't have enough data. The pivot-based support and resistance channel suffices to define the likely trading range until it is, in turn, broken.

You leave the pivot-based horizontal support and resistance zones in place until you get a new swing bar that is substantially higher or lower than your pivot support and resistance zones. Notice that on the chart in Figure 9-7, you do get a matching high to the pivot bar. What's important about the pivot-based support and resistance lines is that they effectively outline a period of activity where traders don't know the trend. Bulls try to make a new high and get only a few cents worth. Bears try to make a new low but fail to get a close under S2.

Then the price convincingly breaks below the second support line. Almost the whole bar is below the line. This is a breakout of the pivot channel and usually a sign that you can now go back and start a new directional channel, either hand-drawn support and resistance or a standard error channel.
In Figure 9-7, a new standard error channel is started, and notice that it's drawn from the highest high, not from the breakout point. At this time, you can discard the pivot channel — or you can leave the support line on the chart. Remember, old support often becomes new resistance.

Part IV
Dynamic Analysis Using Indicators

Glenn Lumsden

'Maths-based indicating formulas can be somewhat intimidating. These may help.'

In this part . . .

*M*aths-based indicators have become enormously popular since the advent of the personal computer. Their purpose is to refine and better quantify the same questions asked in all technical methods: Is the security trending? How strong is the trend? Is the trend ending?

Indicator formulas can be intimidating, but underneath the conventions of how maths formulas are presented is nothing fancier or more difficult than various ways of adding up or comparing characteristics of the price bar over time. In this part, we walk you through the most commonly used indicators and show how they capture one or another aspect of crowd behaviour.

Chapter 10

Using Dynamic Lines

. . . .

. . . .

Moving averages are the workhorses of technical analysis. Just about everybody starts out in technical analysis with moving averages, and some traders never see a need to look into any other technique — that's how successful moving averages can make your trading.

A *moving average* is an arithmetic method of smoothing price numbers so that you can see and measure a trend. A straight line (refer to Chapter 8) is a good visual organising device, but a dynamic line — the moving average — more accurately describes what's really going on and is often no less valuable a visual organiser. In addition, you don't need to choose starting and ending points, removing that aspect of subjectivity, although choosing how many days to put in your moving averages is subjective. In this chapter, we discuss several different ways you can calculate and use moving averages to get buy/sell trading signals.

Visually, a moving average depicts the trend in a useful way, but you have to be careful not to attribute a forecasting capability to the moving average. Moving averages are *trend-following*. The moving average is a lagging indicator — it can still be rising after your price hits a brick wall and crashes.

The Simple Moving Average

You know what an average is — you measure ten of something, add up the measurements, and divide by ten. Here's how you get the average 'moving': Start by finding the average of a number of prices — say ten. The next day you add the newest price to the total and subtract the oldest price, keeping the total number of prices constant at ten. Most traders pick the closing price for moving averages because it's the summary of the period's action and sentiment. (For more on closing price sentiment, check out Chapter 4.)

Yes, using the moving average means re-calculating the whole thing every time you have a new price. Before PCs, it was a laborious process. In fact, a preference for the 10-day average started in the 1930s, because it's easy to calculate by hand (plus it measures two weeks), and it remains popular today. (For a discussion on choosing the number of days to use with a moving average, see the section 'Fixing lag', later in the chapter.)

Figure 10-1 displays a 10-day simple moving average of the closing price of a stock. It's termed *simple* because you haven't performed any adjustments on it. We discuss adjustments later in this chapter.

Figure 10-1:
Simple
moving
average.

Right off the bat, you can see that the moving average clings to the prices and represents their movement better than a straight line and, at the same time, smoothes away the occasional erratic price. You almost stop seeing price variations after you draw the moving average on a chart.

Starting with the crossover rule

When the price is moving upward or downward, so is the moving average line. After a price turning point, the price crosses the moving average line. At the V-shaped bottom on Figure 10-1, for example, prices are below the line until the swing point (ellipse), and then prices cross above the line.

The crossover rule states that you buy at the point where the price crosses above the moving average line, and sell at the point where it falls below the moving average line. In practice, you execute the trades the next day at the open if you're working with daily data.

On the chart in Figure 10-1, you can tell from just eyeballing the moving average that it captured the trend, and the crossovers captured the reversals in the trends. The result is buying at lows and selling at highs. The moving average crossover rule generates a profit. What could be better?

Right about now, you may be tempted to shout 'Eureka! I've discovered a systematic, objective trading system'.

Not so fast. For one thing, the price doesn't always obediently stay above the moving average after an upside crossover (or below the moving average after a downside crossover). See the pair of price bars marked 'Outlier'. First you get a close above the moving average and then the next bar is almost entirely above the moving average. An *outlier* is just what it sounds like — a data point that lies far off the average. This particular chart is tidy — it only has a pair of outliers. Usually you see a lot more.

If you use the crossover rule to buy and sell a security every time the close crosses the moving average, you can get a lot of buy/sell signals that reverse fairly quickly, as this one does. In Figure 10-1, you don't know at the time it's happening that the outliers are abnormal. For all you know, the crossover above the moving average is a genuine indication of a reversal. You know only after the price resumes the downmove that they were outliers.

Table 10-1 shows the gains and losses from buying and selling at the open on the day after a price crossover of the moving average in either direction. Notice that we include the short side — a short sale when the price crosses below the moving average. We explain the short sale principle in Chapter 1, but to summarise, just remember that to *sell short* is to sell something you don't own in the expectation that you'll be able to buy it later at a cheaper price.

To sell short is only to reverse the normal order of the buy-sell equation. Usually you buy before you sell, but if you see a price clearly trending downward, in many cases you can sell it today and buy it back later for a profit. Even if you never sell short, it's important to calculate total profitability accurately when you evaluate a trading rule like the moving average crossover rule. For one thing, a rule that applies equally well to downmoves as to upmoves is more likely to be correct in all cases. For another, the end of a short sale may be the start of a purchase trade.

To evaluate a trading technique, you judge its effectiveness on the basis of its profitability from identifying trends going in both directions.

Table 10-1	Hypothetical Profit from the Simple Moving Average Crossover Rule			
Date	*Action*	*Price*	*Crossover Profit*	*Buy-and-Hold*
9/8/02	Buy	$70.61		$70.61
28/8/02	Sell	$76.00	$5.39	
28/8/02	Sell	$76.00		
11/9/02	Buy	$76.40	($.40)	
11/9/02	Buy	$76.40		
13/9/02	Sell	$71.50	($4.90)	
13/9/02	Sell	$71.50		
11/10/02	Buy	$62.00	$9.50	
11/10/02	Buy	$62.00		
18/11/02	Sell	$78.50	$16.50	$78.50
Total			$26.09 (37%)	$7.89 (11%)

If you traded every crossover signal as shown in Table 10-1, the return is $26.09 on starting capital of $70.61, or 37 per cent in less than one year. This is more than three times higher than simply buying at the beginning of the period and holding to the end. But in the process of trading the crossovers, you take two losses caused by the outliers. The 11/9/02 trade, where you buy the upside crossover only to sell it again two days later, causes a small loss when you exit the first trade, and another loss on buying and then quickly exiting the outlier trade.

Notice that in measuring the profitability of the crossover rule, we assume a policy of 'stop-and-reverse', which means you close out one trade and put on another in the opposite direction at the same time and at the same price. This is the conventional way to calculate the profitability of a trading rule, at least the first time around. Later you may adjust your entry and exit rules, as we discuss in the section 'Filtering out whipsaws' later in the chapter.

Dealing with the dreaded whipsaw

In technical analysis, generally, a buy/sell signal that's wrong (in hindsight) is called a *false* signal. In moving average work, the false signal is a crossover that reverses within a few days, like the outliers in Figure 10-1. False signals usually reverse fairly quickly, putting you back in the trade in the right direction, but in the meanwhile, you take a small loss, called a *whipsaw loss. Whipsaw* refers to the whipping action of the price quickly moving through the moving average in both directions, resulting in a series of back-and-forth trades. (Traders borrowed the word 'whipsaw' from the American logging industry; in Australia, a whipsaw is known as a 'two-man saw' or a 'cross-cut saw'.) Whipsaws occur in even the best-behaved trend, and are really common in a sideways market where traders can't make up their minds in what direction to take the price. Imagine how annoying (and dismaying) it is to get five whipsaws in a row — they nibble away your profits from the strong trends, sometimes to zero.

Whipsaws have a destructive effect on your profit and loss statement in two ways.

✔ When trading a trend-following technique like the moving average crossover, you make most of your gains by riding big trends, and you accept that gains are going to be reduced by the occasional whipsaw at reversal points, sideways periods and any spiky outlier. But if your big trends also contain whipsaws, you end up *overtrading,* which is to make a lot of trades for only a small net gain or loss.

✔ Overtrading almost always results in net losses, because on every trade you have to pay brokerage commissions and fees. Notice that in all the cases in this chapter, we are conveniently not subtracting commissions and fees, but you should remember that profits are reduced and losses are worsened by them in real trading.

Filtering out whipsaws

Instead of using the raw crossover of price and moving average to generate a buy/sell signal, you can set up additional tests, called *filters*. If the crossover passes the filter tests, chances are it's a valid buy/sell signal and not a flash in the pan. Filters come in several varieties and you can apply any or all of them to reduce the number of trades. Note that filters may delay entry and exit, and therefore may reduce total gains while reducing whipsaw losses. Here's how the main filters work:

- ✔ **Time:** The close has to remain above (or below) the moving average for an additional x number of periods after the crossover date.

- ✔ **Extent:** The price has to surpass the moving average numerical value by x per cent of the price or x per cent of some other measure, such as the trading range of the past y days (refer to Chapter 5 for information on the trading range).

- ✔ **Volume:** The crossover has to be accompanied by a significant rise in volume.

- ✔ **Extreme sentiment:** In an uptrend crossover, the low has to surpass the moving average and not just the close; in a downtrend, the high has to be under the moving average, and not just the close. Check out Chapter 4 for a discussion of the high, low and close.

Any of these filters, alone or in combination, removes the whipsaw trade in the outlier case, but may or may not work to remove whipsaws caused by other kinds of price action, like the little whips you get in a sideways move. The only way to know which type of filter and how big a filter to use is to back-test on historical data.

Using the moving average level rule

Instead of looking at the crossover, you can call the end of an uptrend when the moving average today is less than the moving average yesterday, and you call the end of a downtrend when the moving average today is higher than yesterday's.

In Figure 10-1, look at the prices and moving average in the left-hand ellipse. From the peak close, it takes the price six days to cross below the moving average — and *ten* days for the value of the moving average to be lower than the day before. By the time the moving average puts in a lower value than the day before, it's Day 10 and the price has fallen from $82.49 to $75.38, or by 8.6 per cent.

Folklore versus trading tools

Suppose you see reports that Blue Sky Mining stock just surpassed its 50-day moving average, or its 200-day moving average, or that its 50-day moving average crossed its 200-day moving average. This type of information may or may not be interesting and useful. Maybe the price had been within a few cents of the 200-day moving average for months on end, and just managed to inch over it. Why is this news?

Without a context, a price crossing a moving average of a fixed number of days is just another statistic. Because of research by technical trader Richard Donchian, the 5-day and 20-day moving averages became popular, and that makes sense — 5 days is a week and 20 days is (roughly) a month. But 50 days and 200 days are just round numbers unrelated to the calendar (the number of business days in a year is about 240). And as noted in this chapter, the best number of days to put in a moving average is the *smallest* number that still generates as few whipsaws as possible. By choosing a number as high as 50 or 200 days, you're condemning yourself to an inefficient parameter practically by definition.

But that would be to mistake a barometer for a trading tool. If you're looking for an indicator to describe the general tone of a security or market index, the 200-day moving average is pretty good — mostly because it *is* in vogue. To use a fixed number like 50 or 200 makes sense only if everyone else is looking at the same number, and increasingly, they are. Even people who profess to dislike and distrust technical analysis give credence to the 200-day moving average.

But what *exactly* does it mean? Well, the 200-day moving average doesn't have a precise or proven meaning. A security whose price falls below the 200-day moving average has fallen out of favour with traders, and one whose price is in the process of crossing above the 200-day moving average is back in favour with traders.

A moving average always lags the price action.

But despite giving up 8.6 per cent from the highest close while you wait for the moving average to catch up with prices, to trade *this* stock using *this* indicator during *this* period would've been profitable. (For more on this topic see the section 'Fixing lag' later in this chapter.)

The black arrows on the chart in Figure 10-1 mark the buy/sell entry and exit points using the moving average level rule. You buy and sell at the open the day after the moving average meets the rule. Table 10-2 shows the profit you make by applying the rule. Your gain is $43.07 on an initial capital stake of $71.05, or 61 per cent, compared to 14 per cent if you buy on the first date and account for the gain on the last date.

Accounting for the gain is what *mark-to-market* means in Table 10-2. Cash in the bank from closed positions, named *realised gain,* is the main way to keep score in trading, but mark-to-market is the way to keep score on positions that are still open. It means to apply today's closing price to your position to see how much it's worth in cash terms, even though you didn't actually exit the position today. Mark-to-market gains are named *unrealised,* and it's a good phrase, meaning the gain is only an accounting convention — and not real. Needless to say, a mark-to-market valuation is valid only until the next market price becomes available.

Be on the lookout for system supplier performance track records that rely on mark-to-market for wonderful end-of-period gains. To evaluate a technique, look at its performance on closed trades. Mark-to-market gains are only paper gains and can vanish in a puff of smoke.

Table 10-2		Hypothetical Profit from the Moving Average Level Rule		
Date	*Action*	*Price*	*Level Rule Profit*	*Buy-and-Hold*
12/8/02	Buy	$71.05		$71.05
3/9/02	Sell	$78.24	$7.19	
3/9/02	Sell	$78.24		
15/10/02	Buy	$61.54	$16.70	
15/10/02	Buy	$61.54		
14/11/02	Mark-to-market	$80.72	$19.18	$80.72
Total			$43.07 (61%)	$9.67 (14%)

Dealing with limitations

This is where newbies in technical analysis start getting excited. Who wouldn't like a 60 per cent plus return in four months? But before you go off the deep end, consider that we've rigged the case by finding an ideal chart like Figure 10-1. It wasn't hard to find, but for every ideal situation like this, thousands more can be found where applying a 10-day simple moving average crossover or the moving average level rule results in heartache and losses.

The main virtue of this chart is that the security is trending, and in a tidy fashion. Aside from one outlier, prices don't vary much away from the moving average. But this same security goes through periods when it's neither trending nor tidy. Moving averages lose their power to help you make money when either of these two conditions arise:

✔ **Not trending:** Prices can move sideways for long periods of time while the market makes up its mind what to do next (consolidation). In that instance, the moving average is pretty much a horizontal line. It's handy to have confirmation of consolidation in the form of a flat line, but you can't trade it, at least not using a trend-following technique. Figure 10-2 shows a moving average in a sideways consolidation. This particular one is tidy, too — no outliers. But a sideways movement defeats trend-following by definition. No buy/sell guidance here!

✔ **Noisy:** A price series with many prices varying far from the moving average is said to have a lot of *noise,* likening outliers to the static you can get on a car radio as you move out of signal range. The second chart in Figure 10-2 shows a tidy trend, with few outliers. The third chart is the same moving average, but it arises from a price move with many outliers.

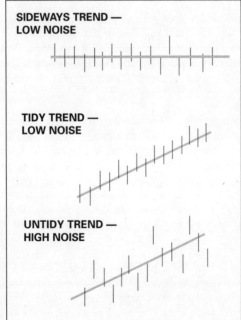

SIDEWAYS TREND — LOW NOISE

TIDY TREND — LOW NOISE

UNTIDY TREND — HIGH NOISE

Figure 10-2: Trend tidiness and the moving average.

Fixing noise

You can't do anything about a sideways move (except perhaps trade the security intraday, on a shorter time frame that may contain minitrends). But you can do something about noise — apply a moving average with more days in it. You want to minimise losses, and a noisy price series makes you vulnerable to false buy/sell signals. When you use a higher number of days in the moving average, say 50 days, noisy outliers get put in their place, arithmetically speaking. An abnormally high or low price relative to the existing average is less important in a 50-day moving average than in a 10-day moving average, because it literally carries less weight in the calculation.

But if you're using a 50-day moving average, your buy/sell signals are even later than the 10 days that cost 8.6 per cent in the case above. Besides, in some periods, the security is tidy, and in other periods, it's noisy, and you don't know in advance which it's going to be.

The conflict between short or long moving averages is the central challenge of working with moving averages, and why moving averages have launched a gazillion hours of research.

Fixing lag

Often you can see a dramatic price move but you know it's going to take days for the moving average to catch up. You're disciplined and committed to following the crossover rule, but potential profits are going down the plughole while you impatiently wait. Why not simply reduce the number of days in the moving average? A short moving average is more sensitive to recent prices.

As a general rule, you want to use as few days in the moving average as possible without running into a high level of wrong signals. When you use a very short moving average, like three days, you not only lose the descriptive visual power of the line on the chart, you also get a lot of whipsaws. In fact, using a three-day moving average on the same data in Figure 10-1 cuts the profitability to under 5 per cent — worse than if you used the buy-and-hold approach. Changing the number from ten days to three days more than doubles the number of trades and increases the number of wrong (unprofitable) trades.

No single number of days is best for a moving average. The best number is the one that fits how noisy the prices are. If your prices are so noisy that you would have to use a high number of days in the moving average, resign yourself to getting late exits long after the price peak. Or you can find a different, more orderly security to trade.

Magic moving average numbers

Some technical traders think that securities prices move in cycles that are relatively fixed, such as three-to-four weeks, three-to-four months (and its double, six-to-eight months), and three-to-four years. Therefore, they imagine that you should gear the number of days in your moving average to these cycles. But while cycles do exist, too many of them exist. They overlap and nobody can agree on a single one that rules securities prices all the time, or which one is ruling the market at any one time. You won't find statistical proof of cycle theories consistently working in securities markets and you will certainly see thousands of situations that don't conform to them.

As noted in Chapter 2, it doesn't matter whether fixed-length cycles are true. If a sufficient number of traders believe they're true, sometimes the traders act in such a way as to cause the predicted cycle to occur. Popular moving averages are 28 days and half of 28 days (14 days), and the combination 5-10-20 days, or a variation, 4-18-40. The 28-day number was devised as a monthly number in apparent disregard of the trading month having 20–22 days compared to the lunar or calendar month. Systems designers joke that the 4-day moving average was devised to ace the people using the 5-day, and the 9-day to get in front of the traders using the 10-day moving average.

Our experience in fixed-length cycles tells us this: Be skeptical of buying into a magic number. The spirit of technical analysis is empirical: What does the data say?

Many technical traders agree, however, that one moving average really does stand out — the 20-day and the 21-day, which for the sake of convenience we refer to as the 20-day. When a security is trending, the 20-day moving average often works the same way a support line works — sellers stop selling when it's reached. Less often, the 20-day moving average constitutes resistance. (Support and resistance are described in Chapters 7 and 8.) The virtue of a moving average that works as support or resistance is that you don't have to choose a starting and ending point — the moving average is plotted as a non-judgemental, 'objective' line. It doesn't hurt to plot the 20-day moving average on your charts, if only to get a feel for what other traders in the market may see as a benchmark level.

You will also see that the 20-day moving average frequently tracks the linear regression, and sometimes falls directly on one of the linear regression channel lines, usually support (refer to Chapter 9). When you see this tracking, you get a sense that maybe the market has some underlying order, after all. Beware superstition! The sense of orderliness may not be an illusion in any particular case, but remember that no trend lasts forever. At the turning point, the 20-day moving average is dead wrong, so enjoy it while you have it.

Adjusting the Moving Average

You can adjust the moving average to make it track current prices more closely without sacrificing all of the benefits of the averaging process.

Moving averages are often abbreviated. You'll see SMA and wonder what that is. It's the *simple moving average* (and you feel like an idiot after you finally figure it out). Likewise, the moving averages we cover in the following sections are also often abbreviated: WMA refers to *weighted moving average,* EMA refers to *exponential moving average* and AMA refers to *adaptive moving average.* The EMA is probably the most-used of all the versions.

Weighted and exponential moving averages

Instead of reducing the number of days in the moving average, a different way to make the moving average more responsive to the latest prices is to weight the latest prices more heavily. You get the *weighted moving average* by multiplying each price in your series according to how fresh it is. In a 5-day moving average, for example, Day 5 (today) would be multiplied by 5, Day 4 by 4, Day 3 by 3, and so on. Remember to divide the total by the sum of the weights, not the sum of the days ($5 + 4 + 3 + 2 + 1 = 15$).

More popular than the weighted moving average is the *exponential moving average.* This is hard to calculate and, fortunately, all the charting software packages can do it for you. The principle is to subtract today's closing price from yesterday's exponential moving average.

When you begin, you start with a simple moving average. You multiply the difference between today's price and the moving average by a constant smoothing factor (the *exponent*). The factor is determined by the number of days you're using in the moving average, say 10 days. The exponent is calculated by dividing 2 by 10, yielding 0.2 as the factor. If you're using 20 days, you divide 2 by 20 and get 0.1 as the factor.

- The factor minimises the change between the existing moving average and the latest price, creating a smaller bridge than in a simple moving average, which has to bridge the entire distance between today's price and yesterday's. This gives the moving average a numerical value closer to the last price and makes it more representative of recent prices.
- The fewer the number of days in the moving average, the bigger the factor. This closes the gap between the moving average and the latest price even more.

Adaptive moving averages

You always want a moving average to be as short as possible to identify the beginning of a trend quickly, but as long as necessary to avoid whipsaw losses. In other words, sometimes you want the moving average to contain a small number of days and other times you want it to contain a higher number of days, and you don't want to be forced to select the number yourself, because you have no way of knowing in advance which is right. You want some automatic mechanical adjustment to kick in when variability changes, to adapt the moving average to the new condition. You can't change the number of days according to conditions, but you can get the same effect by making the moving average adaptive.

A trading systems designer named Perry Kaufman devised an ingenious way to achieve this adaptiveness for trading purposes, and called it the *adaptive moving average*. It is abbreviated KAMA, for Kaufman's adaptive moving average, while other versions of the adaptive moving average are usually named just AMA or have the inventor's initial, like Richard Jurik's JAMA. The Kaufman process of performing the adaptive calculation begins with a concept called an *efficiency ratio,* which measures how straight a line prices follow as they move from one point to the next.

Efficient prices follow a straight line. They receive an efficiency rating of 1. Prices that are inefficient resemble the meandering path of a drunken sailor. They get an efficiency rating of zero. Most prices are somewhere in-between. The rating is then converted to a *smoothing constant* (which is confusing because in this application, it's not constant, but changes depending on the numbers; *constant* is a term used by mathematicians for a term in a formula because it's constantly there, whatever its numerical value). As the smoothing constant gets closer to 1, the moving average tracks the prices more closely. When the smoothing constant is zero, the moving average value doesn't change and is carried over unchanged from yesterday — in other words, a spiky outlier is simply ignored.

The adaptive moving average works like a long-term moving average in that it diminishes the effect of outliers, but without sacrificing sensitivity to trended prices.

Choosing a moving average type

Traders debate which type of moving average is the best. Figure 10-3 shows examples of all four of the moving averages described in this chapter, and that doesn't come close to exhausting all the possible modifications.

Each version of moving averages has strengths and weaknesses. The weighted moving average is the most sensitive to the latest price moves, followed by the exponential moving average. Notice that the KAMA is the best at chopping off the spiky outlier prices that make the price series noisy. That means it works best at reducing whipsaw losses, too. But it gives a value of zero to the breakaway gap like the last bar on this chart. (Refer to Chapter 5 for a discussion of gaps). In a trend reversal like the one depicted on this chart, that's a drawback. You enter the new trend later than if you used a non-adaptive technique, but as an offset, you don't get very many false signals.

Don't endow the moving average with magic properties. It's only arithmetic. A moving average can't capture every important move and, in fact, rides roughshod over some important chart events, like breakaway gaps. The moving average is a repackaging of the price series, not the price series itself. It often pays to remove a moving average from the chart and look at prices without your eye being under the influence of the moving average.

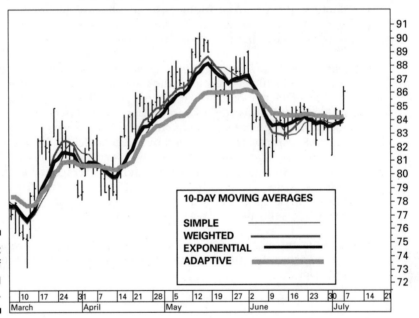

Figure 10-3:
Types of moving averages.

Multiple Moving Averages

You like a short moving average because it responds quickly to new conditions, and you like a long moving average because it reduces errors. So why not use both of them? Or three — a short-, medium- and long-term moving average?

Using two moving averages

Here's where the crossover concept comes back into the picture, and it shines. Instead of looking for the price to cross a single moving average, you look for a shorter moving average (say 5 days) to cross a longer moving average (say 20 days).

When the shorter moving average crosses the longer moving average on the upside, you buy. When the shorter moving average crosses the longer moving average on the downside, you sell.

When you use 5 and 20 days, you're charting a one-week moving average against a one-month moving average. After the advent of a personal computer on every desk, of course, traders were free to vary the number of days in the two moving average crossover model. This is like setting loose a bunch of kids in a lolly shop. Trading systems based on the moving average crossover, with and without filters and other bells and whistles, multiplied. At a guess, traders have written more about moving averages than other single indicator. And why not? A moving average crossover is a chart event on a par with a breakout of a support or resistance line. In fact, you sometimes see a moving average crossover referred to as a breakout.

In the preceding paragraph we refer to the two moving average crossover model. Where does the word model come from? In this context, a *model* is a conceptual framework consisting of certain processes, in this case calculating two moving averages, into which you can put varying values to get different outcomes. For example, you could use the 6-day moving average together with the 21-day moving average, but the principle of the moving average crossover generating buy/sell signals is the same as when you use 5 and 20 days, or 4 and 18 days, or wilder numbers.

Before getting into how to customise the two moving average model, look at Figure 10-4, which shows the same security and time frame as in Figure 10-1, only this time with two moving averages, the short one at 5 days and the longer one at 20 days. You buy when the short-term moving averages crosses above the long-term moving average, and sell when it crosses below. Again the arrows mark the buy/sell crossovers.

You're probably noticing the similarity of the buy/sell arrow placement on Figure 10-4 to those in Figure 10-1. But you can also see that the problems present on the first chart are absent from this chart. The outlier is still there, but the short-term moving average is clearly below the long-term moving average, so you don't care. You hardly see it. On the right-hand side of the chart, some prices close below the short-term moving average, and again, you don't care. The short-term moving average remains nicely above the long-term one, and in fact, you can see a fair amount of daylight between the two moving average lines.

The more open space — daylight — you see between two moving averages, the more confident you can be that the signal is correct and will continue. When the two moving averages converge (as they do near the outlier, for example), you have less confidence that the signal is going to last.

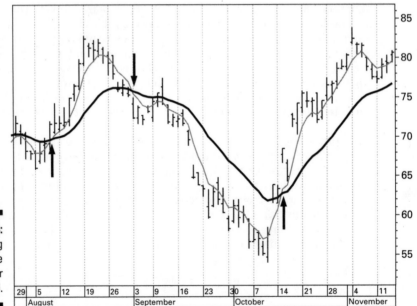

Figure 10-4:
Two moving
average
crossover
model.

If you trade the two moving average model, your gain is $25.31 on an initial capital stake of $70.61, or 36 per cent, as shown in Table 10-3. This is considerably less than the 61 per cent you can make using the moving average level rule, as shown in Table 10-2, but consider the advantages of the two moving average crossover:

> ✔ You can *see* the crossover and don't have to calculate the numerical value of the moving average every day, which is a nuisance. You still may want to add a filter, such as waiting a day or two after the crossover to put on the trade or qualifying the crossover by a percentage amount.

> ✔ The two moving average crossover is more reliable than the single moving average in that it's less sensitive. It lags more, but is wrong less often. You're swapping risk for return, as usual.

Table 10-3   Hypothetical Profit from the Two Moving Average Crossover Rule

Date	Action	Price	Profit	Buy-and-Hold
9/8/02	Buy	$70.61		$70.61
3/9/02	Sell	$74.20	$3.59	
3/9/02	Sell	$74.20		
16/10/02	Buy	$66.60	$7.60	
16/10/02	Buy	$66.60		
14/11/02	Mark-to-market	$80.72	$14.12	$80.72
Total			$25.31 (36%)	$10.11 (14%)

Trying the three-way approach

If two moving averages are good, three must be better. For example, you could plot the 5-day, 10-day and 20-day moving averages on a chart, and you would consider a buy/sell signal to be confirmed only when both the 5-day *and* the 10-day cross the 20-day moving average. If you're always a buyer and never a short-seller, you can add a qualification that a sell signal occurs when the 5-day moving average crosses *either* of the other two moving averages.

This approach is the belt-and-suspenders school of trading, where you're willing to accept a lot of delay in entering a new trade in exchange for hardly any wrong signals.

The three moving average model has one very useful feature — it keeps you out of a trade if the price movement stops trending and starts going sideways, or if it becomes very choppy and volatile, so that you would need an exceptionally long moving average just to see the trend.

In the conventional two moving average model, you're always in the market. When you sell, you not only get rid of the security that you bought, you also go short. But when the security enters a sideways or choppy period, you're going to get chopped up on whipsaw losses. The three moving average model overcomes that problem by refusing to give you a confirmed signal. You stay out of the security and out of trouble.

Figure 10-5 illustrates a three moving average chart. The first arrow on the left marks where the short-term moving average rises above the medium- and longer-term moving averages. The arrow in the centre marks where the short-term moving average crosses below the medium-term moving average — and you're out. You don't enter short at the same time, as in the two moving average case. If you had entered short, you would have been whipsawed several times over the next few weeks. Look at how choppy the prices became, up and down by large amounts over a short period of time. Finally, near the end of the chart, the short-term moving average crosses above both of the other moving averages and you get a buy signal.

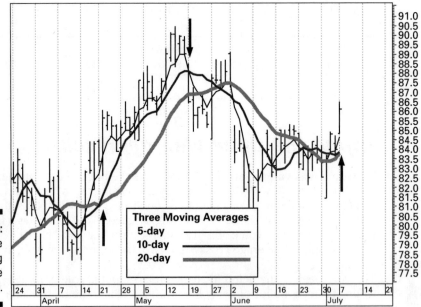

Figure 10-5: Three moving average model.

Moving Average Convergence-Divergence

When the price crosses over a moving average, or one moving average crosses over another, you have a chart event with an embedded trading decision. But the crossover is a blunt instrument. You can often see a crossover coming, but if you're following rule-based discipline, you're twiddling your thumbs waiting for the actual crossover.

If you look at any two moving average crossovers, you see that at a turning point, the short moving average converges to the price and a bit later the long-term moving average converges to the short-term one. By the time the crossover actually occurs, the price peak (or trough) has already passed. This is the lagging nature of moving averages. Similarly, after a crossover, the two moving averages diverge from one another. Wouldn't it be nice to quantify the convergence and divergence? Then you'd have a measure of market sentiment. You could say that sentiment is turning against the current trend when the moving averages are converging and market sentiment is confirming the current trend as the moving averages diverge.

- ✔ **Convergence:** When two moving averages converge, the trend may be coming to an end. Convergence is therefore an early warning. Because moving averages are always lagging indicators, measuring convergence is a way of anticipating a crossover.

  At a peak, one way to look at the convergence is to say that short-term demand is faltering — traders are failing to produce new higher closes. The trend is still in place, as shown by the long-term moving average. At a price bottom, you can interpret the short-term moving average falling at a lesser pace as selling interest (supply) faltering.

- ✔ **Divergence:** When you can see a lot of daylight between two moving averages, they're diverging, and that means the trend is safe from a crossover, at least for another few periods. In practice, abnormally wide divergence tends not to be sustainable and can be a warning of prices having reached an extreme ahead of reversing.

Calculating convergence and divergence

To calculate convergence and divergence, you simply subtract the long-term moving average from the short-term one. That sounds backwards, but stop and think about it for a minute. If the price and moving averages are rising, the long-term moving average is a smaller number, say $10, than the shorter-term moving average, say $15. The short average minus the long average equals $5. Now the price passes its peak and falls. The shorter-term moving average loses steam and the next day it is $13, while the longer-term moving average is still climbing. Today's price drop is a drop in its bucket. The long-term numerical value is $12. Now the difference is only $1. From $5 to $1 is convergence.

The inventor of the moving average convergence-divergence indicator (MACD), Gerald Appel, designed it to use exponential moving averages of 26 and 12 days, although the MACD is a model into which you can insert any moving average that suits your fancy and back-tests well on your security. (We discuss back-testing in Chapter 14.)

The chart in Figure 10-6 shows a 12-day and 26-day moving average in the top window. In the bottom window is the result of subtracting the 26-day moving average from the 12-day moving average, which is the convergence-divergence indicator. When the indicator line is rising, the two averages are diverging. When the line is falling, the averages are converging. At zero difference between the two averages, you have the crossover. You can verify this by checking the actual moving averages on the price chart.

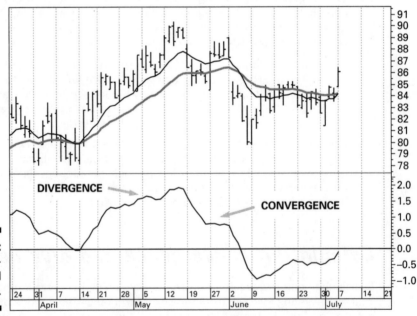

Figure 10-6: Convergence and divergence.

Creating a decision tool

So far all we have is an indicator line. To transform it into a trading tool, you need to give it a trigger. Appel designed the trigger to be a moving average of the indicator, superimposed on top of the indicator. Normally it is a 9-day exponential moving average. The full MACD indicator is shown on the next chart, Figure 10-7.

The arrows again show where you would buy and sell. In the MACD indicator window, notice that the crossover of the trigger and the MACD indicator occurs earlier than the crossover of the two moving averages in the top window. Looking from the left, the MACD tells you to buy two days earlier than the moving average crossover. The real benefit comes at the next signal — the exit. Here the MACD tells you to sell over two weeks ahead of the moving average crossover, saving you $4.68, or almost 5 per cent. Finally, at the right-hand side of the chart, the MACD tells you to re-enter, while the moving averages are still plodding along and haven't yet crossed.

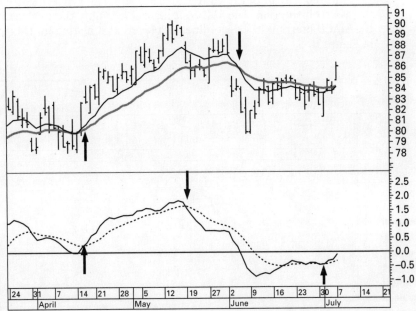

Figure 10-7:
MACD
indicator.

A refinement in applying the MACD is to note that last upside crossover, but to wait until both the indicator and trigger lines are actually above zero to make the buy trade.

The MACD seems to have predictive power, because it gets you out of the trade ahead of the big breakdown, more than two weeks before the shorter moving average crosses the longer moving average to the downside. The plain moving averages don't save you from the gap, either. The MACD's forecasting ability makes it one of the most popular indicators today. But watch out for attributing too much to it — this is only arithmetic. A shock can come along and cause the price to vary wildly from the trend. Then the tendency to converge or diverge becomes irrelevant. A new price configuration develops, and because the MACD is comprised of moving averages, the indicator still lags the price event like any other moving average.

Refining the MACD

Another refinement of the convergence-divergence process you can use is the MACD histogram. The *MACD histogram* is simply the difference between the MACD line and its trigger line, displayed as a histogram chart, as shown in Figure 10-8.

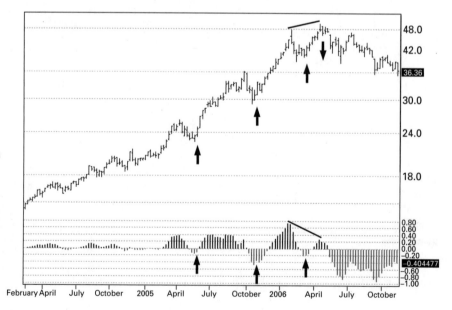

Figure 10-8: A weekly bar chart and MACD histogram of Woodside Petroleum stock.

In Figure 10-8, each bar in the histogram represents the difference between the MACD line and the trigger line on that date. At zero, the MACD line and the trigger line have the same numerical value — they have zero difference between them. As the bars grow taller, the difference between the MACD line and trigger line is increasing (divergence), and this favours the trend continuing. When the bars stop growing and start to shrink, the MACD line and the trigger line are converging — watch out for a signal change.

When the MACD histogram bars begin to move up from below the zero line, the signal is to buy. When the bars begin to move down from above the zero line, the signal is to sell.

You can use divergence between the peaks and troughs of price action and the peaks and troughs of the MACD histogram as buy and sell signals, just as you do with momentum oscillators, such as the RSI indicator (see Chapter 11).

The weekly chart of Woodside Petroleum in Figure 10-8 shows how effective the MACD histogram can be as a tool to time entry and exit trades in line with the overall trend. From February 2004 to April 2006, Woodside was in a very strong uptrend. The MACD histogram gave three excellent buy signals to add to long positions in May 2005, November 2005 and March 2006, as shown by the up arrows. These trades would have been made at $24.50, $33.60 and $42.40 respectively. The signals to go long were given by the MACD histogram turning up from below the zero line. Look at what happened in April 2006! The divergence between the price action and the MACD histogram was an excellent signal to take profits on those long trades. That signal was at $46.80 and delivered profits of $22.30 (91 per cent), $13.20 (39 per cent) and $4.40 (10 per cent). That's what makes the MACD histogram one of the most popular indicators used today.

Chapter 11

Measuring Momentum

· ·

In This Chapter

▶ Figuring out what momentum means in trading

▶ Going over the maths

▶ Using momentum

▶ Getting to know the relative strength index

▶ Introducing the stochastic oscillator

· ·

*M*omentum is another word for the rate of change of an object moving through space and time. In this case, the 'object' is the price of a security. *Momentum* is also a generic term covering a number of technical indicators calculated in various ways. You can measure momentum in many different ways because you have four price bar components to work with and various definitions of the high-low and open-close range to use for context. In this chapter, we introduce you to some momentum indicators and review how to use them.

You can use momentum indicators to generate buy/sell signals directly, but just as often, you use them to evaluate or confirm buy/sell signals generated by other indicators. Momentum is a leading indicator and can be used to offset the lag inherent in trend-following indicators like moving averages. Momentum indicators excel at spotting an impending move when the market is moving sideways, and certain momentum measures are central to recognising when a security is overbought or oversold. (Refer to Chapter 2 for a discussion of overbought and oversold.)

Exploring the Concept of Momentum

The purpose of momentum measures is to identify the pace of market action. The pace is fast during a rally or sell-off and slows down when the price reaches a new high or low. A momentum indicator compares the price today with the price *x* periods ago, so a higher number means a faster speed. In fact, the momentum calculation removes directional bias and displays *only* speed. This takes some getting used to. Your eye is used to interpreting a line pointing upward as meaning a higher value, but in a momentum indicator, the line refers to the pace of the price change, not the price itself.

To get the momentum concept, think about driving. You know how much pressure to put on the accelerator to get up to speed when you turn onto a main road. Take the analogy another step. In Figure 11-1, you start the car from a standstill and accelerate to 60 kilometres per hour. You maintain a steady 60 kilometres per hour for a while, and then you decelerate as you turn off the road. When you're travelling at a steady 60 kilometres per hour, you're covering one kilometre per minute. How many kilometres are you travelling when accelerating and decelerating? You don't know, you don't care — and you don't have to know or care in technical analysis, either.

When working with momentum, you're not concerned with the absolute *level* of prices, only with the *process* of speeding up or slowing down — relative prices.

Figure 11-1:
Getting on
and off the
road.

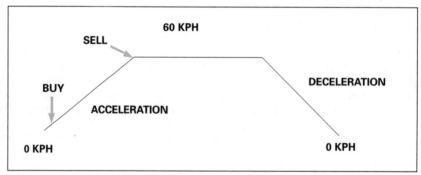

Now switch mental gears and imagine that Figure 11-1 represents the rate of change of the price of a security. It would be great to buy just as the price is accelerating to higher levels and to sell when the process of acceleration stops and the speed levels off. Consider the rise in kilometres per hour as equivalent to a rise in the price. You want to sell at the levelling-off spot, because you can take the money off the table and put it into a different security, one that is still accelerating. Such a trade is therefore efficient in capturing the biggest piece of the price move in the shortest time.

Doing the Maths

In this section, we show you how to come up with several different types of momentum indicators, including two basic versions — *rate of change* and *momentum* — and a useful variation — *percentage rate of change*.

The terms *momentum* and *rate of change* are used interchangeably in technical analysis. The indicators look almost identical on a chart. Unless you plan to write formulas, the tiny differences don't affect your analysis. But we do take a minute to show you the arithmetic behind each one. We use the general term *momentum* throughout this chapter because it's easier.

Calculating rate of change

The rate of change is the easiest version. To calculate the basic *rate of change,* you take the closing price and subtract the closing price from (say) 10 days ago. When you repeat this process every day for a month, you get an indicator like the one shown in the top window in Figure 11-2.

You can choose any *lookback* period when calculating rate of change and other momentum indicators. We use 10 days for the illustration, but you'll usually see 12 days — the standard parameter used in most software.

At point A, you see that the indicator is falling below the horizontal line. The horizontal line is marked zero, so when the indicator is there, the price is equal to the price 10 days ago. Zero refers to *zero change.* When the indicator crosses below zero, it means the price on that day was lower than the price 10 days ago. On the chart, the price continues to fall until point B. Notice that the momentum indicator stops falling only two days later than the actual lowest close. (Refer to Chapter 4 for a refresher on the bar components.)

Now the price starts to rise and so does the indicator. It heads up to point C, where it crosses above the zero line again. Ignore the one-day pop above the zero line just before point C. This is called a whipsaw and we're going to ignore it because the crossover lasted only one day (see the section 'Filtering momentum' later in this chapter). At point C, the indicator above zero means *only* that the closing price is higher than the price 10 days ago. The rising slope, though, implies that it will continue to rise.

When the momentum indicator crosses above zero, the price trend is upward, and the indicator is signalling you to buy. When it crosses below zero, the trend is downward, and the indicator is signalling you to sell. If you were using the rate of change alone as a buy/sell indicator, you'd buy the security at point C — and be vindicated on the last day, when the price rises above your entry level, giving you a profit.

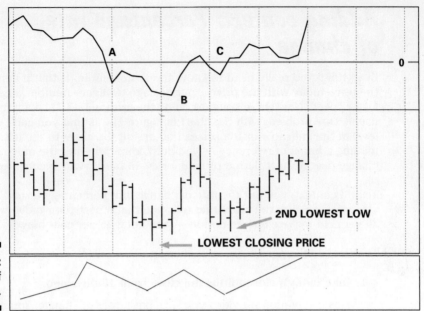

Figure 11-2:
Price rate of
change.

Within the figure:

A   C   0

B

2ND LOWEST LOW

LOWEST CLOSING PRICE

Figuring momentum

As we mention earlier in this section, rate of change and momentum are almost identical, but the maths is a bit different. To create the momentum indicator:

1. **Divide today's close by the close 10 days ago.**

2. **Multiply that number by 100.**

The result is information presented as a ratio rather than the simple difference between the two prices. If today's price is equal to the price 10 days ago, the centreline now reads 100, meaning the new price is equal to 100 per cent of the price 10 days ago, which is the same as saying that there is zero change between the two prices. As a practical matter, you don't care whether the dividing line is labelled zero (rate of change) or 100 (momentum). You may see other versions of the formula used to calculate rate of change or momentum.

Adding context: Percentage rate of change

Everything you really need to know about momentum is that it compares the price today with the price *x* periods ago. A higher number means a faster speed. Now we're going to refine the arithmetic to make it more useful. One problem with the chart in Figure 11-2 is that you can't see the level of the indicator or the prices that are off the chart to the left. You're missing a frame of reference — you don't know whether the move is a huge change over a short period or a minor event hardly worth considering.

To add context, you put the rate of change into percentage terms. Then you get a scale on the chart that tells you that a particular move was a 20 per cent move over the period — and not a 75 per cent move.

To calculate the per cent rate of change:

1. **Take today's close minus the close from 10 days ago.**

   This calculation provides you with basic rate of change. You can use the close from any day in the past, but we've chosen 10 for this example.

2. **Divide the difference from Step 1 by the close from 10 days ago.**

3. **Multiply the answer in Step 2 by 100.**

   See the section 'Oscillating' later in the chapter for more information about multiplying by 100.

The resulting indicator looks virtually identical to the rate of change calculated using subtraction alone, but the arithmetic process converts it to a percentage basis. If you're using charting software, it puts numbers on the vertical axis of the chart denoting that a move is (say) 15 per cent from 10 days ago, or 30 per cent from 10 days ago.

By observing momentum, you discover the maximum speed that any particular security is likely to reach in a 10-day period. You may, of course, choose 3 days, or 5 days or any other number of days. Most charting software allows you to back-test historical data to find the optimum number of days that would have generated the most profit when using rate of change as a buy/sell indicator.

Suppose your security typically doesn't reach a speed of more than 30 per cent in any 10-day period before pausing or retracing. This is because the short-term traders in that security tend to take profit or to cut losses after acceleration or deceleration of that extent. This is a useful ingredient for predicting a new move, and it makes momentum a leading indicator. When you see the indicator reach the 30 per cent mark, you expect traders to do what they usually do; cause a price pullback by taking profit. You can anticipate them and exit early, join them at the same time or wait it out, depending on the other conditions on the chart and your trading plan.

Oscillating

Most technical traders prefer the version of momentum that uses a base of 100. To multiply by 100, called *normalisation* in statistics lingo, keeps price changes in perspective. A price that moves $2 from $12 ten days ago has the same momentum as a price that moves $4 from $24 ten days ago. The normalisation process removes consideration of exact dollar levels, allowing comparison among different securities. In this case, both the $12 security and the $24 security are behaving the same way from the point of view of momentum. You have no reason to prefer one to the other on momentum grounds. You probably prefer the cheaper security but, if the momentum is the same, there's no more profit in either one. In fact, if the $24 security is showing more momentum than the $12 one, you should prefer the more expensive one, because the higher momentum suggests you can make profit at a faster pace.

When you benchmark an indicator by multiplying by 100, you create what's called an *oscillator*. This intimidating term means that the indicator values are limited to a particular range relative to the starting point, either the difference or the ratio between today's price and the price *x* number of days ago. For example, say the price moved from $5 to $15, or a difference of $10. If the price difference tomorrow is $12, momentum rises to 120, representing a 20 per cent increase from the now-benchmark $10 difference.

From a jargon point of view, 'normalising' the result of an arithmetic calculation to derive an 'oscillator' is about as bad as it gets in technical analysis.

Pondering the Trickier Aspects of Momentum

When you see a momentum indicator on a chart, your eye automatically tries to line it up with the price move. Because the most noticeable thing about a price series is its direction, you may think you see a correlation between the indicator and the price. Sometimes this is true and useful, but sometimes it's an illusion and may lead you to wrong inferences. To help you avoid mistakes, we describe some of the trickier aspects of momentum in this section.

Detrending the price series

The momentum calculation removes trendedness (direction) and displays only speed. When your momentum indicator line is horizontal, you may think that momentum has stopped. This isn't so. *Acceleration* has stopped.

To return to the car-driving analogy, when the car is at a steady 60 kilometres per hour, it's still going forward. It's just doing it at the same speed, or rate of change. In calculating momentum, if you use a 10-day basis and on each day the price rises by the same amount, say $2, on the 11th day when it rises by the same amount, the indicator stops rising and becomes horizontal. The price put on another $2 and you're $2 richer for holding it, but momentum doesn't show a rise until the next price shows a change different from $2. Momentum rises if the price rises by $3 on Day 11, and it falls if the price gain falls to 'only' $1 on Day 11. Again, you're $1 richer, even though momentum fell. This is one of the hardest aspects of momentum to grasp. Tricky, isn't it?

Smoothing price changes

When you look at Figure 11-2, you probably notice that the momentum indicator looks a lot like the price series, only smoother, and with the indicator's highest highs and lowest lows a day or two off the price's highest highs and highest lows.

Momentum sometimes mirrors the price move. This is because, like a moving average (refer to Chapter 10) the momentum indicator is tracking the close relative to the close a certain number of days back. The more days back you go, the smoother your momentum line is. Unlike the moving average, momentum doesn't include all the days' closes in between, and by omitting that extraneous information, you get a smoother line. However, if you have a one-day price spike, ten days later you're going to see a spike in the momentum indicator, too. (Check out Chapter 5 for a definition of a spike.) This is when it pays to look at the price bars and not just the indicator. If the spike was a one-day anomaly, the information you think you're getting from momentum can be misleading.

Momentum isn't a trend indicator like a moving average, and yet it seems to track the trend. How can this be? The answer lies in the nature of price moves, which are caused by human beings and all their emotions (refer to Chapter 2). When a price starts to rise, traders jump on the bandwagon and cause the price to move to higher prices at a faster pace. So it's not surprising that the slope of the price move often steepens at the same time as the slope of the momentum indicator. When traders stop adding to positions, closes may still be higher, but by less than they were at the beginning of the move. The trend remains in place and is still delivering profits to you, but at a slower pace.

Filtering momentum

A smooth line is visually more helpful, but you may want momentum to be more responsive to price changes. Therefore, you shorten the number of days in the comparison from ten to (say) three. A 3-day momentum indicator is more sensitive, but it also crosses the zero/100 line repeatedly when the price isn't trending, or is trending only slightly, generating small losses called whipsaws. (We cover whipsaws in detail in Chapter 10.)

The standard solution to whipsaws is to filter the signal. Instead of making the zero/100 line the buy/sell rule, you can say the indicator has to rise (say) 2 per cent over the zero/100 line for a buy and fall 2 per cent under it for a sell. You can also delay accepting the buy/sell signal for one or more days, as in Figure 11-2. You can back-test both kinds of filter using historical data.

Depending on the security, upmoves and downmoves aren't ordinarily symmetrical in size, duration or speed. In Figure 11-3, check out the chart that displays momentum. You can easily see that the scale goes to 130 and more on the upside, but to only 70 on the downside. This means that upmoves accelerate more than downmoves decelerate in this security. Remember, every security has it owns habits.

A drawback of filtering momentum to get better buy/sell signals is that filtering may obscure the seeming cyclicality of the price series that momentum identifies.

Seeing cycles and questioning them

You can back-test momentum like any other indicator. Normally you'd back-test using daily data. In the case in Figure 11-3, we fancied up the back-test by using the *weekly* price of IBM stock (main window) and the 12-week momentum indicator (top window). On such a long-term chart, the momentum line jiggles around too much to draw any inferences from it. To smooth momentum, we imposed a 3-week moving average of the momentum indicator on the indicator. The result is an indicator that appears to cycle from lows to highs and back again. Momentum indicators are sometimes called cycle indicators because of this effect. You can easily see the apparent cycle.

On the chart, the price rises to a peak in 1999 and then falls (albeit not in a straight line) for the rest of the period shown. If you had bought the stock at the beginning of the period and were still holding it at the end, your return would be 49.4 per cent over 5¾ years, or about 8.6 per cent per year. If you had bought and sold the stock every time the momentum indicator crossed the centreline, your return would have been 115 per cent, or 27 per cent per year.

Momentum does work as a stand-alone buy/sell indicator, but you must admit that the most intriguing aspect of this chart is the appearance of what looks like cycles.

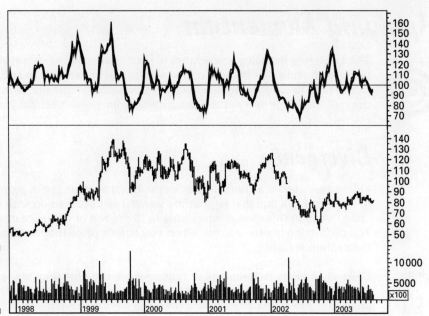

Figure 11-3:
Momentum
cycle.

As mentioned in the 'Filtering momentum' section earlier in the chapter, each security tends to have its own momentum habit. For example, if a security usually delivers a momentum reading of plus 130 to negative 130, this means that the price tends to speed up or slow down by not more than 30 per cent over the course of any 10-day period. Some securities are like old Holden utes — their momentum lumbers from negative 120 to plus 120 over several months, whereas other securities are sprightly Ferraris that alternate between negative 150 and plus 150 in the space of a few weeks. Many commentators speak of a *momentum cycle* as though it were a scientific fact of life. You must make up your own mind on whether price cycles are real, and if they *are* real, whether they're useful to your trading, but look at Figure 11-3 again. The momentum indicator does have an eerie regularity, doesn't it?

Applying Momentum

The basic rule for using momentum in your trading is to buy when the momentum indicator crosses above zero to the upside and to sell when it crosses below zero to the downside. But because momentum is measuring the rate of change and not the price itself, it has some peculiar properties.

Divergence

Momentum can be a confusing indicator, because your eye is accustomed to interpreting a line that is pointing upward as having to do with the dollar value, when in this case it refers only to the speed of the price change. The distinction is driven home when you have a price that is rising while momentum is falling.

Divergence refers to momentum that moves in the direction opposite to the direction of the price trend. Divergence also refers to momentum higher or lower, but less high or low than a previous peak or trough, while the price trend is making a new higher high or lower low. Technically, they're both going in the same direction, so it's a misnomer to call it a divergence, but when momentum falls proportionately short of the price move, you can think of it as a failure to confirm (see Figure 11-4).

In Figure 11-4, the price is making a series of new highs, but about midway through the rise, momentum stops making new highs and starts going in the other direction. Notice that momentum crosses the buy/sell midline on the very next day after the highest price high. This is an ideal example of using momentum as a buy/sell indicator in its own right. If you sell when the momentum indicator crosses the buy/sell line, you're exiting near the peak.

Figure 11-5 shows a chart of Lihir Gold stock. The downtrending move from 1999 to 2000 in price action was not matched by the momentum indicator. The momentum indicator was making higher troughs, reflecting the loss in momentum in Lihir Gold as the lows around 50 cents were made. Following the divergence, the trend in Lihir Gold turned around and touched $1.60 by mid-2002 ($1.10 profit on a 50-cent trade). Divergence in momentum from price movements can be a powerful trading tool.

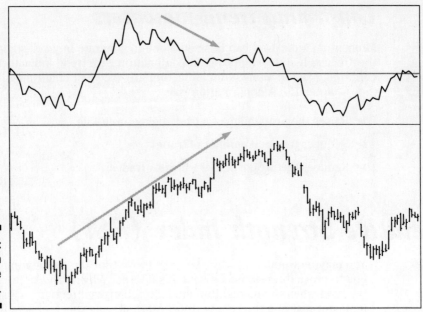

Figure 11-4:
Momentum
and price
divergence.

Figure 11-5:
Momentum
and price
divergence
example
from Lihir
Gold.

Confirming trend indicators

Momentum indicators can be used alone to generate buy/sell signals, but they're also helpful when used in conjunction with trend indicators as a confirming factor. Momentum indicators are excellent confirming indicators. (See Chapter 15.) A confirmation rule

✔ Raises the probability of a trade being profitable

✔ Reduces the total number of trades

✔ Reduces the proportion of whipsaw trades.

Relative Strength Index (RSI)

You may be wondering why you have to wait for the momentum indicator line to cross the zero line, even if it's filtered. Why not make the buy/sell decision when the momentum indicator changes direction — just after the indicator makes a top or a bottom? After all, we expect a move to keep going in the same direction after it starts.

A technical trader named Welles Wilder answered the question. He pointed out that you want to make the trading decision at the change of direction only by ensuring that the *average* upmove is greater than the *average* downmove over a certain number of days (or the other way around for a sell signal). In other words, the average momentum is relatively higher (or lower), hence the name relative strength.

Calculating the RSI

The relative strength index uses averages over several days instead of single price points. However, it uses the ratio method, like momentum. To figure RSI, do the following:

1. **Divide the average upmove over a number of days — say 14 days — by the average downmove over the same number of days.**

2. **Divide 100 by the number resulting from the calculation at Step 1.**

3. **Subtract the whole thing from 100.**

By doing so, you create an oscillator that is limited to a range of zero to 100.

The relative strength index and indeed most oscillators seldom go all the way to zero or 100 per cent, but rather vary between 30 and 70 per cent of the entire range. In some instances, you may find that between 20 to 80 per cent is better, or even 10 to 90 per cent.

Picturing RSI

In Figure 11-6, the RSI is shown in the top window, with the momentum indicator in the second window, and the price chart itself in the main window. The grey trendlines are hand-drawn, just for orientation.

On the left of the chart, as the price is rising, the RSI and momentum rise, too. RSI, however, hits and surpasses the 70 per cent limit and starts turning down the very next day after the highest close. Momentum also turns down, but doesn't cross the centre sell line for another two whole weeks. The RSI then falls to the bottom of its range at an index reading of 30 per cent.

Because you're using averages, the indicator has a normal range of between 30 and 70 per cent of the maximum range. When the RSI's range is higher or lower, it can signal the following:

- **Overbought:** When the RSI is at or over the 70 per cent level, the security is considered overbought (described in Chapter 2). An overbought condition is when the security has moved so far and so fast that traders want to take profit. You can automatically sell when the security becomes overbought (when it crosses the 70 per cent line), or you can use the line as a confirming indicator with other indicators.

  In Figure 11-6, using the crossover of the 70 per cent line as a sell signal on its own is the right trading action.

- **Oversold:** When RSI hits the 30 per cent level, the security is considered oversold. A security is oversold when everyone who was going to sell has already sold, and the security is now relatively cheap (inviting buyers back in).

  But notice that the RSI in Figure 11-6 first hits the oversold level about two and half weeks before the price itself actually makes its lowest low. That's because the price was making new lows, but the 14-day *average* downmove was getting smaller each day — the downmove was decelerating. In this instance, the RSI was giving a premature signal and it would've been better to consider crossing the oversold line as a warning instead of a sell signal.

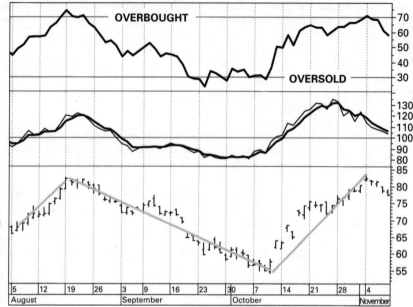

Figure 11-6:
Relative
strength
index.

A divergence between the price and the indicator is a warning sign that the price move is coming to an end. In the place on the chart between the overbought and oversold areas, the indicator is going sideways near the 30-per cent line and the price is still falling. By analysing the internal dynamics of the price (the ratio of average updays to average downdays), the RSI indicator is telling you not to sell the security short at this point, even though the price is still falling, because it is about to reverse to an upmove. (Remember, to *sell short* is to sell the security first and buy it back later at a cheaper price — check out Chapter 1.) If you're a buy-only trader, hang on. Your chance is coming. Finally, an upmove starts again and hits the overbought level on the right-hand side of the chart. Again, the RSI peaks on the same day as the price high. Notice that momentum peaks a week earlier, but has not crossed the buy/sell centreline before the chart ends.

The RSI is much faster than momentum in signalling an impending change.

Sorting through RSI ambiguities

In the example we detail in Figure 11-6, the RSI serves as a sell signal at the overbought level, but doesn't provide an equally clear buy signal when it first meets the oversold level. Instead of reversing smartly, the RSI indicator meanders down around the oversold line for several weeks. So, on one occasion it's a buy/sell signal and on the next occasion, it's a warning.

RSI falls short in the reliability department when it comes to buy/sell signals. For that reason, RSI is used more often as a confirming indicator while other indicators are used to get the buy/sell signal.

The RSI measures the relative speed of price changes. The RSI, like most oscillators, is limited by one of its arithmetic components, the high-low range over x periods. You may have a 75-day uptrend, for example, that has five or six sell signals generated by an RSI that is using 14 days as the base range. They're false signals if you're a long-term trend follower, but splendid opportunities to make profits if you're a swing trader. As we explain in Chapter 14, the trend-follower has one set of buy/sell signals, while the swing trader has multiple entries and exits. The RSI is a top swing trader tool.

The moving average convergence-divergence indicator (MACD), described in Chapter 10, is an oscillator — it uses multiplication by 100 to set the range x periods ago as the maximum. But the MACD isn't range-bound like the RSI and the stochastic oscillator (described in the following section) because its range is a moving average, and therefore adaptive.

Using the Rest of the Price Bar — the Stochastic Oscillator

So far, the momentum indicators all use the closing price. But a lot can be going on in other parts of the price bar, such as higher highs and lower lows. When the close is near the high and each high is higher than the day before, you not only have an uptrend, but an uptrend that is accelerating. In a rally, you expect prices to close near the high of the daily high-low range. In a sell-off, you expect the price to close near the low of the daily high-low range.

Two relationships are particularly important: The high-low range over x number of days, and the relationship of the close to the high or the low over the same x number of days. (If you use the low, the resulting indicator is named the *stochastic oscillator*, and if you use the high, the indicator is named the *Williams %R*, after its inventor, Larry Williams.)

No indicator name is worse than this one. The word 'stochastic' refers to randomness, which of course is the exact opposite of what we're trying to achieve in applying technical concepts — orderliness. It gets worse — the first component of the indicator is named the %K, because that was the letter of the alphabet assigned to the list of experimental formulas by its inventor, George Lane. The second component of the indicator is called %D, for the same reason. The good news: %K and %D appear only in the stochastic oscillator and aren't used anywhere else in technical analysis.

Step 1 (and its logic)

The %K indicator takes the difference between today's close and the lowest low of the past five days, and divides that by the widest high-low range of the past five days. The ratio is then multiplied by 100 to make it an oscillator that ranges between 0 and 100, again with a normal spread of 30 to 70 per cent or 20 to 80 per cent. Five days is the standard parameter used for the indicator, although you can use software to find a number of days that better fits your particular security.

The %K indicator shows you how much energy the price move has relative to the range. If today the closing price is higher than it was yesterday, it's farther away from the lowest low than it was yesterday, too. If neither day put in a new high or low, the high-low range remains the same. Arithmetically, therefore, today's %K is a higher number than yesterday's, and the line on the chart has to rise.

But what about when the price over the past five days ranges from a lowest low of $5 to a highest high of $12, giving a range of $7? If today's close is $12 — the highest high — the top part (numerator) of the ratio is today's close ($12) minus the lowest low of $5, which is $7. This is exactly the same as the 5-day range, and forms the bottom part of the ratio (denominator). As you discovered in primary school doing fractions, $7 divided by $7 is 1, and if you multiply it by 100, your oscillator reading is 100. The indicator is telling you that the price is as high as it gets relative to the range.

And a fat lot of good that does you. You already know that the price made a new closing high today. When that happens, the %K gives a reading of 100 per cent, which by definition is an overbought condition — even if the price is still trending upward! This is exactly what happens in the section of the chart in Figure 11-7 marked by an ellipse. You see that the price has moved smartly up, with several gaps to boot (refer to Chapter 5 for a discussion of gaps).

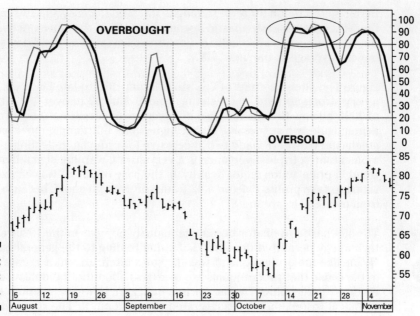

Figure 11-7:
Stochastic
oscillator.

When the %K indicator (the heavy line) reaches 100 per cent, it's telling you that the security is overbought. If you used the %K line alone as a buy/sell indicator, you'd sell at this point — and miss out on another $10 rise in the security.

The stochastic oscillator gives a false overbought or oversold reading at a new highest high or lowest low, because the highest high or lowest low is then used in both the numerator and denominator of the ratio. Therefore, the stochastic oscillator works best in a sideways price movement (as does its inverse, the Williams %R).

Step 2: Refining %K

So far you just have one line in the indicator. What you really want is the equivalent of the zero/100 line in momentum — some kind of crossover guideline to tell you whether to buy or sell, so you don't have to guess by eye. For the stochastic oscillator, the crossover line is the 3-day simple moving average of the %K. This oscillator is named the %D. This combination of oscillators is called the *basic stochastic*. It's very responsive to price changes and is therefore suited to very short-term trading.

Better suited to longer term trading is the *slow stochastic*. In this indicator the %D of the basic stochastic becomes the %K of the slow stochastic, and the %D of the slow stochastic indicator is calculated as the 3-day simple moving average of the 'new' %K.

Figure 11-8 shows a chart of CSL stock. From 1995 to late 2001, CSL was in a very strong uptrend, appreciating from around $2 to over $50. At the end of 2001, a triple divergence (two divergences in succession) occurred. Price action made two successive higher highs in its uptrending move as the slow stochastic indicator made two successive lower highs, reflecting a loss of momentum. A triple divergence is a very strong warning signal that the trend in price action is not healthy. In the case of CSL, it was an excellent signal to take profits ($48 on a $2 trade) or even go short, because CSL fell from over $50 to around $11.

The stochastic oscillator became fabulously popular in the 1990s as technology permitted the spread of swing trading to the general public. 'Trade like the professionals!' was the sales pitch, and an accurate one, too, in the sense that professionals are heartless about not holding a security that isn't performing. The fad for this indicator, however, resulted in some technical writers making exaggerated claims about it. The stochastic oscillator has almost no trend identification capability, and it can signal a premature exit just as a major new trend is starting. Because the first part of a major new trend is precisely where the juiciest profits are usually made, you may feel a conflict between being a trend-follower and being a swing trader. For some technical traders, this can become an endless internal struggle over which is better.

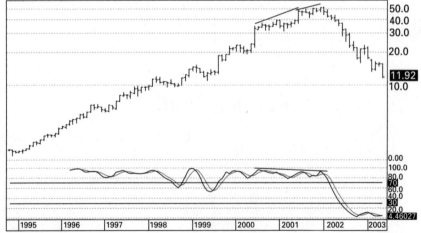

Figure 11-8:
The slow stochastic applied to CSL stock in 2001.

Chapter 12

Estimating and Using Volatility

· ·

In This Chapter

▶ Introducing volatility

▶ Looking at different types of trading

▶ Measuring volatility

▶ Getting the hang of Bollinger bands

▶ Focusing on volatility breakout

· ·

*V*olatility is a measure of price variation. It may be associated with the strength of a trend, but not always. In a sideways price series, volatility tells you whether the crowd is nervous or bored out of its skull.

Because bullish and bearish sentiment in the market alternates, volatility tends to cycle and ricochet between high and low levels and can have value as a forecasting tool (but this is a complicated topic, beyond the scope of this chapter). The thing to note here is that indicators based on volatility work best when used together with other indicators, including standard bar-reading techniques (as covered in Chapters 4 and 5), pattern analysis (Chapter 7) and momentum (Chapter 11).

A change in volatility implies a change in the expected range of outcomes. Therefore, the main reason to keep an eye on volatility is to adjust your profit targets and maybe your stop-loss to reflect the changing probability of a gain or loss in your trade.

In this chapter, we describe three ways that volatility can be measured and discuss some of their virtues and drawbacks. Then we look at the most popular way traders incorporate consideration of volatility in their trading plans — the Bollinger band. At the end of the chapter we introduce another kind of band indicator — the average true range band.

Volatility: A Slippery Concept

Volatility refers to the extent of variation in the price or moves, either as the total movement between low and high over some fixed period of time or variation away from a central measure of value like a moving average. Both concepts of volatility are valid and useful.

Volatility is a slippery concept. Just about everybody uses the word *volatility* incorrectly from a statistician's viewpoint. To the mathematically inclined trader, volatility refers to the standard deviation of price changes (see the section 'Considering the standard deviation' later in this chapter). To other traders and in general usage, volatility means price variance, and that's how we use it in this chapter.

Variance is a statistical concept that measures the distance between highs and lows from the mean (a moving average) associated with each price bar (see Figure 12-1). When you have low variance in a price series, that means it's trending in an orderly manner: Each high and low is a stable distance from the moving average and doesn't differ much from one bar to another.

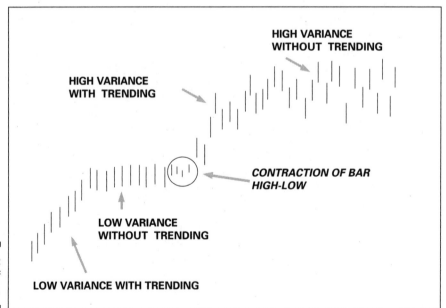

Figure 12-1:
Degrees of
volatility.

In contrast, a disorderly (or volatile) price series has highs and lows that vary and spike a lot from the moving average, so that when you add them up, you get a high gross number. (In fact, the arithmetic process of calculating variance involves squaring the difference between the high and the moving average and the distance between the low and the moving average, which magnifies aberrant prices if they're present in the series.) A disorderly series with a lot of large aberrant prices is considered volatile, or choppy.

Variance isn't used as a stand-alone measure or indicator, and it's not offered in software charting packages. This is because variance isn't directly useful as a separate measure from the standard deviation, which is essentially the square root of variance.

In Figure 12-1, visually it's obvious that the low-variance prices on the left-hand side of the chart are less volatile and therefore less risky to trade than the high-variance prices on the right-hand side of the chart, even when the high-variance prices are in a trending mode. And that's the point about volatility — it describes and measures riskiness.

How volatility arises

Like everything else in technical analysis, it's useful to think of volatility in terms of crowd sentiment. When volatility is high, traders are excited about a new move. They anticipate taking the price to either new highs or new lows, and this arouses greed in the bulls, who put on new positions, and fear in bears, who may try to defend their position aggressively but then may scramble to get out of the way. The start of a new move is when you get either higher highs or lower lows. Volatility (and volume) is therefore typically high as the price takes off in the first big thrust of a new trend, although sometimes volatility is high or low for no price-related reason you can find. Sometimes traders are gripped by a rumour or maybe anticipating volatility in the market.

High volatility means trading is riskier but has more profit potential, while low volatility means less immediate risk, but this is only temporary because low volatility usually precedes a breakout. A breakout is an aberrant price bar and by definition lifts volatility again. Most traders respect breakouts, which often trigger the thrust wave that kick-starts a trend.

Volatility isn't inherently good or bad. Volatility is usually low in a trending price series, for example. So, if you're a trend-follower expecting to hold a position for a long time (weeks or months), low volatility is a good thing. However, as a trend-follower during a low-volatility sideways move, you'll be bored to tears, because you'll have to sit around waiting for a breakout.

You may see advertisements for 'high probability trading' plans that promote particular indicators or trading rules. In practice, only one rule guides *high probability trading* — adapt the amount of money at risk and adjust your stops according to some measure of volatility. Success in trading is a function of risk management, not a function of which indicator to use. And good risk management is a function of understanding volatility, whether the gut-instinct kind or maths-based.

Low volatility with trending

Go back to Figure 12-1. As the price series begins, you instantly see that it's trending upward (note that it has 'broken out' on the topside). Your ability to see the trend is due in part to the orderliness of the move. When your price is trending, you're looking at the trend, not the confusing and spiky variations away from it. Trend-finding techniques like the moving average aren't needed on a series like this.

A trending security that has low volatility offers the best (and safest) trade, because it has a high probability of giving you a profit and low probability of delivering a loss. In addition to being easier on the nerves, here's why:

- You can project the price range of a low-volatility trending security into the future with more confidence than a high-volatility security.
- You generally hold a low-volatility trending security for a longer period of time, cutting down on trading costs like brokerage commissions.

Low volatility without trending

A security that's range-trading sideways but with little or no variation of one price from the next is simply and technically untradeable. You have no basis on which to form an expectation of a gain, and without the expectation of a gain, why would you trade it?

If a price is trading sideways without directional bias but the high-low range of the bars contracts or widens, now you have an opportunity to make money. Range contraction and expansion are powerful hints of an upcoming breakout. You can now start planning the trade. In Figure 12-1, every bar is the same height except the ones in the circle, which are narrowing.

This tightening in range often precedes a breakout, although you don't know in advance in which direction.

High volatility with trending

You may think that the degree of volatility doesn't matter when your security is trending, but an increase in volatility by definition increases the risk of loss. Rising volatility can be scary. You may panic and start fiddling with your indicators to adapt them to current conditions. Tinkering with indicators when you have a live trade in progress is almost always a mistake. A better response to rising volatility is to recalculate potential gain against potential loss, and to tighten your stop-loss, as described in Chapter 17.

High volatility without trending

When a security isn't trending but has high volatility in a wide range, it's rightly called a trader's nightmare. This is the right-hand section of the price series in Figure 12-1. In this situation, you may not be able to identify a breakout of the trading range, which is very wide. Non-trending price action invites traders to try to push the price to extremes to test the range. If the price extreme is solely price-based and has no underlying fundamental news or event, it seldom has lasting power. This results in spiky one- and two-day reversals as bulls and bears slug it out, making it hard to plan trades to find entries or to even set systematic stops.

The best solution to high volatility in a non-trending case is to stop trading the security, or to just narrow your trading time frame down to concentrate on intraday movements. Often you can find tradeable swings within 15-minute or 60-minute bars that can't be seen on the daily chart. (Another choice, of course, is to spread your trading using options.)

Time Frame Is Everything

How you perceive volatility really depends on the time frame you're looking at. This is why you see so many conflicting generalisations about volatility and price trends.

In the following section, we divide the world of traders into trend-followers (long time frame) and swing traders (short time frame). Although the distinction is blurry and not everyone agrees that volatility provides the main dividing line between the two classes of traders, this distinction can be helpful. As we explain in the section 'Embracing volatility' later in this chapter, swing traders focus on short-term minitrends that may or may not be part of a larger trend.

The period over which you measure volatility has a direct effect on how you think about volatility and how you use indicators based on volatility concepts when planning your trade. In fact, it effects what kind of a trader you are. Your trading style isn't only a function of what indicators you like, but also of how you perceive risk. Volatility is a measure of risk as well as an indicator of upcoming price action.

In the short-term chart in Figure 12-2, the security on the left is trending, but with high volatility. The other short-term chart is also highly trended, but with low volatility.

Profiling the position trader

A *position trader* is a trader who buys after a big-picture bottom and sells at a big-picture peak. By *big-picture,* we mean trends lasting weeks and months. In the security in the left-hand chart of Figure 12-2, you buy the security when the price moves above the moving average at the beginning of the chart, and you'd still be holding the position when the chart ends. (For a discussion of using the moving average to get buy/sell signals, refer to Chapter 10.) This security becomes volatile right after the moving average crossover, gets more orderly for a while, and then delivers a fairly hairy downside retracement. To trade this trend is to accept a lot of risk, especially when the price falls back so far — although after the retracement, it makes a new high.

A position trader identifies a trend with the expectation of a long holding period and tolerates high volatility (and directional retracements), because if he enters at the start of a big trend, he hopes to hit a home run in terms of a big one-time profit. Position traders are always trend-followers.

To a position trader, volatility is an annoyance. You select indicators to minimise the appearance of volatility on the chart. One of the purposes of moving averages and trendlines is to divert your eye away from price variance and keep your eye on the big picture — the trend.

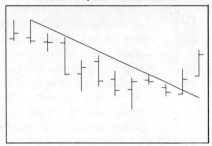

TRENDING, HIGH VOLATILITY   TRENDING, LOW VOLATILITY

Figure 12-2:
Volatility
and time
frame.

Embracing volatility

A large class of technical traders embraces volatility — swing traders. After all, even the most highly trended price action undergoes retracements, and the alternating series of trend thrust and retracement are tradeable as stand-alone minitrends. The high volatility over the life of the trend in the left-hand chart in Figure 12-2 can be broken down into more manageable, bite-sized — and low-volatility — swings. Swing traders can, therefore, be indifferent to whether the security is trending in the big-picture sense or not. Their goal is to pick a low to buy and a high to sell without necessarily knowing or caring about big-picture directional bias.

In Figure 12-2, if you're a swing trader, you would buy the security much earlier than the position trader, right after the second bottom, and hold the position until right after the highest high. Your next move is to go short right after the highest high. This is where the second chart begins. After that, the minitrend move is well-behaved for another eight bars. You see low volatility and therefore a low risk opportunity to trade. You may know perfectly well that the security is on a big-picture uptrend, but you also know that the retracement is like a minitrend and offers an opportunity to make a quick, low-risk buck.

Revisiting the conventional wisdom

The committed position trader never trades countertrend. A position trader sees the same retracement as a swing trader, but because the moving average doesn't give a sell signal, he or she sticks to the technique. The position trader is taking a larger risk in the single big-picture trend trade than the swing trader is taking in the two, smaller swing trades.

If securities move in long-term trends, you make the most profit by hanging on to a position for the entire length of time. You also minimise transaction costs. But as the two charts in Figure 12-2 show, the risk of position trading can be high if your security is volatile. The risk of swing trading this particular security is actually lower, assuming that you can identify the beginning and end of the swing, if only because each leg is shorter. When each swing has low volatility, the swing trader is taking less risk on each successive trade than the position trader, whose single big-picture trade has high volatility. By having a short holding period, the swing trader takes a lower *total* risk on a series of swing trades than the position trader.

This comparison illustrates the point that active trading is the least risky, exactly as the early sages of Wall Street said. Accordingly, the position trader gives back a lot when trend-identification is wrong or the trend abruptly reverses, while the swing trader takes smaller losses.

Measuring Volatility

Volatility is the degree of variation of a price series over time. You can measure volatility in plain or fancy ways. In financial analysis, volatility means one thing — the standard deviation, which we discuss in the section 'Considering the standard deviation' later in the chapter. Before tackling that, we look at other useful measures of volatility.

Tracking the maximum move

One way to measure volatility is to capture the *largest* price change over *x* number of days — the *maximum move,* also called the *gross move.* You subtract the lowest low from the highest high over 10 days or 100 days or some other number of days. The chief use of this measure is to find the maximum move over a fixed period of time to use as a profit target (*maximum favourable excursion*) or as a worst-case stop-loss (*maximum adverse excursion*). See Chapter 17 for information on setting stops.

Similarly, you can find the *minimum move* over a fixed number of days to evaluate whether the security has profit potential worth taking any risk at all. If the security moves so little that the annualised rate of return is (say) 3 per cent when the return on a risk-free instrument like a savings account or bond is 5 per cent, you have no rational financial reason to trade the security.

In Figure 12-3, the top window shows the highest high in a rolling 30-day period minus the lowest low in the same 30-day period — the maximum move. Notice that at the beginning and middle of the chart, you could make as much as $30 in a 30-day period in this stock, but then the volatility of the price change tapers off to under $10 by the end of the chart. At that point, you're taking less risk of a catastrophic drop in the price over any 30-day period, but on the other hand, your profit potential has just been cut to one-third of its previous glory, too — the usual tradeoff between risk and reward.

Maximum move and trend

In Figure 12-3, it's hard to see a connection between the maximum move in the top window and the prices in the bottom window. The straight line starting at the middle of the bottom window is the linear regression of price (refer to Chapter 9). The line slopes upward, meaning the price is in a slight uptrend during the period — but at the same time, volatility is on a downtrend.

The *price* trend can differ in size and slope from the *volatility* trend. Sometimes they're in sync, rising or falling together, or they can move in opposite directions. Knowing something about the trend in the maximum move doesn't necessarily tell you anything about the trend in prices, and vice versa. In other words, volatility is often independent of a price's trendedness.

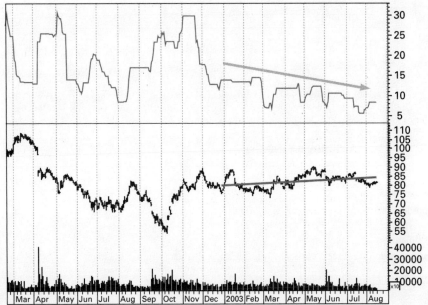

Figure 12-3: 30-day min-max, IBM stock.

Maximum move and holding period

In Figure 12-4, the orderly price series has a net change from the lowest low to the highest high (A to B) of exactly the same amount as the disorderly price series below it. But obviously the disorderly series implies a greater risk of loss *if you have to exit before the period ends.* The trendedness of each security is the same, as shown by the identical linear regression line slopes.

As Figure 12-4 illustrates, measuring the maximum high-low range over a fixed period of time fails to capture the risk of holding a position *during* the period.

Considering the standard deviation

Maximum move measures the gross low-to-high move over a period, but the bottom chart in Figure 12-4 exhibits a different kind of volatility that isn't captured by the maximum move. The disorderly price series has the same degree of trendedness and the same low-to-high outcome over the period, but it's obviously a riskier trend. What, then, is the right way to express that riskiness?

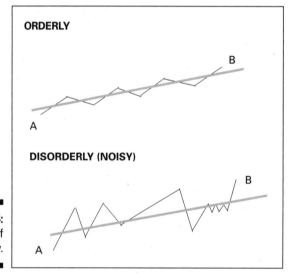

Figure 12-4:
Types of
volatility.

The answer is the standard deviation. The *standard deviation* is a measure of the dispersion of prices away from the average. The wider the spread of prices, the higher the standard deviation. The concept is in the same statistical family as standard error, introduced in Chapter 9. The standard deviation is measured from a moving average and measures the actual variance of each price away from the centerline.

You're probably expecting a chart showing standard deviation about here, right? Well, charting software does offer it but it's not very useful as a stand-alone measure. Hardly anyone actually looks at the raw standard deviation on a chart, because we have other applications for it. See the section 'Applying Volatility Measures — Bollinger Bands' later in the chapter.

Using the average true range indicator

Another way to view volatility is to look at the average high-low range over *x* number of days. The best version of the high-low range is the *average true range,* which incorporates gaps by substituting the close for the gapped high or low. Refer to Chapter 5 for the calculation method and to see expanding and contracting ranges. To review:

- ✔ **Range expansion:** The highs and lows are getting farther apart; volatility is rising. Range expansion provides a bigger profit opportunity and an equivalent increase in risk of loss.

- ✔ **Range contraction:** The highs and lows are moving closer together, and you may think that risk is lower, too. But this is true only up to a point — the point of a breakout.

An indicator like the average true range is helpful in making trading decisions, but don't forget to look at the price bars directly for a pattern that may explain *why* the average true range is expanding or contracting.

In Figure 12-5, the average true range indicator in the top window expands on a one-day increase in the size of the bar. The indicator continues to rise and so does the price, but then it falls precipitously even though the price trend goes up, retraces and goes up some more. Right after the indicator reaches a new low again, the price makes a new higher high. You should be suspicious when the indicator falls while the price is rising. Look more closely — the close on the highest high bar is at the low of the day. Sure enough, the day after the highest high, the price gaps downward.

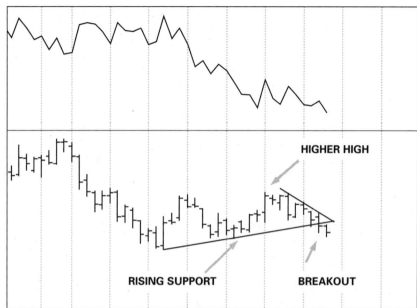

Figure 12-5:
Average
true range
indicator.

HIGHER HIGH

RISING SUPPORT

BREAKOUT

Applying Volatility Measures — Bollinger Bands

Technical traders have devised dozens of indicators incorporating different measures of volatility. The most popular by far is the Bollinger band, named for its inventor, John Bollinger. He charted a simple 20-day moving average of the closing price with a band on either side consisting of two standard deviations of the moving average, which effectively captures most of the variation away from the average. Conventional statistics says that two standard deviations capture 95 per cent of the variation in prices, although in securities, in practice it's a somewhat lower amount (see Figure 12-6).

Bollinger bands are used to display the price in the context of a norm set at a 20-day moving average, which is the number of days that Bollinger's research showed is the most effective in detecting variance. The bands serve to display *relative* highs and *relative* lows in the context of the moving average — they're adapted to the movements in price by the amount of the standard deviation. The bands are, so to speak, moving standard deviations.

When a price touches or slightly breaks the top of the band, this is a continuation signal. Often the price continues to *walk up* or *walk down* the band, as shown in Figure 12-6. A Bollinger band breakout is just like any other breakout — you expect the price to continue moving in the same direction as the breakout.

At some point, every price thrust exhausts itself. Momentum falters, and you expect a retracement or a reversal. Bollinger bands display the end of the upmove in two ways:

- ✔ **The price bar stops hugging the top band in an upmove, and slides down to the centre moving average (or further):** In Figure 12-6, the retreat to the moving average occurs at the ellipse. As a general rule, the failure to make a relative new high signals the end of the move, although this time, the bulls made a second effort to keep the rally going. In this particular instance, the price was forming a double top (check out Chapter 7 for a description of this pattern).

- ✔ **The bands contract:** When the bands contract, the range is narrowing. Traders are having second thoughts about the trend. They aren't willing to spend cash to test a new high, but they aren't willing to go short, either, and thus new lows don't appear.

A narrowing of the trading range implies a pause before an impending breakout. The narrowing of the band is named the *squeeze*. Note that breakouts can occur in the same direction as the original move as well as in the opposite direction. Figure 12-6 displays a reversal, but a reversal isn't the inevitable outcome. In this case, the downside breakout of the bottom of the band occurred only three bars after a failed upside breakout of the top band. This is unusually speedy.

A rapid break of the opposite band is sometimes a *false break*. In the case of a downside move like the one in Figure 12-6, traders could have been overly exuberant in taking profits after such a big run up to the high. See the upward pullback (otherwise known as a short squeeze) from the downmove in the two circles. Sometimes pullbacks keep going and the price resumes the uptrend — although hardly ever after breaking the bottom band like this one. To detect false breaks, use Bollinger bands with other confirming indicators, especially volume indicators. Other momentum indicators such as the relative strength index and MACD (discussed in Chapter 10) will always relect the Bollinger band because they're also based on momentum.

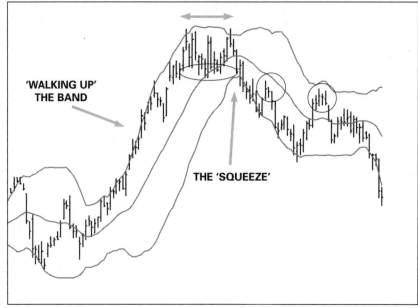

Figure 12-6:
Bollinger
bands.

Reviewing Another Volatility Breakout Idea

Bollinger bands are generally not used to set stops. The bands are equidistant from the centre moving average, so an upside breakout has the same statistical strength as a downside breakout. This means they're not very helpful in determining whether a specific breakout is significant or not, and may be sufficient reason to consider another type of band, as observed by system designer Steve Notis.

To use a band for a stop, you want the band to be asymmetrical, so that in an uptrend, a downmove has to be more severe than recent upmoves to trigger your stop. But you can't filter the equidistant Bollinger bands. This issue can be resolved by using a band made up of the *average true range* (ATR) on either side of the moving average and adjusting the size of the band according to which way the price is trending: Here's what to do:

✔ **Uptrend:** Widen the distance of the lower band from the average.

✔ **Downtrend:** Widen the distance of the upper band from the average.

The greater width of one of the bands from the centre moving average separates corrective moves from real reversals. Of course, before you can widen either band, you need to be sure of the trend direction.

In Figure 12-7, the price makes a bottom on the left-hand side and starts an upmove. The centreline is a moving average of the *median price,* or the average of the high, low and close. The bands are formed by taking a moving average of the ATR and adding and subtracting it from the moving average.

This process puts one whole ATR unit above and below the moving average. Any break of either line means aberrant prices and abnormally high volatility. When the price starts a new uptrend, the price breaking the upper band confirms that you have identified the trend correctly. When the price breaks the band on the downside, though, you need to worry that it's a reversal.

A downside breakout has to pass a higher test in an uptrend. Accordingly, you widen the lower band by adding a percentage of the ATR to it. On this chart, the lower band is 50 per cent wider than the upper band (it's 150 per cent of the ATR). The last bar on the chart breaks the band. This is no mere retracement! The move qualifies as a downside volatility breakout. Notice that the support line was already broken a few days before.

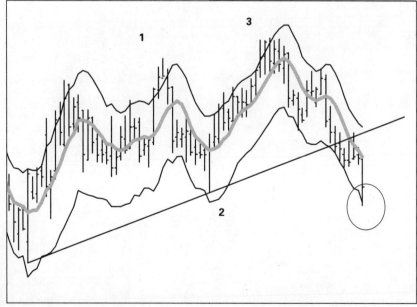

Figure 12-7:
Average
true range
band.

Another feature of the ATR band is that in an uptrend, you get only a few breaks of the upper band before the price retreats to a more normal volatility level, and this often implies to the swing trader that it's time to take profit and enter in the opposite direction. In the centre of the chart, the upside break labelled 1 is followed by a swing down to 2. If you're a swing trader, you're counting on that move to short the security. Then, at point 2, you buy again with the intention of taking profit at point 3.

Chapter 13

Point-and-Figure Charting:
Taking Time Out

- -

- -

*P*oint-and-figure charting filters or strips away time to leave only the significant price moves on the chart. *Significant* price moves are those that exceed the average daily trading range by a certain predetermined amount. By recording only major moves, you ignore minor moves and swings — literally, you don't even record them on the chart. The point-and-figure chart filters price *action* so you don't see a price move in the opposite direction of the current trend until it's meaningful, the definition of which you set yourself. This allows you to place confidence in an accurate reversal signal, uncluttered by the 'noise' of minor moves.

With the point-and-figure method, you can also easily identify patterns on charts, especially support and resistance, and therefore, breakouts of support and resistance. Point-and-figure charts look very different from standard bar charts, and after you get used to them, you may find their directness and simplicity addictive.

Filtering What's Important

Technical indicators aim to identify trend turning points and if a trend exists, how strong it is. But all charts contain a lot of data that isn't meaningful — it's filler, or what we call 'noise'. For example, a standard bar chart has an entry every day, even when nothing interesting or significant has happened. What if you could isolate just the juicy nuggets of price information and forgo the noise?

Displaying the price only when it makes a significant move is the basis of point-and-figure charting. If no noteworthy price action happens on a particular day, you put nothing on the chart. Because chart events like a breakout or reversal often follow real-world events (breaking news, for example), the point-and-figure chart can be considered event-driven.

While cumbersome if done by hand, the technique has held its own since before the turn of the 20th century, and today's charting software allows point-and-figure capability with a click of the mouse.

The point-and-figure method of displaying data takes time to get used to. Although it may initially look weird, after you get used to it, the clarity of the method becomes apparent.

Doing nothing is okay

When a price is trading sideways — not making either a new high or low — nothing significant is happening to the security and according to the point-and-figure method, nothing is worth noting on the chart. This is exactly what point-and-figure charting measures — it adds nothing on the chart when the price fails to surpass the previous high or makes a lower low. All inside days (refer to Chapter 5), for example, are defined as non-events under the point-and-figure methodology.

Putting each move into a column

In point-and-figure charting, you mark a price entry on the chart only if the price is higher than the previous high by a certain minimum amount or lower than the previous low by a certain amount. For a high that is higher than the previous high, you enter an X. For a low that is lower than the previous low, you enter an O.

Remember:

- ✔ **X:** New high
- ✔ **O:** New low

You place the Xs and Os each in a separate column that represents a continuous move, either up or down. In practice, the point-and-figure chart contains alternating columns of Xs and Os, where each column is either a move up or down. A column of Xs is an upmove and a column of Os is a downmove. Each X column is reserved for rising prices and each O column is reserved for falling prices. You don't put an X into an O column or an O into an X column.

Picturing the point-and-figure chart

Say you're considering a security whose price has been rising. The high today is $9. You start a new chart and enter an X next to the $9 label on the vertical axis, as shown in Figure 13-1. The next day, the price high is $10, so you enter an X *in the same column* at the $10 level. When the high reaches $12 the next day, you add another two Xs to denote the move from yesterday's $10 to today's $12. You keep adding Xs in the same column until the price rise stops. In the example in Figure 13-1, the price stops climbing at $13. You see a column of Xs that represents the price rise from $9 to $13 in a single move.

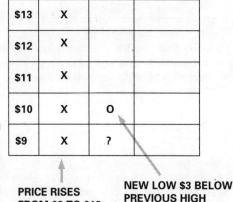

Figure 13-1: A basic point-and-figure chart.

PRICE RISES FROM $9 TO $13

NEW LOW $3 BELOW PREVIOUS HIGH

When the upmove is over and the price makes a new low below yesterday's low by a specific amount, you *must* start a new column, using an O and placing it at the dollar level of the new low. (We talk about this topic in the sections on the 'box size' later in this chapter; for now, consider that the new low suffices to indicate that the upmove is over.) Figure 13-1 tells you that the new low came at $10. You now expect the next entry to be another O where the question mark is placed on the chart. Note the switch from an X column to an O column may be a pause in the uptrend or a trend reversal. Either way, the formation of a new column alerts you to a change in the price dynamics.

You're concerned only with the high or the low of the day compared to the previous high or low. You pay no attention to the open or close.

Each column on the chart represents an upmove or a downmove, regardless of time. On a daily chart, a column can represent 2 days, 10 days, 100 days or some other number of days. You start a new column only when the last directional move is over. On the chart in Figure 13-1, you have an upmove from $9 to $13 and thus five Xs, but that doesn't mean it took five days. It may have taken 30 days, because on days showing no new high or low, you didn't make a chart entry.

Most trading software displays dates at the bottom of the chart along the horizontal axis. These dates aren't spaced evenly at regular intervals as they are in the usual chart format. In fact, the dates are there only for convenience — they don't actually measure time. This is because:

- ✔ When the price action doesn't qualify, you make no entry on the chart. The chart merely skips over that date.
- ✔ On dates when a new high or low appears, you add the entry in the column vertically if it's in the same direction as the last entry, not horizontally. You start a new column if the price action is in the opposite direction, but again, a new column builds vertically. In point-and-figure charting, the date is irrelevant and only price action matters.

Defining the box size

The horizontal axis suppresses dates and so doesn't show time, but the vertical axis is spaced in the conventional way. In the days when traders used actual graph paper, they filled in the little boxes of the grid with the Os and Xs set at some appropriate dollar amount, such as $.50 or $1. In futures markets, traders use the number of points corresponding to dollar amounts. The choice of spacing on the vertical axis is still called the *box size,* even if you're using a computer program and not graph paper.

So make up your mind already!

Traditional point-and-figure charting uses the high and low alone to make chart entries and thus to make trading decisions. To put all your attention on the high and low is exactly the opposite of candlestick charting, which downplays the high and low and concentrates on the open and close. It's also varies somewhat from standard bar reading, in which the close has pride of place as the most important bar component. For a refresher of the four price components, refer to Chapter 4, and check out Chapter 6 for candlestick.

As noted in the Introduction, newcomers to charting may sometimes feel frustrated by the apparent lack of agreement on 'standards', including what's more important, the high-low or the open-close. If technical analysts can't agree on something as simple as that, how can you trust any technique? The answer is that there's more than one way to cook and omelette. Point-and-figure charting emphasises a shift in the price *range* as the basis of trading decisions, which is in keeping with the idea of measuring crowd behaviour. Point-and-figure is just a method of displaying prices that embodies the trading rules in a compressed and simpler manner. Besides, you don't have to use the high and low — you can use the close as your benchmark if you want to in constructing your point-and-figure chart. The purpose of the display method is to filter out irrelevant prices to isolate the core trends, and in the case of a new trend, the close tends to be at or near the high or low, anyway.

Point-and-figure analysis is suitable for trading that has a medium to long-term holding period — weeks and months. The only way to know whether point-and-figure is best for you is to try it out on your chosen securities and see what gains you would've made, how many trades it requires of you, and so on. In general, point-and-figure charting on a daily basis is the easiest technique of all and the best way for a beginner to start getting a feel for making rule-based trading systems.

The *box size* is the minimum amount that the security needs to move above the recent highest high (marked by the last X) or below the lowest low (marked by the last O) before another entry is made on the chart. A good shorthand for establishing a box size is to ask yourself what would be the minimum price move that would concern you — and then to use that figure to define your box size.

When your security has a highest high of $10, for example, and it regularly varies by $.50 per day, you might set your box size at $1 as a mark of significant price action. If today's new high is $12, you acknowledge that this is a price extreme — four times the usual daily trading range — and deserves a new X in the X column. In fact, in this case, the new high is a full $2 over the last high, so you fill in two $1 boxes with the X notation. What happens if the price changes by $.98? Nothing. The new price is close to the box size of $1, but close doesn't count.

Choosing a box size

When you select a small box size, you're really asking to see a lot of detail, including minor retracements. By increasing the box size, you're filtering out filler price action, just as when you make a rule that requires a price to cross a moving average by *x* per cent (refer to Chapter 10 for a discussion of filtering). This simplification is a way to clarify your analysis.

The smaller the box, the more sensitive the chart is to price changes. The bigger the box, the less sensitive is the chart. Opinions vary about box size. If you're risk-averse, you may prefer a small box size. If you want to see only the big picture, you prefer a bigger box. Table 13-1 contains the standard guidelines, but don't feel bound by them. Rather, consider these guidelines a starting point.

Table 13-1	Approximate Guidelines for Box Size
Security Price	*Box Size*
$5–20	$.50
$20–100	$1
$100–$200	$2
$200–300	$4
$300–400	$6

Note that computer programs adjust the box size to fit the screen if you leave the program in default mode. You may wind up with an 'odd' box size of $.67 or some other arbitrary number. Box size is too important to leave to a program, if only because many other traders are using a standard round-number box, like $.50 or $1, and it's good practice to watch market action as other people do. Because software adjusts box size to accommodate the amount of data you select, you get different point-and-figure charts (and hypothetical trading decisions) depending on how many months or years of data you display. Most software usually displays the box size that fits the highest range in the data series in order to get all the information neatly on one chart. Of course, the trading range of any single security changes over time, sometimes gradually, and you may want to take note of that rather than let software obscure the changing range. By fixing the box size when you use charting software, you know when the range is expanding — the columns of X's and O's get taller — or contracting — the columns get shorter and there are more of them.

Adding the reversal box size to the picture

The purpose of the box size is to note a significant change in price. But how do you know how far a price has to move below the X (upward) column to warrant starting an O (downward) column? For that, you establish a second criterion, the *reversal amount*. The traditional reversal amount is three boxes. If your box is $1 and you're currently in a rising X column, you have to get a pullback in price that's $3 (or boxes) lower than the low today to start a new O (downward) column.

You can back-test a variety of box sizes and reversal amounts to arrive at the best box size and reversal amount to use for any particular security. Usually, though, point-and-figure chartists recommend sticking to the three-box rule for reversals but adopting a box size for your chart entries, depending on the absolute level of the prices you're tracking.

The appropriate box size for a security selling over $200 is $4. With a three-box reversal, the amount of movement before you start a new column works out to be $12. If you have 100 shares, you would exit on a reversal of at least $1,200, which is a fairly hefty sum of money. If you use the three-box reversal as the signal to stop (see Chapter 17 for stops), you have to accept a loss of $1,200 when the price goes against you. If you judge that $1,200 is too big a loss to take on a single position, you shouldn't be trading such a high-priced security, and you need to go find a cheaper one. The other option is to set your reversal amount at one or two boxes, a temptation most professionals warn against.

Drawing a point-and-figure chart

To draw the chart, every day you check the highest high and lowest low of the day. Ask yourself, is the price higher than the previous high by $1? If so, enter another X above the last X in the column. Has price turned back from its highs by more than $3? If so that's the three-boxes we recommend as the reversal amount, and you start a new column, entering the O at a level just below the last highest X. Because it's a reversal, now you expect the next entry to be one box lower. The next day, is the low price lower than yesterday by $1? If so, enter another O. If it's higher, it has to be higher than today's high by $3 to abandon the falling-price O column.

If you see a cluster of reversal columns that contain only one entry, chances are your box size is too small — or your reversal amount is wrong.

What if you get a new high by one box and on the same day, also get a new low by the reversal amount — three boxes? This is called an *outside* day (see Chapter 5). The new low trumps the new high and you should start a new column of Os. After all, you're looking for a threat to the trend (and your trading income). A new low by the reversal amount constitutes a serious threat to any prior trend and is often warning of a new (down) trend.

Simple point-and-figure trading rules

In point-and-figure charting, you buy when the new price surpasses the highest X in the previous X column, and you sell when the new price surpasses a previous low O in the previous O column. When the price surpasses a previous high or low, you have a breakout. (Check out Chapter 9 for a discussion of breakouts.)

Applying Patterns

Patterns pop out continuously in point-and-figure charts, especially support and resistance, but also other simple patterns like double and triple tops and bottoms.

Support and resistance

Point-and-figure charting offers two versions of support and resistance, the horizontal historic-level version described in Chapter 17 and the other conventional version of trendlines that slopes along a series of either highs or low, as described in Chapters 7 and 8.

Horizontal support and resistance

In Chapter 17, we discuss the importance of historic highs and lows. Traders remember the *highest high ever* or the *lowest low in three months* as benchmarks when the price approaches the same level. In point-and-figure charting, the horizontal line that you draw to mark the top or bottom of columns is also the recent-history support or resistance. In point-and-figure charting, you often get a series of columns that all end at a floor or a ceiling, regardless of whether they're Xs or Os. This is a function of filtering out price moves that don't rise to the reversal amount, and very handy both for spotting a breakout and setting a stop (see Chapter 17 for a discussion of stops) if those levels are broken.

In Figure 13-2, the top-left chart shows a breakout X above the resistance line. Using conventional charting, you wouldn't have known that line was there unless you were on the lookout for *historic* highs and lows. But point-and-figure chartists draw them all the time to denote where supply becomes abundant or demand falls short, halting a price rise.

Conventional support and resistance

On a standard bar chart, you draw a support line along a series of lows or a resistance line along a series of highs. These lines almost always have a slope that describes the trend and are hardly ever horizontal except in a sideways consolidation. You can draw sloping support and resistance lines on point-and-figure charts, too, but the lack of horizontal scale means that the sloping lines give you no useful information.

You trade point-and-figure support and resistance the same as you do when using conventional support and resistance — a breakout to the upside triggers a purchase and a breakout to the downside triggers a sale. As with conventional support and resistance lines, don't erase a support line after it's broken — it has a good chance of becoming the new resistance line. An old resistance line may become the new support line, too.

Because a point-and-figure chart filters out noisy prices and compresses time, often your chart displays authentic long-term support or resistance that you'd miss on a regular daily bar chart. You may also see *triangles,* which are support and resistance lines that converge. Chapter 7 covers triangles.

The top-right chart in Figure 13-2 shows a conventional support line. You could have a conventional (sloping) resistance line, too. Notice that if your boxes are perfectly square, you can draw a 45-degree line and extend it out into the future by starting with just two columns when one of the columns is one box higher or lower than the other. This allows you to start a support or resistance line more simply and sometimes earlier than in conventional bar charting. The upward-sloping 45-degree line is named a *bullish support line* and a downward sloping 45-degree line is a *bearish resistance line.*

Double and triple tops and bottoms

Double and triple tops are formed when demand falls off on nearing a previous high. When bulls fail to get a breakout above the established high, it's a pretty good sign that sellers are happy to unload the security at that price. See the double top Figure 13-2.

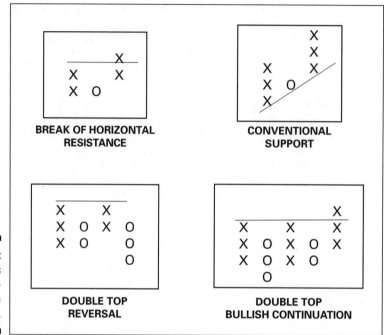

Figure 13-2:
Patterns
on point-
and-figure
charts.

When you get more than one low at about the same levels, it's a double or triple bottom, and to understand it you turn the supply and demand dynamics upside down to — at those low levels, buyers think it's a bargain, and chances are, the price is going to rise as buyers take up the 'cheap' price. (Refer to Chapter 7 for a discussion of double and triple tops and bottoms.)

In regular bar charting, a confirmed double top has a high probability of resulting in the price falling. Equally, a qualified double bottom leads to a price rise. They're both reversal patterns. In point-and-figure, however, chartists find that in an uptrend of Xs, if the intervening Os are on a rising line (the lowest low in the last O column isn't as low as the lowest low in the previous O column), a double top may turn into a triple top and then an *upside breakout* — in other words, a continuation pattern. This configuration is shown in the fourth pattern in Figure 13-2. If the opposite-direction columns line up horizontally, though, the traditional reversal interpretation is probably the more correct one. The columns of zeros in the fourth pattern in Figure 13-2 are not horizontal. In fact, they hint at the continuation of the upward trend.

A double or triple top or bottom can be either a reversal pattern or a continuation pattern in point-and-figure charting, depending on the behaviour of the opposite-direction columns and, of course, the direction of the breakout. In conventional time-based bar charting, you have to wait for confirmation of these patterns — chewing up time. Point-and-figure, therefore, can speed up the process of helping you decide whether you're facing a reversal or a continuation pattern with a breakout to follow

Projecting Prices after a Breakout

Point-and-figure chartists can forecast prices after a breakout using the box count, either vertically or horizontally. However, vertical projections work more often than horizontal projections.

Using vertical price projection

Say that your security has just made a double or triple top continuation breakout like the one shown in Figure 13-2. You want to know how high the price is likely to go. Alternatively, say your security has fallen to a new low but is now rising up from it. You want to know the potential gain if the bottom is really in place and if the upmove is likely to continue. You know that the price will retrace to the downside over the course of the move, but what you don't want to do is mistake a retracement for the end of the trend. If you have faith in the forecast price target, you'll ride out the retracement.

Point-and-figure chartists calculate the forecast price target in each case with an ingenious version of momentum. Here are the steps:

1. **Find the bottom of the last X (upward) column if you have an upside breakout (or the bottom of the lowest X column if you suspect a reversal to the upside).**

2. **Count the number of boxes in the column.**

   Assume that the column contains four boxes.

3. **Multiply the number of boxes by your chosen reversal amount (refer to the 'Adding the reversal box size to the picture' section, earlier in the chapter).**

   We'll stick with the standard 3.

   $4 \times 3 = 12$

4. **Multiply that product by the box size.**

   $1 is the standard.

   12 x $1 = $12

5. **Add the product to the lowest low in the starting column to get your new upside price target.**

   If the lowest low was $10, you add $12 and your price target is now $22.

Figure 13-3 shows a sample vertical point-and-figure target projection.

VERTICAL PROJECTION

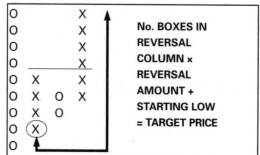

No. BOXES IN
REVERSAL
COLUMN x
REVERSAL
AMOUNT +
STARTING LOW
= TARGET PRICE

Figure 13-3:
Vertical
projection.

The target price objective is only a guide. The actual new high may fall short of $22, or it may be a great deal more than $22. Regardless of prices under or over achieving their target, you don't automatically sell at $22 if the price is still making new highs. But you may want to evaluate the risk-reward ratio in terms of the price projection (the reward) and the lowest low in the starting column (where you should initially place your stop). As discussed in Chapter 17, you should always manage the trade so that the expected gain from a trade is higher than the worst-case loss your trading plan will allow.

To estimate how far a downmove may go, do the process in reverse. Start from the highest high box before the downmove column begins, count the boxes, multiply by three, multiply again by the box size, and voila! You have an estimate of where the drop may stop.

Using horizontal projection

You use a horizontal count to project the price target of a breakout from a consolidation pattern. Say, for example, the price has been going mostly sideways for some period of time. In doing so you see the familiar alternating X and O columns, and with your eye you detect a base, or bottom formation. (In the case of a downside breakout, you need to see a top formation.)

Figure 13-4 shows a base forming after a downtrend over the course of five columns before an upside breakout. To calculate the projected price, follow these steps:

1. **Identify the number of columns in the base, which is the sideways pattern before the breakout. Exclude the breakout column.**

   Say 5 columns.

2. **Multiply by the number of columns in the pattern by the reversal amount you've chosen.**

   We use the standard 3-box reversal in this example.

   5 x 3 = 15

3. **Add the product to the lowest low in the base to get a price target.**

   Say the lowest low is $10.

   Now you have a price target of $10 + $15 = $25.

HORIZONTAL PROJECTION

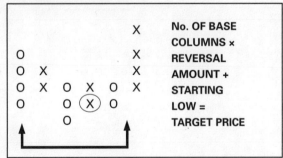

No. OF BASE
COLUMNS x
REVERSAL
AMOUNT +
STARTING
LOW =
TARGET PRICE

Figure 13-4:
Horizontal
projection.

Part V
Using the Tools of Technical Analysis

Glenn Lumsden

'We need to find trend indicators that best match your personality. I'm just not seeing 'stupefyingly wacky' on this chart.'

In this part . . .

*V*isually reading the charts displaying the movements of a security can be as revealing as mathematical analysis. Combining the indicators you know and understand can reveal further information and simplify the analysis you have to carry out to make a trading decision. If you're mathematically competent, you can take a giant leap into system building and remove most of the day-to-day judgemental decision-making that trading involves.

Before you plunge into risking hard-earned cash on securities trading, you have to realise it's not the security that counts, it's the trade. You have to select the indicators that match your personality and preference for risk. But most people don't know their own risk preference when they start out securities trading. In this part, we steer you in the right direction.

Chapter 14

Using Technical Indicators

In This Chapter

▶ Cutting out the emotion with indicators

▶ Choosing indicators

▶ Optimising and back-testing indicators

*I*ndicators are a shorthand mathematical way to identify and measure market sentiment in a different way to just looking at price charts. They give you a framework for making rational and objective trading decisions, cutting out the greed, fear and other confusing emotions that accompany trading — you can exploit crowd emotions without giving in to your own. In this chapter, we discuss how best to use technical indicators to trade systematically.

Traders who use technical indicators believe that systematic trading has a better chance of making significant and sustainable profits in the long run. Technical indicators use mathematical formulas to avoid the hit-and-miss trading that's contaminated and influenced by emotion. Having said that, note that indicators don't always work, and we discuss the right time to use them later in this chapter. To overcome the potential unreliability of indicators, a structured money management plan may also be necessary. Chapter 17 discusses safeguarding your investment.

Squelching Emotion

Trading is about money, and money charges emotions. Many people confuse the ends with the means. To speak of trading as simply based on greed and fear, as many commentators do, is to short-change the depth of emotion in trading. Trading is also about personal success and failure. As a trader you may encounter feelings of regret, shame, frustration and despair, as well as swings of hope, joy and satisfaction.

Traders using technical indicators go to great lengths to remove the emotion and impulsiveness from their trading decision-making process. The chief tool for squelching emotion is the use of rules-based technical indicators.

An *indicator* is a formula calculation based off your market chart to identify chart trends or market turns. Such indicators include the degree of strength of the trend, and whether a trend turning point is being reached. The basic purpose of indicators is to clarify and enhance your perception of the price move. They essentially come in two varieties.

- **Judgement-based indicators:** This group includes visual pattern-recognition methods such as bar, line and pattern analysis, as well as candlesticks (refer to Chapters 6 to 10). These indicators can be time-consuming to draw. They may also be hard to translate into software formulations so that you can back-test them to see how they would've worked over the price history of your security.

- **Mathematical-based indicators:** This alternative group includes moving averages, regression, momentum and other types of calculations (check out Chapters 11 to 15 for more details). You can calculate maths-based indicators by hand, but most traders use spreadsheet software or special-purpose charting programs. This saves time and allows you to concentrate on trade planning and decision-making. Also, you can then back-test the indicator over the run of historical data to discover how well it predicts future price action. A mathematical indicator removes more emotion from the decision-making process than a judgement-based indicator does.

You may think that visual-recognition techniques are too time-consuming and so decide to jump straight into maths-based indicators because they're faster, cleaner and 'scientific'. But maths-based indicators do the same job as judgement indicators — they display price data in different formats to assist you in making a trading decision. Just because they're based on maths though, doesn't mean they're objective. *You* determine the specifications of maths-based indicators in the first place (such as how many days are in a moving average), and *your* specifications may contain preconceived biases. And when you interpret trading guidance from maths-based indicators, you may find yourself using personal judgement again. Using maths-based indicators may involve just as much personal judgement as outright judgement-based indicators. The key to making the most of the 'science' is to test your rules (to verify their basic reliability) and then in the act of trading to stick to the rules you have made and avoid the common mistake of 'manual over-ride'. Even the best models can be applied erratically and that largely destroys their value.

If mathematics isn't your cup of tea, don't worry. You don't have to use formula-based indicators to become a proficient technical trader. Technical analysis provides a diversity of tried-and-true methods, such as visual pattern recognition methods that involve no maths. (Support and resistance is one example of such an indicator.) Also the maths involved in most technical analysis isn't all that difficult — for now, don't worry about this and don't let it intimidate you. You can apply maths-based techniques without understanding their inner workings as long as you understand the behaviour of the market that the indicator is identifying, and how to apply the indicator. A relevant analogy is knowing how to drive a car without being its mechanic.

Using a simple rule based on a single indicator to guide your trading (whether judgement- or maths-based), can make or save you a bundle. For example, buying when your security breaks a resistance line or selling when it falls below a moving average may help you make good decisions, fast. Remember in this business, complexity is not necessarily rewarded.

Classifying indicators

In Chapters 1 and 2, we point out that securities prices are sometimes *trending* — prices are moving strongly in one direction — and that sometimes trends are punctuated by *retracements,* or small moves in the opposite direction before the trend resumes. At other times, prices go into prolonged sideways conditions, called *range-trading.* Finally, there comes the time when trends end, and after they end, they may reverse and go in the opposite direction of the prior trend. Given these different movements, there are five conditions you want your indicators to identify (and some different indicators you can use to help identify these movements):

- A trend is beginning (moving average crossover indicator, pattern breakout indicator).
- A trend is strong or weak (slope of linear regression indicator or moving average indicator).
- A trend is retracing but is likely to resume (relative strength index indicator).
- A trend is ending and may reverse (moving average crossover, pattern breakout indicator).
- A price is range-trading (slope of linear regression indicator or moving average indicator).

Fading the trend

Price trends don't go in straight lines for long. They usually proceed two steps forward and one step back. Sometimes you see a pause in an uptrend arriving, where early buyers are about to take profit, setting off a domino effect of falling prices. Knowing that the uptrend is well established, but instead of waiting for the trend to end, you sell out of your position and even may go short with the intention of exploiting just this one small retracement downmove (short selling is described in more detail in Chapter 8). It sounds counterintuitive to sell into an uptrend. But in practice, retracements are fairly reliable. Trading the retracement is called *fading the trend,* and it has become very popular in recent years, especially in futures. It works best if the countertrend trade is very short-term (hours or days).

When you fade the trend, you're breaking a cardinal rule of technical trading — to trade with the trend, based on the Dow principle that when a trend is established, the probability is high that it will continue. Therefore, to fade the trend should be regarded as a purely opportunistic action based on an understanding of crowd psychology and a careful reading of price behaviour. It also illustrates that the frame of reference of technical trading isn't the security and its fundamentals, but the short-term timing of crowd behaviour. Just remember, swing trading against the trend requires quick execution of trade plans, total concentration, nerves of steel and, most important of all, tight capital management rules.

Each indicator usually works best in one situation and less well in others. Technical traders argue the merits and drawbacks of indicators in each situation, and if you ask ten technical traders to list their top indicator for each task, you'll get ten entirely different lists. This does not necessarily mean one is right and the others are wrong, it just shows that various indicators suit some people's goals and trading styles better than others. For example, in the preceding list, we suggest some indicators that may be useful, but other indicators are equally valid to identify that particular condition. To a large extent, the indicator you choose for each task will depend on the security and also on your choice of analytical time frame.

Choosing a style that best suits you

Unless you're building a trading system, as we describe in Chapter 16, the trend is usually the focus. In a perfect world, you first determine whether your security is trending or range-trading sideways, and then you apply the appropriate indicator for that market condition. In practice, you may not always find it easy to classify price moves as either trending or not trending in a neat and tidy way. At the very least, prices usually have an identifiable range of movements, whether they're trending or not. In addition, the minor and temporary movements against the trend (retracements) always create doubt, dogging the mind of the trader: Is it a momentary correction or a reversal?

The way you deal with these small price movements against the trend, depends on your trading style. Successful traders identify and stick with a trading style. The two distinct categories are

- **Trend-followers:** These traders like to trade trends and may wait out retracements and sideways range-trading situations until they resolve themselves, or break out, back into a trend. Some trend-following traders may also choose to modify their position when the long-term trend of a market is or becomes unclear, using momentum indicators. For example, when a security appears overbought or oversold a trend-follower might take some profit as a hedge but leave some funds invested in case the trend continues. (Refer to Chapter 2 for a definition of overbought and oversold, and Chapter 12 for a selection of overbought and oversold indicators.) Figure 14-1 illustrates a trend, complete with minor retracements within it, and shows how a trend-following trader makes decisions.

- **Swing traders:** These traders operate whether a trend is present or not. Swing trading is usually more short term in focus and is more flexible than trend-following, because you can apply swing techniques under different market conditions based on the current 'swing' underway. However, to succeed it needs to be traded more often, closely watched and carefully managed.

   Swing trading is about buying at relative lows and selling at relative highs, regardless of whether the price is trending. A swing trader may know that a price is downtrending, for example, but may still be willing to buy it for a short-term profit opportunity when a momentum indicator says it's temporarily oversold and likely to enjoy a temporary bounce upward. Figure 14-2 shows how a swing trader tries to capture every move, including the retracements. (Note: This is the same chart as in Figure 14-1.)

If you intend to mix trend-following and swing trading indicators, be careful: You may end up getting confused. Often one indicator tells you to buy exactly when the other one says 'sell'. One example of this is when a downtrending price becomes temporarily oversold and is now bouncing upward. You may engage in a little wishful thinking that you see a trend reversal, and you become a buyer of what you think is a new uptrend.

To avoid making this mistake, you need to select a core trading principle, either trend-following or swing trading (for more information about combining techniques, see Chapter 15).

If you choose the trend-following style, you're choosing to suffer through the downward retracements in an uptrend (or the upward retracement in a downtrend). You're going to have to wait it out, and if you have correctly identified the trend, your patience will pay off when the trend resumes. If you choose swing trading as your style, you need courage and a keen sense of timing, because this style sometimes demands you to trade against the trend.

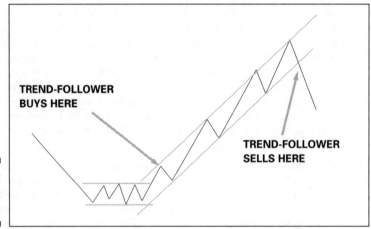

Figure 14-1:
Trend-following.

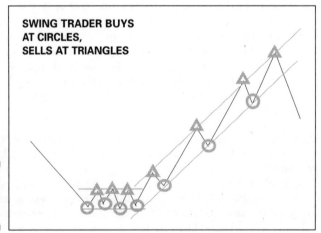

Figure 14-2:
Swing trading.

Your choice of using trending or swing trading indicators determines your holding period. Because trends occur over time, trending indicators generally keep you in a trade for longer than swing trading indicators.

The best principles to employ when selecting a trading style are the ones that you can understand. Simple, old-fashioned techniques, such as bar reading and pattern identification, are powerful because they relate to the raw numbers and give the same results regardless of your trading style. Maths-based indicators are powerful, too, because they're objective by definition. However, if you find that you can't get a 'feel' for the market — what the crowd is feeling and how the price trend is unfolding — from a maths-based indicator, don't use it. Stick to things that make sense to you, otherwise you'll get lost.

Examining How Indicators Work

Indicators aren't inherently tied to particular time frames, nor do they have a single correct interpretation. For example, the standard momentum indicator described in Chapter 11 uses 12 days, and the standard interpretation is that you buy when the indicator is over zero and you sell when the indicator is under zero. But you could use 5 days or any other number of periods for the indicator, and you could also sell when the indicator turns downward even when the value is still above zero. In the following sections, we describe the general way indicators work. Be aware, though, that technical traders are a diverse bunch and use indicators in an infinite variety of ways.

Selecting the relevant time frame

Most indicators measure price and volume changes relative to previous prices and volume over a specific *look-back* period, such as 12 days or 21 days. You can use larger or smaller time frames to suit your trading horizon, which could be hourly or even weekly. If you compare the trend-following chart in Figure 14-1 with the swing trading chart in Figure 14-2, you can easily deduce that trend-following is going to use indicators with a relatively longer time frame than swing trading.

With the exception of 'historic' highs and lows, most indicators have a range of time in which research shows they work best. (For more on historic highs and lows, see the section 'Establishing benchmark levels' later in the chapter.) This is why charting software comes with preformatted indicators that have default parameters, such as 12 periods for the momentum indicator.

In the momentum example, 12 periods is the default because researchers in the past have found it the best number over hundreds of thousands of price series. To adopt the default parameter does *not* mean that you must trade every 12 days if you use the momentum indicator to guide you. It means that looking back 12 periods from today tends to give you useful information. It's a starting point, and if 12 periods doesn't work for you, you're welcome to use a different number of periods. Refer to Chapter 11 for more on momentum.

Some indicators and patterns can stretch from a few days to many months or even years and still be valid and useful, but most maths-based indicators have an associated fixed time frame, from very short-term to very long-term.

- ✔ **Intraday:** Entry and exit on the same trading day

- ✔ **Short-term:** 3-12 days (average 3)

- ✔ **Intermediate-term:** 12-45 days (average 20)

- ✔ **Long-term:** More than 30 days

Notice that a long-term time frame includes some of the intermediate-term. Don't fret — defining time frames is arbitrary and really up to you. Because definitions of time frames and trading horizons are an individual preference, you're welcome to create your own. Technology offers further flexibility. You can put an indicator on screen that traditionally used (say) 12 days — but today it can be 12 periods, and the period could be hourly or as short as 5 minutes. (Refer to Chapter 6 for a discussion of intraday time frames.)

The ability to apply any indicator over any time frame is one of the great features of technical analysis. Price patterns and trends can be found in any price/time horizon, be it hourly, daily, weekly or even monthly. Thus intraday bars are like microcosms of daily bars, and daily bars are like microcosms of weekly or monthly bars. Traders respond to price changes in regular, consistent and repetitive ways whatever the time frame, and you can trade on those patterns at your discretion.

So how do you pick indicators to go with your time frame? Where do you begin? First, you must discover the time frame you really want to deal in. This means getting rid of the idea that you already know your time frame. You may think you're a long-term trader but then discover a real affinity for an indicator that works stunningly on your favourite securities at 20 days. Don't dismiss an indicator that you think 'belongs' to a different time frame. The indicator may well be more flexible than you first think. You can use short-term indicators to make long-term trades and vice versa. Technical traders all over the world are inventing new twists and tweaks on indicators all the time, and you can, too. If you're a beginner, don't exclude any possibility, even such ugly-sounding things as the stochastic oscillator. (For more about that particular beast, turn to Chapter 11.)

Heeding indicator signals

Indicators are designed to give buy and sell signals. The art of charting is to determine when to treat the signal as a warning and when to use it as a black-and-white rule. In the interest of objectivity and to remove emotions from trading, your best move is to act when the indicator says so. Indicators generate signals in two ways.

Crossover signals

The term *crossover* refers to one line crossing another line. Crossovers include:

- ✔ **The indicator crossing the price or the price crossing the indicator.** (Check out Chapters 8 and 11 for support and resistance lines and moving averages. Also, there is an example of a moving average crossing the price line in the section 'Optimising: The Necessary First Step' later in this chapter.)

- ✔ **One line of a two-line indicator crossing the other.** (See information on the moving average convergence-divergence indicator in Chapter 10.)

In most instances — but not all — the price crossing an indicator is called a *trading signal,* one of the most important concepts in technical analysis. Usually, a crossover signal is arithmetically measured and objectively observed. If the indicator line is, say, at 10, and the price goes to 10.5 from below 10, it's a (crossover) trading signal. Even if the price goes up only to 10.05, it's also a trading signal (in this case a 'buy').

Range limits — oscillator signals

Oscillators are trading formulas designed to describe where today's price stands relative to its recent trading range, as we describe in Chapter 11. Oscillators are usually (but not always) based on an index of zero to 100 on the upside and zero to minus 100 on the downside. Zero is neutral or the middle of the range reading. Thus the theoretical range can oscillate between −100 and +100 (hence the name oscillator). In practice, traders find that most of the time, the scope of the price range trades well away from the outer limits and doesn't vary by more than 20 per cent to 80 per cent of the total possible range. Thus, they draw a line at 20 per cent of the maximum range and another one at 80 per cent (or 10 per cent and 90 per cent, or some other variation). When the indicator approaches one of the lines, you know that the price is nearing an extreme of its recent range.

This is a warning of a market nearing its overbought or oversold condition and thus possessing the potential to retrace or reverse, soon. Depending on your risk appetite and whether you're a trend-follower or a swing trader, you may alter the amount of your position or alter your stop (see Chapter 17). If you're a swing trader, you may even use an actual crossover of the range lines as a buy/sell signal.

Convergence and divergence

Convergence refers to two indicator lines coming closer to one another, much like when a support line and a resistance line converge to form a triangle (refer to Chapter 7) or two moving averages get closer together (refer to Chapter 11), indicating less difference between their numerical values. Convergence is most often seen in indicators on the price chart, and generally means that the price action is starting to go sideways or has a narrower high-low range, or both. A sideways move, in turn, generally precedes a breakout.

Divergence, on the other hand, refers to two indicator lines moving further apart — for example, when the spread between two moving averages widens. Divergence also refers to an indicator and the price going in different directions, and this is the most common and useful type of divergence to observe. Momentum indicators, for example, display the rate of change of a price. The slope of a momentum indicator displays the strength of a trend. It is useful to know when the strength of a trend and the trend itself begin to diverge. For example, a price may still be rising (making new highs) but the speed of its rise may be slowing. In that case, the momentum indicator turns down and starts to fall. The fact that the price and indicator are diverging is an important sign that the upward trend in the price is probably about to peak and reverse (refer to Chapter 10).

Establishing Benchmark Levels

Some characteristics of the price chart are inherent to the chart and not deliberately placed indicators. Every chart has historic highs and lows, for example. Technically, these aren't indicators, and yet they may serve to indicate future price action. You've probably heard the phrases '52-week high' or '52-week low', meaning the security is reaching a one-year high or low. A new one-year high or low has no analytical value to the technical trader — unless it's also a historic high or low. A *historic* high or low is an absolute level that's remembered by traders and becomes a market benchmark.

Examples of historical highs are the all-time high in the NASDAQ tech stocks of 5,048 set on 10 March 2000, and the all-time high in spot gold at $850 in January 1980.

When a price makes a new historic high or low and then retreats from it in the opposite direction, years can pass before this benchmark is surpassed. In the meantime, intermediate highs and lows emerge and become minor benchmarks (alternatively resistance and supports) in their own right. At the time they occur, they seem 'historic'. After a bounce up off a new low, traders may hesitate to break it, but after they do, the price accelerates to the next low. The same thing happens on the way up to new highs. Profit-taking after a high causes the price to retreat, as traders hesitate to breach the new 'historic' high.

Hesitation ahead of the breach of a benchmark price can be prolonged and is often accompanied by a gap (refer to Chapter 5 for more about gaps), demonstrating that traders are aware of these historic benchmark levels, and avoid being caught with a trading position near them.

Historic levels are both a cause and an effect on indicator behaviour. If an uptrending indicator like the moving average flattens out mysteriously, widen the time frame on your chart to check whether the price is near an historic level. The market, in this case, is preparing the ground to test the old high. If the test fails, you should expect a retracement and maybe even a significant reversal. If the price passes the test and makes a new high, you can expect the price to accelerate quickly and deliver a substantial profit. See the discussion on momentum in Chapter 11.

Historic levels usually override all other technical factors. Say you calculated the average of all the retracements in a very long uptrend and you came up with 15 per cent. When you see a retracement starting in your security and you project the same 15 per cent drop from the last high (refer to Chapter 7 for more on this projection). But a 15 per cent drop would break a previous 'historic' level. If the move you've identified is truly a retracement and not a full trend reversal, expect the drop to stop short of its usual 15 per cent.

Round numbers also tend to have a magical effect on traders, who seek them out and name round numbers as price targets or support and resistance more than chance would allow, probably because they're easy to remember.

Choosing Indicators

The good news is that everything works. Moving average indicators work (refer to Chapter 10). Channel breakouts work (refer to Chapter 9). Trading in a three-to-five-day time frame with candlestick analysis works (check out Chapter 6). But indicators only *indicate*. They don't *dictate* the next price move and at the end of the day, price action has supremacy over all other aspects of your analysis. If your indicator disagrees with a price, then your indicator is wrong, not the market.

All newcomers to technical analysis (and many old hands as well) tend to lose sight of the limitations of indicators. According to trading folklore, technical traders seek the Holy Grail — the perfect indicator or combination of indicators that are right 100 per cent of the time. The Grail does not exist. One of the reasons it doesn't exist is that *you* are different from the next trader. Equally important, *you* (like the market) will change over time. The 'ideal' indicator that delivered great profits ten years ago is one that you should now avoid.

One old joke hits the nail on the head: 'Give 12 technical traders a new indicator and a year later you have 12 different track records.' The joke is perfectly accurate because how you use an indicator isn't set by the indicator itself, but by the trading rules you apply to it. Indicators and trading rules have a chicken-and-egg relationship. The process of selecting and using indicators involves not only the characteristics of the indicator, but also your trading rules and personal risk appetite. There's no guarantee that some other guy's system actually suits you. For example, you may like an indicator but find it generates too many trades in a fixed period, so you don't execute every single signal. Someone else may use the identical indicator, but instead of overriding indicator signals with personal judgement, he modifies the exact timing of trades by using a second indicator. We talk about combining indicators in Chapter 15.

Modifying or adjusting indicators with trading rules is *always* better than overriding them. To override your indicator haphazardly is self-defeating. In effect, you're letting the emotional element back into your trading. Plus, you won't get the expected result from the indicator — tempting you to blame the indicator. Fortunately, most indicators are fairly flexible. They can be adapted to fit the trading rules you prefer, such as the frequency of your trades. Indicators are about price-move measurement, you and your tolerance for risk. The trading rules you choose, though, must be appropriate to the indicators you use them with. In short, don't pick indicators that you can't follow, like a momentum indicator that gives ten trading signals per month when you don't have the time or inclination to trade that frequently.

Optimising: The Necessary First Step

Using a single simple indicator can make money or preserve capital from losses. Take a look at Figure 14-3. The chart is of QQQ, the tracking stock of the NASDAQ-100 Index (technically an exchange-traded fund that incorporates the 100 largest and most actively traded non-financial stocks on the NASDAQ). QQQ more than doubled from March 1999 to the all-time high in March 2000. If you'd used a 50-day moving average crossover indicator to signal when to sell, you would have sold QQQ seven days after the peak. (We discuss the 50-day moving average in Chapter 10.)

Of course, every trader would like to improve on that, too. You could have saved even more money if you had sold a day or two after the peak, instead of seven days afterwards. Fifty days is an oft-used parameter for the moving average, but you need to find out whether it's the best one for your particular security. Who knows? Maybe 36 days, 77 days or some other number of days works better.

The first step in seeing whether a given indicator can work for you is to test out how it would have worked in the past. You expect price patterns to repeat, because crowd psychology doesn't change much.

Optimisation is the mathematical process of testing a hypothesis on historical data to see which parameter would've worked the best. In the case of the 50-day moving average, your hypothesis is that some number of days inserted into a moving average would reliably and consistently deliver to you the very best or *optimum* level to exit ahead of a crash, or the very best entry ahead of a big price rise.

Optimisation is a necessary first step. It's necessary because when you're starting out to trade a new security, you have no idea of what indicators to use or what parameters to put into the indicators. In keeping with the scientific approach of technical analysis, you want to try various indicators and different parameters in the indicators to see what works best. We say that optimisation is a necessary first step because common sense tells you that conditions are never exactly the same, and what worked on historical data may not work in the future. Back-tests designed to find good indicators and optimum parameters can give you a sense of accuracy and reliability that may be false. Here's why:

✔ The future *will* differ from the past. Price patterns repeat, but only in a general way. Any number of equally probable outcomes are possible in any specific situation. What worked in March 2007 may get disastrous results when applied in 2010 or 2012. It's hard to follow trading rules built on past patterns when you know the future will be different.

    ✔ The real world will always differ subtly from tests. The assumptions that you make when designing a back-test can't deal with the variety of market practicalities you encounter when you apply the indicator. For example, you won't be able to act immediately when the signal occurs and the delay may cause 'slippage' — loss of opportunity — between the order signal and the actual price you get.

Both problems relate to the how you make decisions given the practical limits of the information provided by indicators. Note, however, that every trader using charts can tell you that there are far bigger challenges in trading than just picking indicators.

Constructing a back-test optimisation

The chart in Figure 14-3 displays a back-test (a test on historical data) of the single moving average crossover rule on IBM stock.

Assume you have traded IBM stock on and off for a number of years, and you want to try your hand at applying an indicator-based technical trading rule. Here's the hypothesis: If you buy IBM stock every time the price crosses above the x-day moving average and sell it every time the price crosses below the x-day moving average, it'll consistently and reliably be a profitable trading rule.

The goal of the optimisation back-test is to find x, which is the number of days in the moving average. Just about every software package allows you to search for x. In this case, the software delivered a result in less than 15 seconds. We told it to try every moving average from 10 days to 30 days over the past 1,000 days. The most profitable moving average would've been 15 days. Figure 14-3 shows the 15-day moving average and the buy/sell signals that the indicator would have generated at every crossover.

In the top window, take a look at the *equity curve,* which shows the cumulative running total of the profit you would have made if you had been buying or selling at each arrow. From a starting point of $1,000 in capital, you now have $2,443, or a gain of 144 per cent. Because 1,000 days is about 4 years, that's an annual return of 34.5 per cent — better than the return on a risk-free bond and a whole lot better than the loss you would have taken if you had bought $1,000 worth of IBM stock on Day 1 of this test and simply held to Day 1,000. The stock fell 30 per cent during the 1,000 days.

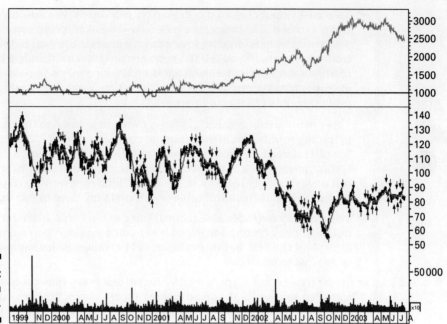

Figure 14-3:
Optimisation
back-test.

Indicator testers often compare the indicator outcome to the return on the risk-free bond and/or the buy-and-hold strategy. This isn't an adequate measure, however, because it fails to account for the risk you *are* taking. We don't have the space to get into this, but be aware that statistical measures are available to give you a risk-adjusted way of comparing the return on a hypothetical back-test like this one (or actual returns) to other indicator returns.

Take another look at this picture

Look at Figure 14-3 again, and you can quickly see that this case illustrates the general objections to the back-testing process.

- Notice the horizontal line on the equity window at $1,000. Now see that one month into the test, your equity fell below its starting point. The indicator drew losses straight away. In fact, it had a few more draw downs in its trading lifecycle, too. In real life, you'd probably not stick with a trading rule that failed to show an interesting amount of profit for almost two full years.

✔ To actually apply the 15-day crossover rule would've caused you to trade a total of 119 times, or every 8 days on average. In some cases, you would've been trading every day. Of course, the cost of those trades isn't zero. If you tell the software program to include a cost of $10 for every purchase and another $10 for every sale, no moving average crossover parameter from the 10- to 30-day set would have been profitable. Read that sentence again!

This phenomenon is called *slippage*, the term applied to the reduction in trading profits that arises from the cost of trading. It includes the bid-offer spread, commissions and fees (before taxes). When doing any testing, always look at the performance track record of an indicator back-test *after* slippage. This can make all the difference between a profitable trading rule and an unprofitable one. It certainly does in this example.

✔ The majority of trades lose money. You can't see that from the chart, but most back-testing software shows you a *system report* summarising aspects of the test. In this example, of 119 trades, 82 lost money and only 37 were profitable.

✔ To get these results, you would've had to sell every time the indicator signalled sell, and at the same time go short the stock (check out Chapter 8 for an explanation of going short). In practice, most people can't short equities, although it's an everyday occurrence in the futures market.

In this case you can always tell the software that you're only a buyer when the indicator signals a buy and you never take a short position when the indicator tells you to go short. Because the stock was a net loser over the entire 1,000 days and buy-and-hold would've returned a big loss, you can guess what the outcome is — only a 15 per cent return over the 1,000 days, or about 3.6 per cent per year. Factor in the cost of commissions at $10 per trade — and you would have lost a disappointing 100 per cent of your starting capital.

Finding the silver lining

This particular moving average rule didn't work after you factored in realistic market factors, such as paying commissions and not being able to take a short position. But the case does exemplify one characteristic we're seeking in a trading rule: The average profitable trade is much higher than the average unprofitable trade (over $75 in this case versus an average unprofitable trade of $26.67). Winners were almost three times the size of losers. This yields a win/loss ratio of 2.8, or $2.80 in profit for every $1 in loss. Moreover, the average winning trade lasted 19 days, while the average losing trade lasted only 4 days. Even though the trading rule didn't work, it does meet a second winning characteristic of technical trading that you seek from your indicator: 'Let your winners run and cut your losses short.'

The goal of every indicator-based trading rule is to get more profit from winning trades than you lose on losing trades. The goal isn't to have a higher number of profitable trades than losing trades, although that's nice if you can get it.

Fixing the indicator

This case illustrates common problems you encounter when you begin back-testing indicators to find the optimum parameter.

Overtrading

An unadjusted indicator often results in overtrading — it generates too many trades overall. *Overtrading* is trading so often that slippage reduces profits or even eliminates them. You therefore need to find adjustments to the indicator to reduce the number of trades, without damaging the returns from the winning trades at the same time.

You can *filter* the buy/sell signals by specifying that you want the software to generate a buy or sell signal only if the price is *x* per cent above or below the moving average or has been above/below the moving average by *y* amount of time. When applying filters be careful not to make conditions too fancy or too numerous. You get no prizes for complexity. It's possible to fix the 15-day moving average trading rule with filters to reduce the number of trades so that profitability is high enough even to absorb trading costs. But you may find that filter fixes aren't robust, meaning that they back-test nicely but then fail to deliver the expected gain in real-time. This is because the volatility of the security changes over time. (Check out Chapter 12 for more on volatility.)

The bottom line is this: Keep indicators and their trading rules as simple as possible.

Losing trades

You have to accept that most indicators generate more losing trades than winning ones, and the reason the indicator works is that the winning trades are bigger in money and percentage terms than the losers. But, of course, you still want to reduce the losers. The single best way to do that is to add a confirmation requirement, or a filter, such as one of the momentum indicators. In fact, requiring that the moving average indicator be confirmed by a simple momentum rule (refer to Chapter 11 for more on momentum) reduces the number of losing trades from 82 to 32 and improves profitability by another $1,200, even after the $10 commission. That said, you could still end up having more losing trades than winning trades in absolute numbers, but the average win-loss ratio improves to 7 to 1 ($7 in gain for every $1 in loss).

Adding judgement calls

In many instances, when you look at the chart itself, you can see where some bar configuration or pattern would've kept you out of a losing trade or gotten you into a winning trade sooner. For example, the price may break a trendline (refer to Chapter 8) or show a gap (check out Chapter 5). If you do go down this route you can't systematically include judgement calls like this in a back-test of a maths-based indicator unless you're mathematically very advanced and adept. In most instances, to specify a condition like a gap as qualifying a trading rule would require you to create a very long and elaborate formula, which arguably really only makes your model more complex, not necessarily profitable.

Applying the indicator again

After successfully back-testing a given indicator, your job isn't quite finished. Back-tests are hypothetical. You don't actually make those trades. To get a more realistic idea of how an indicator-based trading rule works, you should back-test the rule on historical price data and then apply it to out-of-sample data. That is, simulate the model using price data that was not originally used in the back-testing to check that the parameters you have selected are authentic. In the IBM case, for example, you'd back-test the rule for the years 1999 to 2003, obtain the 15-day parameter, and then see how it worked in 2004. If the results are about the same on the fresh data, you should consider your rule to be *robust,* meaning it works across a wide range of conditions.

After optimisation, you can further test an indicator by *simulating.* In this process, you take the indicator and use it on the market, either on untested data or on real-time market rates, but without necessarily committing money to the trade. Also called *paper trading,* simulating is your second chance to test your indicator before you spend your first cent.

Back-testing is still risky

Back-testing sounds tedious but it's a valuable exercise because it delivers a measure of how well an indicator parameter might work — in a situation where you otherwise have no other evidence that the indicator might be effective to signal profitable trades. Back-testing is better than eyeballing a dozen versions of the indicator on a chart — it quantifies your observations without using emotion in your decision-making process.

But back-testing has risks and can give you a false sense of certainty. The parameter you use in the indicator may have been effective in the past, but that's no guarantee it'll be effective in the future.

The flaw in optimisation is that the 'ideal' parameter for an indicator is ideal only for the past. Critics of back-testing name the example in Figure 14-3 as a perfect case of how *not* to build an indicator-based trading rule. The minute you add one or two more days of price data, the back-test outcome can fall apart. If you run the same simulation again next week, the optimum number of days to put into the moving average may be (say) 21.

The principle of using a moving average is fine — but to alter the indicator, with or without filters, is to risk *curve-fitting*, which means making the indicator only perfect for the past. The probability of it being perfect for the future is then low because, of course, the market changes. Instead you should apply the moving average principle in a more flexible way by making it adaptive (see Chapter 11), by adding confirming factors, by consulting volume and other means. Pretty soon you realise that the exact parameter of 15 days isn't the important characteristic of using a moving average indicator.

You shouldn't count on finding a magic number to put into your indicators. The default parameters that you find in books and software can often be used without harm to your performance — if you have good indicators for the security and you apply your trading rules with care, discipline and consistency.

Chapter 15

Combining Techniques

*U*sing one indicator helps you time your trade's entry and exit. Good timing increases profits and cuts losses. Combining two indicators improves your trading performance more. Indeed you can add as many indicators and trading rules to your charts as you manage in your head or program into your computer. This chapter looks at some popular combinations of techniques and offers guidance on the process of putting techniques together to forge a systematic approach to trading. In the next chapter, we talk about considering a full-scale trading system but before that, you need to examine the compatibility of indicators. You also need to realise that adding indicators multiplies the difficulty of the trading decision.

Simple Ideas that Last

If you happen to meet a professional trader, you may be astonished to hear exactly *how* many pros make a living — by applying the same simple indicator and the same simple rule, over and over again, on the same small set of securities. 'It can't be that easy!' you think. But it can be. Professionals have a disciplined ability to focus on a single, narrow set of circumstances. They know from experience that the indicator and rule produce a profit most of the time. If it fails to produce a profit this time, too bad, that's part of the business. They put it behind them and move on to the next case. Because the professional considers that losses are a necessary part of trading and controls them ruthlessly, and doesn't dwell on a loss, he's ready for the next trade with a clean mental and emotional slate.

Reviewing two classics

One of the oldest trading concepts is also one of the simplest — Richard Donchian's 5/20 system, which uses a trend-following principle (see 'A case study in complexity' later in the chapter). The 5/20 system basically has you buying when the 5-day moving average crosses above the 20-day moving average and sell when the closing price crosses below the 5-day moving average. Both the buy and sell crossover signals are qualified according to additional filtering criteria, specifically that a crossover has to exceed the level of the previous crossover in the same direction, proving its street credentials, so to speak. (See Chapter 10 for information on moving averages and filtering.)

Another simple but effective one-rule concept is to buy when the price moves above the range established in the first *x* number of minutes of trading. This is called the opening range breakout by its inventor, Toby Crabel. The *opening range breakout* is a bit unusual, because it considers the opening price to be the important component of the bar, rather than the close. The opening range breakout is a volatility based breakout system (see the section on 'Efficient Entry and Ruthless Exit — The Setup' later in the chapter). With the opening range breakout, you can improve the odds of getting a successful trade by adding one or more confirmation qualifiers, such as:

- ✔ The preceding bar was an inside day, or doji (refer to Chapter 6)
- ✔ The opening range over the past 3 to 10 days was narrowing
- ✔ The opening is a gap from the day before (refer to Chapter 5).

Confirmation is critical

As the two classic cases illustrate, even the simplest trading rule based on a single indicator uses confirming filters, patterns or another indicator.

Another example is in 'Finding the silver lining' in Chapter 14, where adding momentum to a moving average indicator improved the gain/loss ratio from 2.8:1 to 7:1 (which means you get a $7 gain for every $1 loss, instead of a $2.80 gain for every $1 loss).

But which two indicators should you choose? Or should you choose three or four or more? Because technical analysis has produced over 350 stand-alone indicators and at least that many patterns, the number of possible combinations and permutations is in the thousands. By the time you add time constraints, such as 'Buy 30 minutes after the open if *x, y,* and *z* occur', the number of potential trading regimes is in the hundreds of thousands.

The key reason for adding confirming indicators is to overcome the inconvenient little fact that every indicator fails some of the time. By requiring a second indicator that gives the same buy or sell signal, you increase the probability that the trade you take is profitable.

Introducing Complexity

You use setups like the opening range breakout (which is covered in the 'Reviewing two classics' section earlier in this chapter) to take a hit-and-run bite out of a price move. To use technical analysis for the longer term and to be in the market more of the time, you can follow indicators in a continuous way. As we describe in Chapter 14, most price moves usually last weeks and months, and different indicators and patterns have greater or lesser ability to identify trend turning points and the strength of a trend.

Most technical traders use one or two indicators to capture a turning point for their entry into the trade, and then different indicators to identify the strength of the trend, with perhaps yet another indicator or two to identify their exit point, which may or may not be the actual end of the trend. (As we point out in Chapter 12 on volatility, when a trend becomes choppy, you may prefer to exit the trade even if the trend is still in place, because the increase in volatility raises the risk of loss relative to the trade's profit potential.)

Traders tinker endlessly with combinations of indicators. Tinkering is irresistible when you see, or think you see, additional techniques to speed up the process, improve total profitability or reduce losses. But this complexity is not always useful.

Adding complexity is tricky, though. When you combine indicators, you may discover that they contradict one another. One indicator says buy, while a different indicator says sell. This type of conflict is very common.

The price, for example, has crossed above its moving average and you bought the security. The trend has been in place for a while. Now one of the momentum indicators is signalling that the security is overbought and will retrace. You don't know if the retracement will be minor or transform itself into a full-blown reversal. You know that the moving average lags the price action — no help there. Do you accept the sell signal from the swing indicator?

No single correct answer exists. Sometimes momentum indicators are wrong, and the retracement doesn't occur at all, leaving you with the problem of where to re-enter your trend, which is now running away without you. But even after the most exhaustive back-testing and observation, you'll still be wrong some of the time no matter which decision you make. The purpose of combining indicators is to improve the odds of being right about the next price move, even if does not work out in every case.

The only way to know whether two or more indicators work well together is to back-test them together, with the trading rules meticulously stipulated and adhered to. You can easily back-test a single indicator to find out whether a simple trading rule can make money. Testing multiple rules for various contingencies, though, is a difficult job. The minute you start back-testing on historical data to see how this indicator or that condition affects the outcome of a trading rule, you're jumping in the deep end of the pool. The more decision rules you pile on, the more questions you raise — and the more need for back-testing and the more call on your time

Choose a ruling concept

The moving average versus momentum case above demonstrates that you have to choose a ruling trading style — be it trend-following or swing trading — and stick to it. From there, you select one or more confirming indicators from a different style category. Finally, you choose an exit rule based on either the same principle as the trading style or a different one. See Chapter 14 for a discussion of indicators and the different trading decisions of the trend-follower and the swing trader.

A common mistake in technical trading is to switch from a trend-following style to a swing style depending on what mood you're in — or even in mid-trade. This is really another excuse to override your original trading style. You can't evaluate an indicator properly if you don't apply it consistently, and you can't evaluate your skills as a trader if you switch styles on a whim.

Trend-following

Trend-following techniques include the moving average crossover concept (Chapter 10) and pattern work (Chapter 7), and usually involve holding a position for the medium and long term. This is also called *position trading* and is based on the Dow dictum that a trend tends to stay in place until something big comes along to stop it. When your security has a habit of trending, position trading based on trend-following is a profitable ruling concept and less nerve-wracking than other trading styles. However, it can also deliver horrendous one-time losses, because some trend-following techniques, such as the moving average, tend to lag the price action.

When the price runs sideways or into a choppy range, it takes a few days for a moving average to catch up. Moving averages are slow to identify trend turning points. A momentum indicator or pattern can help you exit more efficiently than the same trend-following indicator.

Swing trading

Swing trading combines elements of trend-following and elements of breakout trading (as well as certain original indicators like Martin Pring's KST indicators, which are a little too complicated to go into here). Momentum indicators tell you where the price lies in relation to its recent high-low range, and because many momentum indicators seem to cycle between relative highs and relative lows, they're also called *cycle indicators*. A cycle is like a minitrend that captures the action-reaction character of price moves. Momentum indicators include the relative strength index, the stochastic oscillator, Bollinger bands and other indicators that display the price relative to its recent high-low range.

In cycle trading, you trade the short-term minitrends whether or not you have a breakout and sometimes without regard for the big-picture trend, assuming there is one. In other words, when a cycle indicator bottoms and starts turning upward, you're a buyer in anticipation of an upside breakout. If the price is already in a big-picture trend and the cycle bottom was just a pause, you're well-positioned to ride a resumption of the uptrend, as well as the cycle upturn. If the price was in a big-picture downtrend, to buy at a cycle low is to take advantage of a retracement. This means you're trading counter-trend. Pure cycle trading is the least intuitively obvious of the techniques, and cycle traders often puff up the quality of their analysis with fancy maths.

Breakout

Breakouts occur in both trend-following and swing-trading indicators and styles of trading. Breakouts are usually considered events that mark the start or end of a trend, but you can use them at other times, too. A flag or a pennant, for example, may help you evaluate the momentum versus moving average puzzle we mention at the start of this section (see Chapter 7 for a discussion of flags and pennants).

Breakouts are also the key factor in a subset of swing trading, *setup trading.* See the section 'Efficient Entry and Ruthless Exit — The Setup' later in this chapter. In general, to emphasise breakout concepts implies that you have a shorter holding period and thus trade more frequently. The breakout doesn't stand alone. You seek confirmation of a breakout signal from a trend-following or cycle indicator. Say you have an upside breakout of a resistance line. You get confirmation that you have a high probability trade when a momentum indicator tells you that the security is coming up off an oversold condition. A breakout signal can trigger a trade that lasts anywhere from a few minutes to many days or even weeks.

A case study in complexity

A trend-following concept like the moving average crossover accepts late entries and lower profits, because moving averages always lag the price action. Say you now decide that you want to improve the moving average system, so you add two additional indicators: You want to enter earlier, so you add a momentum indicator. You want to exit closer to the high, so you also add an overbought indicator.

In Figure 15-1, the main window shows the primary trading concept, the moving average crossover. You buy when the 5-day moving average closes above the 20-day moving average (the thicker line) and sell when the price closes below the thinner 5-day moving average. Technically, the entry rule (the crossover) is a form of breakout, so you're already using a breakout signal concept to enter. Say you now want to identify the entry sooner. You complicate it a little by adding a momentum indicator at the bottom of the chart that tells you when momentum is also on the rise, giving you an earlier entry than the moving average by three days. At the top is a different momentum indicator (relative strength) telling you when the price is coming down off an overbought level. This gives you an exit one day earlier.

Using the moving averages alone makes you a profit of 3.9 per cent in three weeks, or 67.6 per cent annualised. When you accelerate the entry and exit by using the additional indicators, you increase profitability by over 50 per cent.

	Buy	*Sell*	*Profit*
Moving Average Concept	$64.35	$66.86	$2.51
With Momentum and Relative Strength	$63.38	$67.32	$3.94

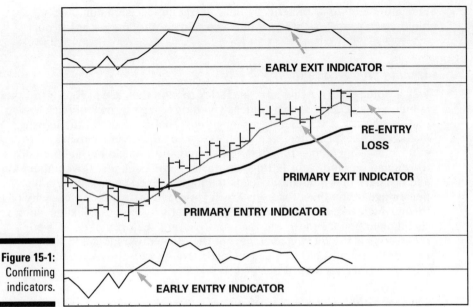

EARLY EXIT INDICATOR

RE-ENTRY

LOSS

PRIMARY EXIT INDICATOR

PRIMARY ENTRY INDICATOR

Figure 15-1:
Confirming
indicators.

EARLY ENTRY INDICATOR

At a glance, the case in Figure 15-1 seems to be a successful integration of three indicators that accelerates entry and exit and makes you more money. But in reality you may have opened a can of worms and may not even be making anymore money. Here are some examples of problems that can arise when you combine indicators.

Trading decisions multiply exponentially

What if the momentum indicator gives you a false reading? As we mention in Chapter 14, indicators are often wrong. This time the early entry worked, but plenty of times it doesn't. So you need a stop-loss exit rule for that one aspect of the trade, the early entry. You can't use the primary technique, the moving average, because it hasn't told you to enter yet!

Now you need two stop-loss rules, one for the now-incorrect entry based on momentum and another one for the real exit, which can be based on either the ruling principle or the second, the more agile relative strength indicator. This gives you a back-testing headache. You have to specify that one stop applies if the trade is only *x* days old and the ruling concept hasn't yet given you an entry signal, and a different stop applies if you do have a confirmed entry signal from the ruling concept and the signal is a little older. Because prices often jitter around ahead of a trending move, you can enter and be stopped out several times before your trade rules gets around to delivering the entry signal.

Indicators add up arithmetically but the trading decision complexity multiplies exponentially every time you add another indicator to your system.

Trading styles can clash

Pick a ruling style for the entry and stick to it. In the case in Figure 15-1, you shouldn't have entered early unless you'd done a great deal of back-testing on this security and found that momentum reliably precedes the moving average crossover in this security. It's okay to adjust your moving average entry rule using momentum, but you should know ahead of time the odds of the momentum indicator letting you down. If you back-test the combination and discover that momentum leads the moving average crossover a high percentage of the time, the odds are in your favour (in which case, why have the moving average indicator at all?). Alternatively, if your back-test shows that momentum failed to lead the crossover in a majority of cases, your ruling style is the moving average, not the momentum indicator and you're better off without it. This time you made money with the early entry, but next time you may lose more.

Concepts can mirror each other and waste your time

In the case of Figure 15-1, the confirming indicators match one another. The relative strength indicator in the top window looks suspiciously like the momentum indicator in the bottom window. And it is. A technical trader named Tushar Chande studied the correlation among various momentum concepts. He found that momentum and the relative strength indicator shown on this chart (Mr Chande's own version) are over 90 per cent correlated. (See Chapter 11 for a discussion of all the guises momentum can assume.) When two things are highly correlated, it means they move more or less in lockstep, in which case one or the other is redundant and a waste of your time to use.

The purpose of using multiple indicators is to get confirmation that a signal is likely to be correct. Obviously, if you're using a momentum indicator, you don't get independent confirmation from another momentum indicator, because they're both using the same style or conceptual principle.

Additional entry and exit issues

On the right-hand side of Figure 15-1, you've exited. But in the next few days, the price rises back above the short-term moving average and closes at new highs. You think that the uptrend is resuming and you want to get back in the trade. You still have 'permission' to buy from your original primary indicator, the 5-day moving average being above the 20-day moving average.

What indicator do you use to re-enter after having exited with a profit? Does a re-entry rule differ from a first-time entry rule? Well, there are two possible and conflicting answers to that question:

- ✔ **No, you shouldn't get back in.** You have a triple sell signal, from your primary model as well as both confirming indicators. You know that the moving average is slow to respond to new prices, but the relative strength indicator tends to be a leading indicator, and it leads you to believe this is no longer a viable trade.

- ✔ **Yes, don't waste a perfectly good trend.** Just find a new confirming indicator. This is usually something as simple as 'Re-enter in the same direction when the close surpasses the most recent highest close (or when the high surpasses the previous highest high)'. For all you know, the seeming resurgence of the uptrend after your exit is telling you that the downmove was only a minor retracement. You'd get this answer from a professional trader, by the way. But remember, the professional's holding period tends to be very short, and he's willing to exit the renewed position on the same day.

When you violate your trading rules, you're trading emotionally and relying on luck, not skill, to trade.

Okay, you still have one condition that leads you to believe that the trend remains in place — the 5-day moving average is above the 20-day, which was your original buy signal. But you have a sell signal from your confirming indicators as well. Unless you have back-tested the specific security and how it behaves in exactly this situation, to re-enter on a higher close or higher high is to violate the spirit and the letter of trading on indicator-based rules.

And now you need a new rule to exit on a stop-loss or to take a new profit. You still have the original moving average, but your confirming indicators are now out of sync. How do you know when to exit the second trade? Well, you can go back to the original trading rule of exiting on the price crossing below the 5-day moving average. This is exactly what happens at the end of the chart. Now pretend you re-enter at the highest high and exit at the cross of the price below the short-term moving average. The amount of your loss is marked by the two horizontal lines. This loss, of course, reduces the gain you previously made when you were following the moving average model.

Golly, all you wanted to do was improve a simple moving average system, and suddenly you have four or five new indicators, each needing a new application rule and each needing to mesh with the others in addition to being consistent with the primary trading style.

Use the KISS approach — keep it simple, stupid. Especially if you are new to technical analysis, don't add too many conditions and try to account for every contingency.

For every time the security in Figure 15-1 goes on to greater highs while you've exited on a minor retracement, there are other cases in which the security reversed direction and fell into a downtrend. The purpose of your moving average rule was to get you out in case that happens. Don't tinker with a winning trading rule by adding something at the last minute that wasn't back-tested. You may make an opportunistic gain — professionals do — but by acting on impulse, you're just as likely to give back profits that were made systematically.

Expecting a Positive Result

The main reason to add bothersome complexity is to improve gains or reduce losses, or both. But you need to have some idea that the overall conditions are right to make any trade in the first place.

Calculating positive expectancy technically

The first question to ask yourself is whether the security in front of you right now offers an opportunity to make a profit. As statisticians say, you want to have a *positive expectancy* that a gain is possible. Not every security offers a profit potential. If it is range-trading sideways with low volatility (refer to Chapter 12), profit potential is low no matter what techniques you're using.

In general terms, a high-positive expectancy trade is one that

- ✓ Displays a bar configuration or pattern that generates profits a high percentage of the time
- ✓ Has multiple of confirming indicators, as discussed in the section 'Introducing complexity' earlier in the chapter
- ✓ Offers an obvious exit point, like a spike high or the downside break of a support line.

Think of the trade as a *process* in which the evidence mounts that the indicators are correct. Don't neglect the configuration of the price bars themselves as a starting point. Sometimes technical traders become so involved with mathematical indicators that they neglect the hard information about supply and demand embedded in the raw price bars and in hand-drawn indicators. If you prefer maths-based indicators over visual pattern recognition, you can quantify breakouts with formulations, such as 'highest close in *x* number of bars' and the like, although this may become cumbersome.

See Figure 15-2 and take a look at the numbered list below that corresponds to the numbers on the chart.

1. The price puts in three days of higher highs and higher lows, and then rises above a resistance line (refer to Chapter 8).

2. The price gaps to the upside (refer to Chapter 5).

3. At the same time, the price crosses above the 20-day simple moving average inside the Bollinger band.

4. A few days later, the relative strength indicator in the top window crosses the buy/sell line to the upside.

5. A few days later, the MACD in the bottom window crosses its buy-sell line to the upside.

6. Finally, the price breaks out above the Bollinger band top, a continuation signal that suggests the trend will continue upward.

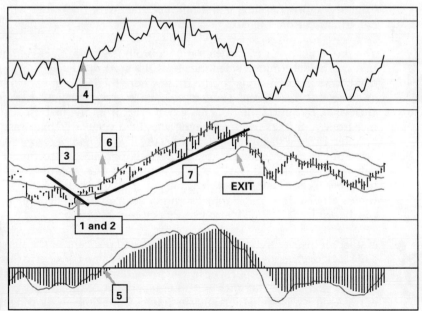

Figure 15-2: High-probability trade.

You can trade this chart any number of equally valid ways depending on your appetite for risk. The key point is that all of the indicators are saying the same thing at about the same time. You can say to yourself, for example, that the first indicator (three higher highs with three higher lows plus break of resistance) gives you a 25 per cent expectancy that the price is going to rise further. The gap gives you another 25 per cent. The cross of the 20-day moving averages gives you a further 25 per cent. You now assign a 75 per cent probability of a further price rise — in fact, a full-blown trend. By the time you get to the fourth confirming indicator, you're now 100 per cent convinced.

Where does the 25 per cent come from? *You* determine it — from experience, from back-testing and from reading other traders' work. Go back and look at the history of gaps in this security. If you're trading a security that has gaps only once a year or so and every time the move continued in the same direction, you're safe in giving it a pro-entry value. On the other hand, you may be looking at a security that gaps a lot without delivering the expected move in the direction of the gap. In that case, be sensible — don't assign the gap any weight towards the trade.

You may not like the number 25 per cent. Okay, pick a different number. Just be careful not to pick such low numbers that you postpone entry until the move is practically over. Each individual views risk and indicators differently. Some traders will enter on the three higher highs (with higher lows), and get in before the break of the resistance line and the gap, for example, improving their gain from this trade over the trader who waits for confirmation from the gap.

The probability of a trade generating a profit isn't an objective number that can be determined scientifically at the start of a trade (because no-one knows before the end of the trend where the last person will buy or sell a security). You can *estimate* the chance of any particular trade being successful by subtracting the margin of error from the historical success rate from your back-tests, assuming you did a very large back-test. (Refer to Chapter 14 for a discussion of back-tests.) The *margin of error* is a statistical concept that programmers are just starting to include in technical analysis software. For example, say that a particular set of indicator-based rules delivered 80 per cent profitable trades over a large number of hypothetical trades on historical data. Your margin of error is 20 per cent, meaning the rule-based trade will deliver a loss 20 per cent of the time.

Maths boffins say that if a technique works 80 per cent of the time on Blue Sky stock over many trials, it should work the same (or nearly the same) on Pink Cloud stock. In other words, the probability of the outcome suggested is a function of the statistics — and independent of the quality or character of the security. Non-mathematicians have a hard time swallowing this one.

You can show identical back-test results for Blue Sky and Pink Cloud, but feel in your bones that you should increase the margin of error judgementally when trading Pink Cloud. Don't dismiss instincts like this out of hand. Maybe Pink Cloud stock has lower liquidity or some other characteristic that is not taken into account in the back-test — leaving it vulnerable someday.

Enhancing probability: Entering at your leisure and exiting at once

The review of the chart in Figure 15-2 discusses the trade in terms of a single purchase and sale. In practice, you can enhance profitability by scaling into the trade. To *scale into the trade* means to add to the position as each indicator confirmation appears. Say you have $5,000 to place on this security. You start by placing a portion of that capital ($1,000) when the first or second indication appears that you've got a winner trade in the making. Then you place additional lots of $1,000 as each benchmark is reached, until you have 100 per cent of the capital allocated to the trade. One clear place to add more to the trade is at point 7, where the price tests support and successfully bounces off it. However, when you exit a trade, you exit all at once.

In Figure 15-2, the price breaks below the support line just before the Exit label. At that precise point, the price also crosses below the 20-day moving average, and the two indicators in the top and bottom windows turn downward. The chart is telling you that the probability is high that the move is over. You exit as shown.

Incorporating sentiment and event risk

Somewhere in the back of your mind you should consider whether the environment is favourable to positive expectancy. Even if your particular security is trending, the market sentiment can be susceptible to shocks and event risk. An example is when your stock is going up but the market index (the all ordinaries or the Nikkei stock, for example) is going down. In equities, when the major indices are going down, you want to know whether sentiment towards your particular security is contaminated. And while you're at it, what are conditions in the bond market? As a general rule, falling interest rates favour stocks, while rising rates are somewhat negative for equities.

Incorporating a quantitative measure for sentiment can be very difficult. Analysts and traders have developed various sentiment-type indicators, but including them into your own trading plan is hard. How much weight do you give them? The same thing is true of calendar effects or seasonal aspects to the market. The popular United States rule, 'Sell in May and go away', may have you out of equities entirely over the northern summer. But what about the company that announces a wonder drug or technological innovation in the height of summer? If you're not trading for the period, you could miss a big gain.

No single correct answer can be given on how to incorporate sentiment and event risk factors. Probably the simplest rule is the best — use them as 'on/off' switches on a trade. That is, trade in the direction implied by sentiment, otherwise don't trade at that time.

You attach the estimate of high or low probability to the trade, not to the indicators. And ultimately, what ensures high-probability of a successful trade is a stop at every stage. At the start of the trade, the stop gets you out at a small loss if price developments fail to turn into a trend. After the three higher highs and the break of the resistance line, for example, the price can fly back down instead of gapping upward. Later, as the trend develops, you place stops to protect gains as they accrue.

Efficient Entry and Ruthless Exit — The Setup

Setup trading is a form of swing trading that's very popular today. A *setup* is a particular configuration of bars, usually with one or two other confirming conditions, such as a pattern or an indicator, that delivers an expected outcome in a high proportion of trades. The opening range breakout described in the section 'Reviewing two classics' earlier in the chapter is an excellent example of a setup. Candlestick trading could be considered setup trading, too (refer to Chapter 6).

Setups usually have catchy names (like *pinball* and *coiled spring*). Do these setups work? If you identify the setup correctly, yes, the price does often behave in the predicted manner. Unfortunately, statistics on exactly what percentage of the time they do work don't exist, but experienced setup traders say that setups work often enough that early entry gives you an edge.

Each setup identifies a specific market condition that can be explained in terms of the psychology of the market. Setup swing trading is eclectic. It borrows from bar reading, pattern identification and indicators. Setups are effective techniques that help you read the supply and demand dynamics on the chart — you can imagine what traders must be thinking, such as the predictable burst of buying after a test of support. In general, you're also counting on the normal swing of action-reaction and the principles of support and resistance.

One benefit of setup trading is that you can be out of the market until you spot a setup situation. You take no risk when you're out of the market and only trade when you think conditions are ideal. Some setup trades are intraday, where you enter and exit the trade on the same day. Other setup trades are more long-lasting because they lead to authentic trends that you stick to until your stop is hit.

Starting off early

A setup identifies the conditions that precede and accompany a price move, giving you a head start in entering a trade. When you correctly identify the setup, the price goes in your direction immediately. And when a strong move begins, the first few days can account for 25 per cent or more of the total move. That's the thrust or impulse aspect of new moves. As a general rule, your goal as a setup trader is to take a profit bite out of a move without necessarily riding the position over the entire move.

Entering early is in stark contrast to trend-following, where you wait until the move has proved itself according to some definition of trendedness before you take a position. In setup trading, you enter a position on the same day or the next day as the chart event, whereas in trend-following, you may not enter until several days later.

The key to setup trading is early identification of a trading opportunity and quick entry into the trade.

Exiting the game

The second part of the trade — the exit — borrows a page from the professional playbook — ruthless stops.

- ✔ If the setup is a dud — it fails or you have not identified it right — you need a stop at a level of loss that you can tolerate. See Chapter 17 on stops. Setup traders always plan and determine in advance the level at which the setup must be considered a failure, and they always place a stop at that level.

- ✔ If the setup succeeds, you keep moving your stop upward to secure each new level of gain as it occurs. Generally you hold until the price moves against you by some specified amount or according to a different bar pattern or indicator than the one you used to enter the trade.

Efficient entries are the hallmark of setup swing trading, but being quick on the trigger doesn't imply that the trader is a wild-eyed risk-taker. Quite the opposite. One of the chief features of setup swing trading is emphasis on risk management.

- ✔ You *never* give up profits by sitting out a retracement (as you often do when trend-following).

- ✔ You absolutely, positively have to use stops and keep them updated.

Working hard while trading like a pro

But here's the catch: Not every setup works every time, and you have to adopt the professional's attitude to a losing trade — get out and ask 'What's next?'. Non-professionals have to swallow hard to adopt this attitude. Amateurs feel an emotional attachment for their securities — pros don't. In the pros' world, the only thing that counts is making money. If a security doesn't offer a good setup today, they abandon it for a new one without a backward look. If your job required you to make a specific sum of money trading *every day,* you'd feel hard-hearted towards securities that fail to offer setups, too.

Other drawbacks include:

- ✔ A setup that you like may not appear every day or even every month. You'd have to memorise a dozen setups if you want to be in the market all the time.

- ✔ If you focus on setups to the exclusion of all the other concepts in technical analysis, you're at a loss for what to do when setups don't appear, and you'd miss out on other opportunities, too.

- ✔ To find your favourite setups, you have to scan a list of securities, and sometimes the best setups may appear in securities that you wouldn't touch with a bargepole on a fundamental or value basis.

- ✔ Setups require intense concentration and often the ability to trade actively during market hours. If you have a day job, this can be hard to do. And remember, active stop management is critical to success, meaning you really should be out of the market altogether when you go on holiday or a business trip. War stories about hair-raising losses usually involve not having placed a stop and learning about some market-moving event only after arriving in an exotic location.

Reading promotions carefully

Because many professionals use setups to make trading decisions, some trading system suppliers play off this nugget of information to claim that they have a 'magic secret' that'll get you trading like a pro. The secret will identify 'high-probability trades', and sometimes the supplier promises that 'You can't lose!'. Experienced traders cringe when they see such over-the-top promotions, even though it's not exactly false advertising, because the statements contain some grain of truth. If you identify a setup correctly, the price often does take off in the direction you expected. If it doesn't, your stop cuts losses. Do enough setup trades with enough discipline for a long enough time, and it's very possible that your gains from winning trades outweigh losses from losing trades.

But be wary of such promotions. For one thing, trading system suppliers who use exaggerated claims aren't showing respect for your brainpower or common sense. Razzle-dazzle ads may intend to deceive and bamboozle rather than to share wisdom. Keep in mind that:

✔ Pros don't have any secret indicators or techniques. All the trading techniques and tricks, including setups, are available to you in books, magazines, newspapers, Web sites, seminars and chat rooms.

✔ As for claims that you can't lose — don't be silly. Of course you can lose. In fact, you will lose on a trade at some point down the track. The point is to lose little and gain big. You don't need to spend thousands of dollars on a program or seminar to grasp the principle of the stop-loss.

✔ If trading discipline is a problem for you, trading psychologists and coaches can help. But discipline is a personal habit that you can't acquire from anyone else — you can only build it internally. The heart of 'trading like a pro' is the trading discipline, not the indicator.

Some reputable technical traders offer follow-along setup trading in seminars or online, for a fee, where you can see the price action on the chart and hear the trader's commentary every few minutes. What you learn from participating in such training courses has less to do with identifying the setup and more to do with sharing the pro's attitude towards exploiting a promising situation but knowing how to retreat from a loser — without regret. Also, it doesn't hurt to compare war stories with other participants to remind you that you're not alone in trying to come to grips with the challenge of trading.

Chapter 16

Building (or Buying) a Trading System

The purpose of using indicators and trading rules is to squelch emotion and to impose discipline on your trading practices. To remove all emotional judgement from trading, some technical traders go the whole hog and design trading systems. A strict, fully mechanical trading system automates the trading process by making *every* decision depend on your indicators and trading rules. You therefore have no discretion over any aspect of any trade.

Although a trading system is the logical conclusion of using technical indicators to guide trading, building a full-bore automated trading system is a huge task. In this chapter, we show that while a trading system relieves you of worry and emotion, it does has its own pitfalls. Developing a trading system is also a lot of hard work and time-consuming. And you'll probably have trouble following it, too! However, if you want to make money and preserve capital, it's a big help to adopt at least some of the principles of trading system design.

Defining Your Trading System

The term *trading system* has different meanings to different people. *Systematic trading* can be as simple as a single indicator and a stop-loss rule (for more on this see Chapters 14 and 15). In fact, most folks in the technical analysis field now refer to any *trading regime* as a *system,* even when it doesn't meet the strict requirement of a fully automated process. In this chapter, we speak of a *trading system* in the strictest sense — where every decision is dictated in advance by the indicators and trading rules that you set down.

Meeting the strict requirements

A trading system is a *mechanical trading system* when it has covered all the bases and dictates every single trading decision, leaving no latitude for the operator to intervene and inject a subjective decision. Definitions vary, but most systems designers would agree on the bare minimum:

- ✔ You need to back-test every indicator and combination of indicators over a large amount of historical data and have a clear idea that the indicator or set of indicators works on the security to generate a favourable gain/loss ratio that's better than 1:1.

- ✔ The system contains enough trading rules so that whatever the contingency, you never need to make a judgement call. The system provides clear directions that you yourself set ahead of time.

- ✔ You must follow the system without fail and without overriding the signals by using emotional judgement. You take every trade that the system signals to you, because you never know which signal is the one that'll generate the juicy profit, and in most systems, the successful back-test track record depends on those big profits to offset many small losses.

Most technical traders use software, which helps remove as much judgement and subjectivity as possible (but remember, it doesn't have to be all computerised to be a system). As we mention earlier in this chapter, in the strictest form of a trading system, everything is mechanised and the program does all the decision-making work, based on your design, and all you have to do is execute the trades.

Make no mistake, building a mechanical trading system is a major undertaking. Balance your need for profits against the time and money required to build your trading system. Such an effort requires knowledge of statistics, computing and risk management as well as technical trading methods. You could spend years developing a comprehensive mechanical trading system, and many people do.

Finding your place on the spectrum

You don't have to embrace a fully mechanised computer program-based system to be a technical trader. You can use some indicators just some of the time. But when you take losses, you sometimes start imagining that some technical indicator and its associated trading rule would've saved you from the loss, so it becomes tempting to try to trade more and more systematically.

Meeting the designers

Books, articles and Web sites abound on the topic of technical trading systems, but who are these gurus and system designers behind it all? Usually they're self-appointed experts who have mastered one or more of the software packages designed solely for technical analysis. Sometimes they program their own software. Gurus and system designers could be maths professors, engineers, medical doctors, economists, historians, musicians and practitioners of hundreds of other lines of work, and they run the gamut from brilliant, insightful and inspiring to self-important, argumentative and petty (just like any other field). The point here is to be careful in choosing your mentor.

System designers are usually adept at mathematics and computer programming, although often they may not be very good traders, as they themselves may admit. This isn't really surprising because maths and computer programming are complex and intricate, while trading can be mind-bogglingly simple. System designers come from all kinds of backgrounds and can't be easily pigeon-holed. Some start with programming and apply it to markets. Some start with markets and use programming as a tool.

It's amusing and intriguing that many technical traders barely passed high school algebra but take home high six-figure profits, while many know-it-all system designers scrape by selling subscriptions and software. After all, if they could design a truly winning system, why would they sell it to you — for any price? To be fair, some system designers simply enjoy the company of like-minded people interested in solving the same puzzles — why the market behaves the way it does. Some enjoy teaching (nothing beats seeing the dawn of 'Got it!' pass over a glowing face).

Why pay attention to system designers if they're not successful traders? Because, as we say in Chapter 14 on indicators, the biggest obstacle to long-term trading success is not your indicators or system, it is you and your emotions. Indicators and trading rules are the tools you use to manage trades and to manage risk. Most technical traders, though, continue to seek ideas from system designers. You never know when you'll get a 'Eureka' moment and discover one indicator or one rule that makes all the difference to your own trading performance. It always pays to have an open mind.

You can start small, building your system slowly. The first step is to review various indicators and their associated trading rules. You can develop a buy/sell system fairly easily, choosing indicators that are logical and workable to you, and then adjust the trading rules until you get a satisfactory mix of hypothetical gain and loss from back-testing.

'Hypothetical' is the right word because the chief reason to combine techniques in a trading system is to back-test indicators and trading rules to see how they have worked in the past. We discuss back-testing in Chapter 14. For all its faults, back-testing is the only way to know if an indicator has worked on your security. After you find good indicators and rules, you can always take them out for a trial run in real time. If your live results are similar to the hypothetical results, you're all set to trade with real capital. Or so you think.

Why Mechanical Systems Fail

Consider this section to be a warning about how hard it is to be a fully systematic trader. The virtue of a well-designed mechanical trading system is that real-time results come in as the back-test leads you to expect. The challenge of a mechanical trading system is and remains . . . you.

You have to trade *exactly* as the system dictates if you're to have any hope of duplicating test results. This can be very hard to do. In fact, it's impossible for most traders because they allow their emotions to intervene with the system. More than one advanced system designer has had to give day-to-day control of trading his system to another party, because he can't help second-guessing it. (And we're not telling you which one of us this was!)

Fooling around with new ideas

Mechanical trading systems sometimes fail because the trader can't resist fiddling with system components — either indicators or rules. Most traders' systems are never really quite finished. They evolve, because technical traders are still devising new techniques as well as reviving old ones, or sometimes the trader himself is changing — for example, his trading requirements for profit or risk may also be evolving. The problem with new techniques is that people are impatient and try to fit the new idea into an existing system without fully back-testing it — or sometimes without back-testing it at all. Even experienced technical traders (late at night, after a few martinis) confess to reading about a new idea or hearing about it at a seminar or conference, and running right back home to trade it — using actual money. Needless to say, this always ends in tears.

Back-testing until you're blue in the face

To find the 'perfect' moving average, you can spend countless hours trying to find the ideal parameter for each indicator (for more on this topic, see Chapter 14). As soon as you discover that 20 rather than 15 days is the optimum number to put into a moving average, the market changes again and the new best number is 21. Market conditions vary. That's why a lot of indicator fiddling is just spinning your wheels. Indicator signal accuracy isn't 100 per cent reliable to begin with, and fiddling with indicators often doesn't cure the inaccuracy problem of most indicators. You have to accept that excessive complexity does not guarantee profitability. Sometimes the simplest model makes more money.

Performing back-testing research while working towards a fully automated trading system has two virtues — you not only find out about indicator effectiveness and reliability, but you also get the opportunity to refine your money management rules, which often yields as much or more profit than simply replacing indicators or adjusting indicator parameters.

Before you spend a zillion hours adding or perfecting indicators, remember that your goal isn't to have the perfect indicator; your goal is to make money. The reward you want is profit, not perfection. Your time is more wisely spent perfecting your money management rules than back-testing indicators until 2 am. Maybe nothing is wrong with your indicators — it's your money management that needs work. *Money management* refers to how you allocate capital among securities (*portfolio management*) and on specific trading occasions (*position sizing and stops*). See Chapter 17 for a discussion of managing the trade.

Not sticking to your time frame

No rule is always right. Technical analysis contains rules that are valid in the context of their own time frame but that may not be valid in a different time frame. For example, your short-term momentum indicators are screaming at you to sell because the security is overbought (refer to Chapter 11), but you're in the middle of a very large and very clear uptrend. The price didn't break a moving average or a support line on the downside. What should you do?

To ask this question at a time when you have money in the trade demonstrates that you didn't plan the trade for all possibilities. You're unable to prioritise your indicators. The short-term indicators tell you to exit. The long-term indicator tells you to hang on. The 'right' answer has nothing to do with contradictory indicators but rather with your choice of time frame. If you're a short-term trader, exit and wait for your short-term indicators to show more promising conditions. If you're a long-term trend follower, and you have back-tested the price series and you know that the probability is low that these setbacks in the trend are going to produce a loss, then you should stick to the trade. You should already have chosen which indicator trumps the others, and that decision should be based on how much money you can afford to lose if you're wrong.

To improvise the decision in the midst of the trade isn't the right way to trade technically. You're using indicators, but you're not trading systematically. In fact, you're in the grip of the very emotions, preconceptions and prejudices that technical trading is designed to avoid in the first place.

Practising self-sabotage

The success of technical trading systems is due to one characteristic — they keep you in winning trades for a relatively long time while getting you out of losing trades relatively quickly, so that over a large number of trades, your profit exceeds your losses. In this sense, fully systematic technical trading is a numbers game based on a series of trades.

While a mechanical system imparts confidence in the eventual profit-and-loss profile over some period of time, it has the drawback of losing on any one single trade — and sometimes you want to override specific trade signals. Don't!

Overriding technical signals is called trading with *discretion*. Discretion is an innocent-sounding word, but in fact, it's dynamite. To exercise discretion means to abandon your hard-earned, high-probability systematic trading signals in favour of personal and emotional judgement (again).

Just about every non-professional technical trader allows himself the luxury of discretion to a greater or lesser degree. Every trader has to pick his own spot along the discretion continuum. Professionals tend to exercise discretion a lot less than non-professionals — professionals tend to follow rules. System purists point out that to override signals is to defeat the purpose of having a system, while experienced traders say they have a 'gut feel' about when a signal is bad. (Gut feel can sometimes be a function of what you had for breakfast.)

You should force yourself to be as strict as possible. Overriding system signals with emotion is the main way that traders sabotage themselves. Sabotage can take the form of overtrading (trading too often) or being unable to pull the trigger (indecisiveness) despite having a clear buy or sell signal.

One of the chief reasons to use technical analysis and a systematic approach to trading is to give yourself a break from emotion. You may get away with a little overriding once in a while if you have good instincts, but if you do it on every trade, you're not a technical trader (and before long, you may not have any capital left, either). It's better to find a fresh technical indicator or rule when you get the urge to override than to give in to the urge every time.

Because you can't back-test judgement, the only way to evaluate discretionary overrides is to keep a trading diary and write down every override you want to do. After a suitable time (a minimum of six months), go back and do an honest review of your judgement. A trading diary is a prose rendering of what you're seeing on the chart, as well as what you're thinking and feeling about it. A good way to check whether you're on the right track is to print out the chart and write your ideas right on it. Then, a few trading periods later, print out the chart showing what happened.

A common outcome of evaluating overrides is that you discover you always want to take profits too soon or take losses right at the worst level. A trading diary has many benefits:

✔ You get ideas about additions to your system to overcome a shortcoming. The diary becomes a wish list. Then, while perusing the technical literature, you can see a gem when you find it — it's the solution to the issue on your wish list.

✔ You may discover that your eye was detecting important patterns that maths-based indicators don't catch. If you had a feeling that you should stop out a position (defined in the following section) but your indicators didn't agree, and in retrospect you can see an island reversal or some other pattern, you may have a hidden talent for patterns that you should work on and develop. See Chapters 5 and 7 for more about patterns.

✔ You discover personal characteristics you didn't know about (and may or may not like). A common finding is that you saw a continuing trend because you wanted to see it, and willfully ignored reversal warnings from other indicators that were present on the chart. 'How did I miss *that*?' you may say to yourself. Another common finding is overtrading. You like the way it feels — the adrenaline rush — to pull the trigger on a new trade. Watch out! You're trading for fun, not to make money.

The trade you dismiss today as holding no promise could be the one trade that provides half of your earnings six months from now. The old joke has it that trend-followers make all their money in three months and spend the next nine giving it back bit by bit until the next big trend comes along. If you're a trend-follower, you can't afford to override the big-win trade.

Besides, refusing to obey your system implies that you lack faith in your own creation (the trading system). Now you're in the dark heart of low self-confidence. You need to think about whether you really want to devote all the time and energy that active trading requires. Remember, trading is a business. You don't have to do it full time but you do have to apply business-like standards when you do.

Following Big-Picture System Rules

Having a positive expectancy of a gain is the key element of taking a trade (for more on this topic, refer to Chapter 15). Whether you're aiming for a full trading system or working more casually towards a more systematic approach, here is a short list of other considerations that have a big impact on overall long-term profitability.

Stopping out versus the stop-and-reverse

To *stop out* of a position means you've attained a profit target, taken as much loss as you're willing to take, or reached a level of risk you can't tolerate. Just because you've stopped out of a position doesn't mean you necessarily want to, or need to, reverse positions and trade in the opposite direction.

You have to decide whether to be in the market all the time, or whether you're willing to stay out of the market under some conditions. Some professionals are required by the rules of their firms to be in the market nearly all the time. They're not 'working' if they're not trading. This is a burden that the individual doesn't have. The flip side is that when you're out of the market, you're potentially missing an opportunity as well as not taking a risk.

If you're building a system, your back-tests must specify the conditions when you would neither buy nor sell, but stay out of the market — to be *square*. This decision has to do with your personal preference for how active a trader you want to be. You need to be realistic about how many trades you want (and can) execute in any one period of time (for more on this topic, see Chapter 14).

Trading more than one security

Up to this point, we have focused on trading systems in terms of a single security. In practice, your real interest is in how much money you make.

You may have a valid and systematic way to trade a single security, but you still face a high risk of loss due to a one-time catastrophe. The obvious solution is to apply your valid and systematic trading regime to a broader array of securities. This diversification of trades also reduces risk. When one security is falling in price, some other security is rising. A solid track record may require offsetting some losses with gains in an inversely correlated or non-correlated security. As discussed in Chapter 15, to be correlated means to move in lockstep. In securities, Security X can be highly correlated with Security Y. They rise and fall together. When you trade both of them, gains are magnified on the way up, but so are losses when they're both falling.

A good portfolio is diversified, so that the price behaviour of each security is unrelated to the price behaviour of the others. Using spreadsheet software (such as Excel or Open Office Calculator), you can easily discover whether your two favourite securities are correlated. In fact, you can plot both securities on the same chart and eyeball whether they move in tandem. If they do, you don't have to dump one, you just have to add something else that is inversely correlated to improve total portfolio performance; this is called *portfolio optimisation*. Portfolio optimisation isn't, strictly speaking, a technical analysis idea. But technical traders use it as a natural extension of the systematic approach to trading.

Optimisation can sometimes make for some strange security bedfellows. Don't reject a non-correlated security on fundamental grounds and pass up the opportunity to smooth your earnings path. You don't have to *like* the security to trade it successfully. When you're building a system, the nature of the security isn't relevant — the only thing that counts is how it adds to or subtracts from your profit performance. If you're building an equity system and find that adding soybean futures would reduce total system risk by half, then find out how soybean futures are traded. It's in your interest. If you build a futures trading system for equity index futures and its performance would get a jolt of low-risk profitability by including the Japanese yen, then it doesn't matter whether you know anything about foreign exchange. Include the Japanese yen in your futures trading system — you're only trading price, after all.

The same thing is true when you buy a system that requires you to trade each security in a basket of securities. If you cherry-pick the securities, you're violating a core principle of the trading strategy, its diversification. See the section 'Buying a Trading System' for more details.

Don't trade on too little capital

A good system designer acknowledges that every system takes losses, and the trader must have enough capital to remain standing afterwards. If the system is capable of generating a $3,000 loss, the minimum capital required to trade the system is obviously higher than $3,000. A *drawdown* is the amount of money you lose on any single trade. Whether you're building your own system or buying one, you must know the expected average drawdown and the expected maximum drawdown, and be prepared for the worst.

As a general rule, the maximum drawdown you should accept in any single trade is 20 to 30 per cent of capital — although you can take only three or four worst-case losses in a row before you're out of the trading business. (For more on stop-loss principles, see Chapter 17.) Professional traders tend not to accept drawdowns of any more than 1 or 2 per cent.

Trading with too little capital is the major cause of system overrides. If you've allocated a sum like $3,000 to your technical system but have built a trading system that routinely generates a $3,000 loss before the system generates a sell signal, you're taking too much risk and can be easily knocked out of the game. Sound silly? Not at all. In commodity and financial futures, where leverage can be 100 or more times your initial capital, a minor swing can cost you your entire stake, or more than your entire stake. Carrying this much risk is emotionally nerve-wracking, to say the least — and as we mention in lots of chapters in this book, a nervous trader is prone to trading emotionally.

Buying a Trading System

You may see ads (and receive solicitations in the mail) for trading systems that promise huge returns, practically no risk, and an 80 per cent accuracy of trade recommendations. These are called *black boxes,* which are systems that claim to select high-probability trades but don't reveal the trading rules and indicators that the system uses. The promotional material may say that the inner workings of the system are self-adaptive (it's a 'neural network' that 'learns' from its own mistakes) and too complex to display.

Even in the case of a self-adapting system, chances are that the system worked well on certain securities in a certain time frame in the past. But that's no guarantee that it is working today, will work in the future, will work on the securities you like, or will work for you. You have to ask yourself why anyone would sell such a goldmine to you (at any price) instead of keeping it to himself. Some very big names in the investment world do indeed use sophisticated and complex self-adjusting systems; they're top secret, and truth be told, the big names aren't disclosing how well they work, either. Always treat claims made by system sellers with caution.

Overcoming phoney track records

If you choose to buy a trading system, be aware that amateurs, crooks and charlatans are found in the technical analysis business just as they are in any other business. You will see fraudulent track records, track records that mysteriously include only certain periods, and other chicanery. One trick is to adjust the track record by excluding the performance of securities in a portfolio when they produce losses in the period, but to add them back when they produce gains. You can see through this financial foolishness by:

- Getting disclosure of all the indicators and rules, and verifying results yourself by testing the system on the same historical data as the supplier's track record.

- Examining the supplier's actual brokerage statements. With today's easy communications, there's no excuse for not making broker statements available. And if the system supplier doesn't actually trade the system, ask why not?

- Asking to see the list of every published trade recommendation for suppliers who publish buy/sell reports. Make sure you get data covering several years, and verify that the trade prices shown actually existed on each trade date. Make sure the market was open on each trade date, too.

Your best bet is to follow the old rule that if something sounds too good to be true, it's probably not . Keep an eye peeled for the one telltale sign that a system is just someone's bright idea — the notification that performance results are hypothetical. Any 12-year old can 'fit' trading indicators to historical data to produce 100 per cent-plus gains. The only question is how the trading system performs in real time.

If you buy a system despite all warnings we provide here, do a pretend-run on paper before committing real money to it.

What to look for in a system

Only a few system suppliers are crooks. Most are perfectly legitimate. Still, you want to get good value for money spent. You should look for:

- ✔ Original ideas that are fully disclosed. In some cases, you could pay $250 to $5,000, only to get nothing more than a formula or two that you could have acquired free from a book or the Internet.

- ✔ *Scalability,* which means that you can trade the system with a variable amount of money, including small amounts. Some trading systems require $50,000 or $100,000 in risk capital, or some other amount that is unrealistically high for a newcomer to technical analysis. Generally, a good reason exists for requiring so much capital — the system depends on diversification among many securities to get the published track record, for example, or the system tends to generate big drawdowns. If you buy a system that is dependent on a large amount of capital to run effectively, and then allocate too little money to it, you must cherry-pick the trades, defeating the core concept.

- ✔ Fully-defined money management rules. Most trading systems don't contain money management rules and leave so much decision-making up to the user that duplicating the advertised track record is virtually impossible. Only a handful of trading systems are truly comprehensive in that they include full money management rules. Also, most systems don't provide guidance on what securities to trade or which securities the system is good for.

Pick the Tool, Not the Security

Say that you just arrived from another planet and you have no attachment to the concept of blue chip stocks and no difficulty seeing soybean futures in the same light as IBM or the Swiss franc. To you, a security is a security, and you care nothing about its underlying value or fundamental characteristics.

Welcome to the world of professional traders, chartists and system designers. They don't look any more Martian than the next guy, but they have a peculiar and wonderful ability to see a price as just a price. Using this mind-set, you pick indicators that combine together really well to generate high profits and controlled losses across a wide range of securities. You trade the system without regard for the nature of the securities or its fundamentals. In fact, you winnow out securities if they don't come up to system requirements, no matter what they are.

You can sit a professional trader down in front of a screen of live prices, and before an hour is out, he's spotted a method to trade the securities. Even if he's an equities trader and you're showing him silver futures, he's still able to 'read' price direction. Prices behave in similar ways, because the human beings trading them behave in similar ways. The same thing is true of an experienced chartist. Hand him a chart with no label and in no time he can tell you whether to buy it or sell it.

Professional traders, technical analysts and systems designers are indifferent to the security or their fundamentals. They care only about the price, where the price is going, and whether they can have confidence in the outcome. So if you like a particular indicator and find it reliable, it makes sense to scan the universe of securities to find what the indicator is saying today.

Picking indicators that fit your system and personal risk profile first and the securities to trade them on second is to reverse the usual order in securities trading. Most people are trained to think that they should know a little something about the fundamentals of a security before they dare to trade it. But when your only goal is to make money using technical indicators, why not reverse the order?

The process goes by several different names, the most generic of which is *scanning*. You scan a universe of securities to find the ones that fit the criteria you specify in your system test. Each technical analysis software package has its own name and method of scanning. Say you want to use moving averages. You can tell the software to search or explore for every security in your database that has just risen above its 20-day moving average. Now you have a candidate list of securities to check out for other technical criteria.

To name a single criterion will probably deliver too many candidates. Here's a set of sample criteria to look for when seeking a good stock to trade:

- **Already high:** Within 10 per cent of the high relative to the past year's high-low range
- **Rising:** Rate of change (momentum) greater than 10 per cent over the past six months and greater than 20 per cent over the past year
- **On trend:** The slope of the linear regression is greater than zero
- **Liquid:** Defined as volume greater than 200,000 shares traded per day on average
- **Not a penny dreadful stock:** Meaning a minimum price of $5 per share

You may also choose software to scan for fundamental criteria, either before the technical scan or afterwards. Scanning all solves the problem of tips, where someone tells you that Blue Sky is going to trade ten or a hundred times higher in a few months. If the security isn't already exhibiting a rising trend with strong momentum, or if it doesn't have the fundamentals to support broader trader participation, the tip is worth what you paid for it — zip, zero, zilch.

Chapter 17

Managing the Trade

. . . .

In This Chapter

▶ Creating trading rules

▶ Knowing when to take the money and run

▶ Keeping losses under control

▶ Getting to know the stop-loss order

▶ Finding out how to adjust positions

. . . .

*I*n technical trading, you use indicators that help you identify what the price is doing — trending, going sideways, making a peak or a bottom and so on. Indicators give you useful information about price dynamics, but it's up to you to build trading rules around them. Indicators are about price changes. Trading rules are about you and your money.

In this chapter, we talk about developing trading rules that match up with your indicator skills, your appetite for risk and your choice of time frame. Special emphasis is on stop-loss rules — don't leave home without one.

It's when you sell that counts. Notice that the focus is on money, not on the security and not on the indicator. To *trade* is to plan the purchase and sale, and to have an emergency exit plan if prices don't develop according to the expectations that your indicators give you. This chapter covers the process of melding indicator-based trading with your own personal risk management.

Building Trading Rules

The technical trader seeks to plan the trade from entry to exit. This is the opposite of traditional investing, where you buy a security for an indefinite period of time and seldom establish in advance the level at which you will sell. But if you want to increase your capital stake or preserve capital, it's when you sell that counts. You sell for one of two reasons — you met a profit target or a loss limit. In technical trading, making money is more important than having indicators that forecast perfectly.

Exits are harder than entries. Brokers say, 'It's easier to buy than to sell'. Nobody knows why this is so. On an entry you have hope and expectation — ideas and feelings — but on an exit, you have either a profit or a loss — cold hard cash.

The paramount rule in technical trading is to control losses. You can pick so–so securities and apply so–so indicators to them, and if you're trading systematically, you can still make a decent net gain if you only control losses. The process of successful technical trading rests on two pillars:

✔ Controlling losses. Any fool can make money in a rising market, however the real test is knowing when to sell. If the market turns against you, and it will from time to time, try not to freeze. Likewise, don't hope that the market will turn around in your favour if you wait long enough. Make a subjective decision based on the charts. If they tell you to sell, then sell. Another trade is always waiting to happen.

✔ Take some money off the table once in a while and put it in a risk-free or low-risk investment, like a term deposit or a savings account. Don't wait for the market to take back what it has given you — it will eventually, if you allow greed to cloud your judgement.

These two ideas are so critical that the rest of the chapter is dedicated to them. First, though, we need to answer some common questions and clarify what a trading rule is and how it works.

Answering common questions about trading

The overall subject of money management is a big one and we can't hope to cover more than some basics here. The first question is usually, 'How much should I put into technical trading? Ten percent of my capital? Fifty percent?' No single correct answer exists. You have to decide this one on your own. However, take a look at the following list for answers to specific questions that we *do* have answers for:

✔ **What should I trade?** Should you trade shares, currencies (Forex), futures or CFDs. The answer lies with the exposure to risk that you're prepared to manage. What you must remember is that the higher the risk the higher the return or conversely the higher the risk the greater the potential loss if you get it wrong. Futures and CFDs are leveraged products and can be very tricky to manage if you're inexperienced. To paraphrase the old saying, 'buyer or seller, beware'.

✔ **How many securities should I trade?** As a general rule, you want more than one as a form of *diversification* (which reduces the risk of losing it all in a single crash) but fewer than 20 (which would require too much analysis even for a full-time trader). Three to five securities initially are about right, especially for a newcomer. This gives you a feel for the market and your trading style. If you wish to trade leveraged products (for example, futures or CFDs) then one trade at a time is much safer.

✔ **With whom should I trade?** Should you trade through a licensed broker who can give you advice on what to trade or should you trade online, using your own judgement, thereby saving money on brokerage fees. The choice is yours and is dependent on how confident you feel. You may wish to start with a broker before moving to online trading after you become more confident. Whichever way, always look at the charts before making a trade.

✔ **Which securities should I trade?** This is trickier.

- Diversification reduces risk, so pick securities whose price moves aren't correlated. To pick two securities that move in the identical way is to get the identical return from trading them, and because you *will* have losing trades, you risk the doubling of losses.

- Pick securities whose moves you have the best chance of identifying, given the indicators you select. If you prefer slow-changing, lagging indicators like moving averages, you want to trade securities that are slow-moving and highly trending. If you like trend-following, don't pick a choppy, high-volatility security, which is better traded with different indicators.

- Use publicly available information or your insight about certain securities or classes of securities to assist with your trading. Farmers, knowledgeable about farm crops, trade cattle or wheat futures. If you can read the mind of the Reserve Bank, trade bond or currency futures. If you know about the mining industry, trade BHP, Rio or Oxiana. It can also pay to supplement technical analysis with the perspective that comes from fundamental analysis gained from research. If you like a security, then look up the security's Web site. Read the quarterly reports, annual report and market releases to gain an insight into what the company is all about.

✔ **How do you allocate your capital among the securities you're trading?** You can divide it up equally, or you can allocate a higher percentage to the security getting the most winning trades over the past 30 or 90 days. You can also allocate more to the security that just gave you a loss — this can be dangerous though, because it may continue to fall. Counterintuitive as this may sound, it's nonetheless one of the top approaches discussed by strategists. You should, however, look for signs that the downtrend has ended before throwing good money after bad.

Establishing your rules

To plan your trades, you need trading rules. A *trading rule* is the specific action you take when certain conditions are met. Trading rules are also called by the fancier names *risk management* and *money management.* At the most basic, a trading rule instructs you to buy or sell when an indicator meets a preset criterion (like the moving average crossover in the case in Chapter 14). Most indicators have a buy/sell trading rule already embedded in them, as we describe in each of the chapters about indicators (Chapters 4 through 16).

Keep in mind that technical trading is a mindset that goes beyond using indicators. The purpose of trading rules is to qualify the action signalled by indicators and to guide you when the market delivers a surprise instead of what you expect. Trading rules improve your trading performance by refining the buy/sell signals you get from indicators. Trading rules tend to be more complex and contain more conditions than indicators. A day trader may buy after the first 45 minutes if x and y also occur. Or, sell half the position when z occurs. Alternatively, a swing trader may buy two days after a new high is made, as long as the price does not fall back to below the point of breakout and as long as the trend is confirmed by indicators.

Having an emergency plan

You can be the best indicator analyst in the world and still be a lousy trader. That's because indicators are only indicators. They're often wrong. Conditions change and contingencies arise, as described in Chapter 3.

Those of us in the technical trading business have heard the story dozens of times — the novice trader transformed $2,000 into $250,000 in his first six months. He then lost most of it, or even all of it, and has been trying for the past ten years to get the groove back. He labours mightily into the small hours over complex formulas. He thinks the magic lies in designing the perfect indicator. He complains that the market is no longer trending these days or that the indicators no longer work.

But there is no magic and there is no perfect indicator. The market didn't change its degree of trendedness, either. The trader is simply failing to acknowledge that he got lucky with the right indicator at the right time on the right security. He's now using different indicators and overriding them willy-nilly. But of all the errors, the biggest was not having a plan to control his losses, which cost him $250,000. You must remember that some indicators work well on a trending market, while others work well when the market trades within a price range. No indicator works well under all circumstances.

You need an emergency plan to take care of these three problems:

- ✔ **The indicator is wrong.** One of the inherent challenges of using indicators is that you have to follow every buy/sell signal that your indicator generates if you expect to get the same or a similar gain/loss profile as you got in your back-test. One reason to create trading rules is to compensate for the possibility of indicators giving you false signals.

  For example, you're using an indicator that's fairly sensitive to price changes, and it gives a lot of false signals. But you like the indicator because it gets you into a new move early. Instead of refining the indicator itself, you can modify the indicator-driven *decision* by specifying that the indicator has to be confirmed by a second indicator. See Chapter 15 for more on confirmation.

- ✔ **The indicator isn't wrong but you think it is.** The urge to override an indicator signal is strong in the face of unexpected conditions and contingencies. Overriding is hard to do unemotionally — after all, your money is being lost. The point is to override an indicator the same way you developed the indicator in the first place — systematically.

  If you're overriding an indicator using fundamental judgement based on news, obviously you can't back-test your decisions. You can, however, develop a list of overriding factors and conditions, and take action only when they're present. At the least, the list limits your ability to override your indicators randomly. For example, you get a new indicator signal at the close on a Friday but you know that Monday is a national holiday and the market won't reopen until Tuesday. Instead of automatically following the signal, spend the weekend going back over the price history to see if the price typically makes jumps before or after three-day weekends. In other words, using common sense and experience, you should question why an indicator is giving a new signal. And you should have a good reason, preferably based on research, to override it.

- ✔ **Catastrophes do happen.** To determine in advance what you will do under various conditions is especially critical when a price makes a very large and unexpected change. As noted in Chapter 3, large and unexpected changes are very common in markets, because the market is a group of people who sometimes fall into the grip of manias and panics. If you're positioned the wrong way when a mania or a panic occurs, you need to get out — fast. For example, 1987 and 9/11 are two classic examples where smart players would have liquidated their trades as soon as possible.

Taking Money off the Table

When you have a gain in a trade, how much is enough? How do you know when to take profits? Unfortunately, few technical traders offer guidance on this topic or describe a take-profit rule. You never know at the beginning of a trend how long it'll last or how far it'll go. It's therefore very difficult to choose a profit target. In practice, each individual trader develops his own technique. The optimum way to take profit is, in fact, one of the great unexplored frontiers of technical trading.

Relying on indicators

Instead of formulating take-profit rules, most technical traders rely on indicators to signal when a move has ended. The signal is the *de facto* take-profit rule. Lagging indicators always force you to leave a little profit on the table, because the indicator signals a late exit after the peak or bottom has already passed. Leading indicators can get your exit closer to the top, but at the risk of missing a breakout and new trend.

Using averages

You can use an average to exit. You look back over historical data, see that the indicators generated an average gain of x per cent for the same period in the same security, and exit when you have reached that percentage gain. A related technique is to note that the market (say the All Ords or the ASX200) has returned an average x per cent in each of the past five years, and when you reach that same level in your security, it's time to go.

To base an exit on an average is to violate the principle that tells you to let your winners run. Perhaps this year the return on that indicator or that market will be double x. After all, the variation around an average can be very large. In general, exiting because an average was reached isn't a good rule.

Securing satisfaction

Every trade has two components: What the price is doing and *you*. Say that a trade has given you a 50 per cent return, or it has reached some specific dollar level, like $10,000. Are you justified in taking the profit? Yes, as long as you're satisfied with the 50 per cent or the $10,000 and won't succumb to remorse over the lost opportunity if the trend keeps going. You may find that keeping yourself in check when this happens is surprisingly difficult to do. A lot of traders reinstate the same position. To exit only to get back in the same trade is obviously inefficient. You miss part of the move, you pay the bid-offer spread and commissions twice, and the only benefit is that you're taking no risk while you're temporarily out of the market.

Worse, to take a profit and then get back into the same trade shows that you don't know why you're trading. The purpose of trading is to make money, but to get back into the trade after making a satisfactory amount of money is to say that you're not treating trading as a way to make money. Instead, you view it as a way to have fun, feel the excitement of the trade and satisfy your ego (for having selected a winning trade).

Controlling Losses

Your level of risk seeking or risk aversion is personal. Therefore, nobody can design rules for you. You must do it for yourself. Ask yourself whether you'd faithfully follow every buy/sell signal generated by a given indicator when the back-test of the indicator predicts you will have some individual trades that entail a loss of 50 per cent of your trading capital. No?

Well, how much of your trading capital *are* you prepared to lose? This isn't an idle question. Put down the book and stare at the wall and think about it. Your answer is critical to whether you can succeed in technical trading. If you say you'll accept no losses at all, forget technical trading. You *will* take losses in technical trading. If you say that you're willing to lose 50 per cent in a single trade — whoa, Nellie! That's too much. Two losing trades and you would be out of business. The right amount to lose on any trade is somewhere between nothing and everything-in-two-trades. Here's help in arriving at your personal number.

Experienced traders ask themselves, 'How much will I lose today?' when they wake up every morning. In contrast, beginners find losses almost impossible to contemplate. And yet if you don't control losses, it's not a question of whether you go broke, but of *when* you go broke (as a famous trader named W D Gann wrote on the very first page of one of his books).

Selling out of a losing trade is the single hardest thing to do in trading. For one thing, it means that your indicator let you down. Maybe indicator-based trading is wrong. No! Indicators are valuable tools — they just can't do the entire job alone. Accept that your indicators have shortcomings and that your job is to overcome those shortcomings by using money management rules.

A bigger problem is your bruised ego. To sell a losing position means you failed. The standard response to a loss is denial. 'It will come back!' you cry. In the long run, this may be true. But in the long run, you may be broke and unable to take advantage of the price coming back. Look again at the table in Chapter 1 that shows the percentage gain that you need to recover a loss. To recover a 50 per cent loss, you need to make a 100 per cent gain.

Every top trader admits to taking bigger losses than they had planned. Many go out of business for a period of time, only to come back later with essentially the same indicators — and better ways to manage the trade. In fact, some investors say that the best time to place money with a professional trader is right after he has taken a fat loss — because then he's a better trader. Note that such investors aren't predicting he will be a better indicator analyst but a better *trader*.

The Stop-Loss Order

The stop-loss order is *the* tool you use for overcoming the unreliability of indicators (as well as your own emotional response to losses). A *stop-loss order* is an order you give your broker to get you out of a trade if it goes against you by some amount. If you're a buyer, it's a sell order. If you're a seller, it's a buy order. The stop-loss order is sometimes called a *protective stop* because it protects you from losing your entire stake.

Stop-loss orders help to protect you from a 9/11-type event or a bad announcement that impacts adversely on a security or the market overall.

Mental stops are hogwash

In keeping with the principle of planning the entire trade, you should enter your stop-loss order at the same time you enter the position. Why some traders don't do this is a psychological mystery. It's probably the triumph of hope of a spectacular gain (glorious wishful thinking) over the fear of a small loss (dreary reality check).

Many traders say they keep a mental stop in their heads, but this is a delusion. Traders who do this con themselves into thinking

- They'll be watching the price every minute the market is open and will have the gumption to sell at a loss if the limit is reached.
- No catastrophic 9/11 shock is going to happen while they have a position.

One of the main reasons to have a stop is to guard against catastrophic shocks; therefore it's vanity to suppose a shock can't happen. In practice, traders with mental stops sit hopelessly by as the trade goes further and further against them. They may pretend that they're busy re-analysing the situation, but analysis-paralysis is a rationalisation.

Other traders say that the security they're trading doesn't lend itself to stop-loss orders, because it's too volatile. Or they're such big traders that the market would find out where their stops are and maliciously target them. The most pernicious of the excuses is that the trader routinely has his stop hit, only to see the price move back in the direction of his original position. This isn't a reason to avoid using stop-losses. It's a justifiably good reason to reset the stop to a better level so this doesn't happen or happens less often.

To pretend that you have a mental stop or to refuse to place stops is to avoid accepting the reality of trading — it's a business, and setbacks happen in business. Setting a stop-loss is like buying insurance in case the store burns down. Not to take out insurance is to treat trading as a hobby and to view the amount at stake as play money that won't be missed if you lose it rather than viewing it as risk capital. Most professional firms use stop-loss orders — and fire any employee who breaks discipline.

Sorting out the types of stops

Technical traders have developed many stop-loss principles. Each concept is either a fixed trading rule or a self-adjusting one. Stops relate to indicators, money or to time, and often these three don't line up neatly to give you an easy decision. You have to choose the type of stop that works best for you.

The 2 per cent stop rule

Probably the most famous stop-loss rule is the fixed 2 per cent rule that was employed by a trading group named the Turtles. The *2 per cent rule* states that you should stop a loss when it reaches 2 per cent of starting equity. If you're trading risk capital of $10,000, you can afford to lose no more than $200 on any single trade if you expect to stay in business for a long period of time. The 2 per cent rule is an example of a *money stop,* which names the amount of money you're willing to lose in a single trade.

Two hundred dollars may sound like a tiny number to you, but in the context of active trading, it's quite large. You need only 50 losing trades in a row to go broke. And 50 trades may sound like a lot of trades, but you'll find that many valid indicators have you trading that often, depending on your time frame. If you're trading intraday or very short term, you could have a lot more than 100 trades in a year.

Also, you may think it would be rare to have 50 consecutive losses in a single security, but if you're trading several securities, 50 is no longer a large number. If you're trading five securities, for example, you go broke after ten consecutive losses per security.

The fact that consecutive losses pile up more quickly when you trade a lot of securities is the chief reason that trading advisers usually recommend that you not trade more than five securities at a time — and that the securities not move in tandem.

Risk/reward money stops

The risk/reward ratio puts the amount of expected gain in direct relationship to the amount of expected loss. Say, for example, that you're buying a Blue Sky stock at $5 and your indicators tell you that the potential gain is $10, which means that the stock could go to $15. You could set your initial stop at $2.50 or 50 per cent of your capital stake, for the chance to make $10. That gives you a risk/reward ratio of 10:2.5 or 4:1. (Strangely, the amount of the gain, the *reward,* is always placed first in the ratio, even though it comes second in the name.) The higher the risk/reward ratio, the more desirable the trade.

But consider the premise that your ending capital will be triple your initial stake. You should always make a trade on a positive expectation of making a gain. But gee, expecting a 300 per cent return is going a bit far, isn't it? Well, it depends on your skills. If you consistently forecast and get 300 per cent gains, time after time, good on you. You may be able to accept a higher initial stop-loss level than other mere mortals. The main reason to avoid aiming for gigantic gains is that the prospect of tripling your money carries an emotional wallop that even the coolest of minds has a hard time resisting.

Calculating the risk/reward ratio and using it to set a stop is dangerous. In the Blue Sky case above, you're willing to lose 50 per cent of your capital. If you lose, you can take only two such trades before you run out of money. Moreover, you can start out with a fixed risk/reward money stop but then change it to an adjustable stop as you modify your idea of how much the trade could potentially gain. Say the price falls from $5, your original entry, to $3.50. But your indicator is still telling you the potential high price is $15. If you buy more at $3.50 and the $15 is indeed reached, your gain is even bigger in percentage terms. This is how traders trick themselves into adding to losing positions, the blackest of cardinal sins in trading.

To apply the risk/reward ratio in a conservative and prudent manner, turn it upside down. Instead of calculating it with your best-case expected gain, use a realistic worst-case estimate of the gain. Your worst-case gain should be higher than your worst-case loss. For example, say you're prepared to lose $2 for the chance to make $4. Your risk/reward ratio is 4:2 or 2:1. If you practise this exercise on every trade, the risk/reward ratio becomes a filter that winnows out trades that may be high probability but with excessive risk.

To analyse risk/reward ratios is a complex task requiring knowledge of statistics and probability, and it's beyond the scope of this chapter. But remember that in technical trading, the general rule is to take small losses and aim for bigger gains, not to take big losses and aim for gigantic gains.

Maximum adverse excursion

Maximum adverse excursion is a concept developed by John Sweeney. Using this method, you calculate the biggest change in the high-low range over a fixed period (say 30 days) that's equivalent to your usual holding period. Actually, you need to calculate the maximum range from the entry levels you would've used. Because you know your entry rules, you can back-test to find the maximum range that was prevalent at each entry. The *maximum adverse excursion* is the statistically-determined worst-case loss that might occur during the course of your trade, although you may choose to adjust (tweak) the stop according to changes in the volatility of the range as they occur. For example, if the security never changes from high to low by more than $10 over the period, you would set your stop at $11. Over time, you should see a regular pattern between the maximum adverse excursion and your winning and losing trades. In fact, you can use the inverse of the adverse excursion, the *maximum favourable excursion,* to select trades in the first place. Refer to Chapter 12 to find out more on dealing with volatility.

Trailing stops

Trailing stops use a dynamic process that follows the price: You raise the stop as the trade becomes more profitable. This means calling the broker or re-entering the stop electronically every day, depending on how you execute trades. The important point is that you keep the stop updated to protect gains and to guard against unacceptable losses. A trailing stop is set on a money basis — you maintain the loss you can tolerate at a constant dollar amount or percentage basis. You could, for example, say that you're not willing to part with more than 20 per cent of each day's gain, so you'd raise the stop every day to include 80 per cent of today's gain.

Some traders object to the trailing stop on the grounds that the normal average daily trading range will almost certainly encompass the trailing stop level on many occasions. A random event can cause a small spike, for example. Trailing stops are highly protective, but you risk being stopped out on an arbitrary price event that isn't really related to the overall price trend.

Trailing stops are easily back-tested. Some securities are highly trending and lend themselves to trailing stops, and other securities are volatile and don't. Of course, the trending security can also alternate periods of high and low volatility, so conducting a back-test can get a little tricky.

Indicator-based stops

Indicator-based stops depend on the price action and the indicators you use to capture it. Indicator stops can be either fixed or self-adjusting. We mention them at various places throughout the book; here are some important ones:

- ✓ **Last-three-days rule:** The most basic of stop-loss rules is to exit the position if the price surpasses the lowest low (or highest high if you're going short) of the preceding three days. This sounds a little corny. However, it fits well with another piece of trading lore that says a trade should turn profitable right away if you've done the analysis right and you're actually buying right after a low or selling right after a peak. If the price first rises for a day or two but can't hold on to the gain, the upmove that you think you've identified is probably a false one. Consider the crowd dynamics (refer to Chapter 2) and how they play out on the price bar (covered in Chapter 4). You need a series of higher highs *and* higher lows to name an uptrend. If you get a lower low in the first three days, the probability is good that the trade is going south.

- ✓ **Pattern stops:** Pattern stops relate directly to market sentiment and are very handy. Most are of the fixed variety. We list a few below.

  - The break of a support or resistance line is a powerful stop level, chiefly because so many other traders are drawing the same lines.

  - The last notable high or low (the 'historic' level; see Chapter 14) or the high/low of an important time period, like a year.

  - You can infer stops from other pattern indicators, such as the centre confirmation point of the W in a double bottom or the M in a double top (refer to Chapter 7). When the confirmation point is surpassed, the probability is high that the move continues in the expected direction. If you're positioned the wrong way when the pattern appears, the pattern confirmation is also your stop level.

✔ **Moving-average stop:** You can also use a separate indicator that isn't part of your buy/sell repertoire to set a stop, such as a moving average (see Chapter 10). You may not use a moving average because of its lagging nature, but it may serve well when it comes to getting out of a position that's going against you. Many traders use the 10-day moving average as a warning to reduce a position, and the 20-day moving average as a stop. It's interesting how often a retracement will penetrate a 10-day moving average but stop just short of crossing the 20-day. A moving-average stop is clearly of the self-adjusting variety.

Volatility stops are the most complex of the indicator-based, self-adjusting stops to figure out and to apply, but they're also the most in tune with market action. Many variations are available. Here are three of particular interest:

✔ **Parabolic stop-and-reverse model:** Invented by Welles Wilder, the parabolic concept is easy to illustrate and hard to describe. The principle is to create an indicator that rises by a factor of the average true range (refer to Chapter 5) as new highs are being recorded, so that the indicator accelerates as ever higher highs are met and decelerates as less high highs come in. In an uptrend, the indicator is plotted just below the price line. It diverges from the price line in a hot rally, and converges to the price line as the rally loses speed, as shown in Figure 17 -1. The parabolic stop is both self-adjusting and trailing; a rare combination.

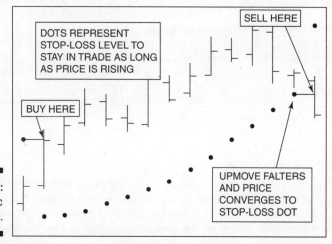

Figure 17-1:
Parabolic
stop.

✔ **Average true range stop:** This stop is set just beyond the maximum normal range limits. The average true range channel is described in Chapter 12. You take the average daily high-low range of the price bars, adjusted for gaps, and expand it by adding on a constant, like 25 per cent of the range. Say your average daily trading range is $3. If the price goes more than 25 per cent beyond the $3 high-low range, you consider it an extreme price and the signal to exit. The average true range stop has the virtue of being self-adjusting, but it also has the drawback of setting a stop that has nothing to do with your entry.

✔ **Chandelier exit:** This stop solves the entry-level issue. Invented by Chuck LeBeau, the chandelier exit sets the stop at a level below the highest high or the highest close *since your entry*. You set the level as a function of the average true range. The logic is that you're willing to lose only one range worth (or two or three) from the best price that occurred since you put on the trade. Like the parabolic stop, the chandelier is both self-adjusting and trailing.

Indicator stops usually entail taking a loss greater than the 2 per cent benchmark rule. This hands you a hard decision. If you take the 2 per cent rule, you have to live with the remorse of exiting trades only to see the price move your way later on. If you take an indicator rule that entails losses greater than 2 per cent of your capital, but have a series of losing trades early in your trading career, you could lose a lot of money before you figure out how to adapt and apply indicators.

Time stops

Time stops acknowledge that when money is tied up in a trade that's going nowhere, it could be put to better use in a different trade. Say you're holding a position with the expectation (from your indicators) that it'll rise or fall — but nothing happens. The price goes sideways. At some point, you lose patience and exit the position. This is reasonable. After all, time is money. The money could be invested in a risk-free asset yielding some return, however small. Alternatively, the money could be put to work in a security that is moving. Professionals keep a list of tradeable securities and rank them according to their trendedness and thus their ability to deliver a profit, mindful that the purpose of trading is to make money.

Clock and calendar stops

Clock and calendar stops pertain to a price event happening (or not happening) considering the time of day, week, month or year. For example, who says the end of the calendar week must be the end of your analytical week? One calendar-based rule, for example, considers that Wednesday is the end of the analytical period. You'd stop out of a long trade if the price fails to deliver a higher close on Wednesday, because the move is weak.

Clock-based rules abound. Some technical traders advise against trading during the first hour in most stock markets, because buy- or sell-on-open orders are being executed then (refer to Chapter 4). Others say that more gain can be had from the first hour than any other hour of the trading day if you can figure out which way the crowd is trading. As we describe in Chapter 15, one setup trader trick is to buy or sell in the direction of an opening gap — and be done for the day an hour later. In foreign exchange, you often see prices retrace at the end of the New York trading day — about 7 am in Sydney — as traders there close positions. This sets a benchmark for the Australian trading day.

Fortunately, if you're into technical analysis, you can analyse all these clock and calendar effects via back-testing. Most good technical analysis software packages come with back-testing capabilities. Be aware, though, that back-testing always show better results than can normally be achieved. This is because you can't always do the perfect trade — there will always be slippage due to your inability to achieve the exact entry/exit price — and broker's commission.

Adjusting Positions

Stops are the first line of defence against indicator failures and market catastrophes. The challenge in following indicators is that they're wrong sometimes and don't respond quickly to catastrophic shocks. But to exit a position is an extreme response when your uncertainty isn't high. A stop is a blunt instrument when more delicacy may be called for.

Many indicators are black and white. You should either buy or sell. They lack nuance. Similarly, stops are a one-way proposition. It's hardly ever appropriate to override a stop, but what if a nice uptrend is in place and you think your stop is wrong? Sometimes you know things (or think you know things) about the security or the market environment that can't be reflected in the indicator or the stop. So, if you spot a situation that you think should trigger a stop — but it doesn't — you have the choice of reducing your position instead of exiting.

Applying discretion is tricky, because you can't back-test it. But if you can't help having insights and you think your gut-feel is more often right than wrong, the solution is to systemise applying discretion. You do this by changing the amount of money you place on the price move, which is called *position adjustment*.

Reducing positions

The safest way to reduce the risk of loss is to reduce exposure to it. If you've bought on an indicator-based signal but you think you know of a fundamental reason why it's not going to be a good trade, the two conflicting ideas may cancel each other out. Similarly, you may have a nicely trending security and get a surprise stop hit that you don't trust, because you think you can identify the cause as an anomaly. Instead of being paralysed or not trading at all, you have a few options:

- Delay following the indicator signal until the non-technical event risk is past.
- Stay in the trade but reduce the amount of money you allocate to it (and perhaps tighten the stop while you're at it).

Some traders advise reducing (or exiting) positions ahead of known event risks, such as central bank meetings, earnings announcements and national elections.

Adding to positions

You can add to a position when your existing position is highly profitable. Statisticians debate whether you should add to winning positions using unrealised profits from the existing trade, called *pyramiding*.

To pyramid is to use hypothetical profits to enlarge your position. Say you started with $1,000 and the trade has now generated another $1,000 in paper profits. Why not borrow against that extra $1,000 to buy some more of this high-performing security? The answer is that if a catastrophe strikes and the trade goes against you, your risk of loss can become huge — more than your original stake if your stop fails (or you didn't place one). Be aware that if you engage in pyramiding, you're taking a higher risk than if you don't. The reward may be there but so is the risk, should the market turn against you. Pyramiding has a compounding effect on the overall profit or loss that you can achieve. So be careful and make sure you have very tight stops in place when you trade this way.

If you want to add to a position, the big question is how to determine the exact amount to add. Just as in determining the amount to allocate to trades in the first place, you can consider the risk/reward ratio — but this contains the wish or hope for the gain and is therefore subjective. You have better options:

✔ If you're using a 2 per cent stop rule, when the existing position has gained a profit that is greater than the 2 per cent of starting capital you'll lose if the stop is triggered, you add the amount of the surplus profit to the position with its own 2 per cent stop. The problem, of course, is that it's awkward to trade in odd lots, and odd lots don't even exist in futures.

✔ For those trading futures or CFDs using *margin* (where the trader puts down only a fraction of the value of the contract being traded), one rule of thumb is to add to the position when the existing trade has earned the cost of the minimum initial margin of the new position. If you're trading on a 50 per cent margin, you add to the position when the existing position has racked up enough paper gain to fund the new position.

This is an especially valuable rule in the futures market, in which the trader puts down only a small fraction of the value of the contract being traded. For example, to trade the ASX 200 (SPI), you may need at least $10,000 deposited with your broker (as of this writing — the exchange changes the amount from time to time). You don't want to add a second ASX 200 contract to your position until the first contract has a profit of $6,000. By then, you figure that the move is well in place. But remember, you have to have one stop-loss order on the first contract and a different one on the second trade.

Pyramiding without proper stops has probably caused more traders to go broke than any other cause. When you're caught trading in the wrong direction, the market can be very unforgiving. You should never bet the bank on a market move. Likewise, if you're *margin called* (required to pay up on a contracted trade), then you should consider liquidating the trade. You're obviously trading against the trend.

Applying stops to adjusted positions

If you're using an indicator stop and it signals that the price rise is over, doesn't that mean you want to exit all positions at the same level as soon as possible? The answer from statisticians is maybe. It depends on whether you're thinking in chart terms or money-management terms. If you're using a breakout concept to set your stop, for example, the price crossing a support line is a sell signal, which would apply equally to all positions.

If you're using a 2 per cent or other rule (such as the chandelier exit) that's calculated specifically with reference to your starting point, you exit each trade according to the rule. This has benefits and drawbacks.

The benefit is that you're still in the trade if the stop was triggered for one trade but the price retracement is only a minor, temporary one. You still have other positions left and if the price makes a big jump your way, you're correctly positioned to take advantage of it. The drawback is that a well-set stop may really identify a change in overall price behaviour (such as the average true range stop). If it's a catastrophic price move, you may not get good execution of your stops and may end up losing more than the amount you planned.

More from the frontier of technical knowledge

Some technical traders say that you can estimate the probability of each trade in advance, and therefore it's not only safe but also wise to vary the amount of your position. In fact, you can probably improve on the expected results of your indicators. Other technical traders feel, usually with vehemence, that it isn't possible to attach probabilities to specific trades. They say that you can attach probabilities to indicators and to overall rule-based approaches, including stops, but not to specific trades. They say that instead of varying position size, you should vary your stop-loss order.

If market conditions are choppy (highly volatile), you might widen your stop even though your own particular security is behaving nicely. In this instance, you fear an overflow effect from the general market to your particular security. You may switch from a money-based trailing stop like the 2 per cent rule to a volatility or pattern type of stop. Notice that to change the type of stop you use now entails yet another back-test.

When you see advertisements that describe a 'high-probability trading strategy' be sure to investigate how the author applies stops and whether position adjustment — with stops — was thoroughly back-tested. You also want to see how it worked in real time. Often the 'strategy' is just an indicator without any accompanying trading rules to control losses.

Part VI
The Part of Tens

Glenn Lumsden

*'I'm using the trading method that
best matches my risk profile . . .
reckless and foolhardy.'*

In this part . . .

No matter how short-term or long-term your orientation, some technical principles are universal, and some characteristics of the successful trader are universal, too. Every trade has two parts — the security with its technical characterstics and you. After you master a few key concepts, exactly how you apply the technical methods is a matter of personal preference — the 'right' method is the one that matches up with your risk profile and that you can trade in a consistent rule-based manner. In this part, we condense the key concepts covered throughout this book.

Chapter 18

Ten Secrets of the Top Technical Traders

In This Chapter

▶ Putting your faith in the chart rather than 'experts'

▶ Understanding the concept that 'the trend is your friend'

▶ Getting to know the virtues and drawbacks of technical indicators

*I*n this chapter, we point out ten issues that you have to face to succeed in technical trading. The old joke has it that 'money is how we keep score', but trading and investing are far more complicated than just making money. Some people value 'not making too many mistakes' (preserving capital) more than they value making a boatload of cash. Some traders are looking for the hurly-burly fun of trading more than anything else. If you trade for a living, 'keeping your sanity' isn't a bad goal, either.

You can trade technically in any number of equally valid ways. In fact, technical traders come in all shapes and sizes, and from all walks of life. Go to any technical analysis conference, and you'll meet people ranging from the geeky maths whiz to the goal-oriented fund manager to the retired schoolteacher. You can't tell from looking at them what technical style they use. Some are quick-trade artists who make rapid-fire trades lasting no more than an hour every day. Other technical traders immerse themselves in chart after chart for hours every day but hardly ever make a trade. Another kind of technical trader is always in the market, either long or short, buying and selling, willing to take big losses for the chance to make spectacular gains. They're all genuine technical traders using technical analysis to understand the charts.

Whatever their style, successful technical traders all have one thing in common: They've each built a trading plan that uses the technical tools that suit their personality and appetite for risk, and they follow it.

What you need to determine is whether you wish to be a trader or an investor. Traders tend to hold their trades for short periods of time (whether for a couple of hours or for a couple of days). Investors tend to hold their trades for longer periods of time or until the trend has clearly changed.

Trust the Chart

The essence of technical analysis is to analyse the price action on a chart to arrive at buy/sell decisions. You determine whether the security offers a positive bias towards making a profit by looking at indicators on the chart, not on the fundamental characteristics of the security itself. This doesn't mean selecting securities without judgement. The world has tens of thousands of securities to choose from. You're welcome to choose your own universe of what you consider to be fundamentally sound securities from which to select high-probability trades. In doing so you need to understand and feel comfortable with the trading style you choose.

After you select your personal universe of securities, every trading decision is based on chart events and not on news developments, fundamental factors, or what some 'expert' says. The chart contains all the information you need to make trading decisions. If information is truly important, the chart will reflect it.

If you want further information on what's behind price movements, check out the company's Web site for announcements. Alternatively, the exchange where this security is traded normally provides such information.

Charts reflect current market information and the market's perception of how that information will impact on the price of the security going forward. Sometimes, unexpected price movements can actually provide evidence of insider trading or the ongoing accumulation or selling of a security, long before the price actually begins to move strongly in either direction.

The Trend Is Your Friend

Many advisers, analysts, brokers, economists, fund managers and journalists are smart, sensible and honourable. They'd never intentionally mislead you about the prospects of Company X or the supply and demand for Commodity Y. But a million factors can influence the price of a security. Any number of bizarre and even unprecedented contingencies can combine to move a security's price straight into a brick wall — or onto a rocket ship to the moon.

The single best way to know what's happening and what's likely to happen to the price of your security is to follow its trends. If you buy when a new uptrend is just starting and sell when the uptrend peaks, you'll make money over the long run. If you're a short-seller or a two-way trader, you'll make money when you sell short at a peak and cover (buy back) at a bottom.

Timing matters. It matters in dozens of aspects of life, and it definitely matters in investing and trading. Timing makes the difference between gains and losses, and the difference between ordinary gains and extraordinary gains.

Stocks are grouped into sectors within the market. These sectors don't always rise or fall together. For example, the finance sector (which includes bank stocks) would more than likely fall during a recession due to problem loans and bad debts, whereas the resources sector (which contains mining stocks) would more than likely rise during periods of high inflation. The end result is that as stocks in one sector fall, stocks in another sector may be rising.

You Make Money Only when You Sell

A policy of 'buy and hold' is the optimum long-term investment strategy, but only if you meet all of the following criteria:

- ✔ You start with a winning period rather than a loss that has to be recovered.
- ✔ You pick securities that survive long term.
- ✔ Your concept of success is the average return against a benchmark such as a stock index over a long period of time.
- ✔ You start early and live a long time.

Many people rode the bull market in the 1990s to great fortunes — on paper. Then, when the crash came, they saw their net worth go down the drain. They were afraid to sell because they were holding onto the idea that to buy and hold is the best rule, always and under every circumstance. Obviously, it's not. No single rule is right in every circumstance. Securities rise and fall according to market sentiment. It's common sense to sell securities when they fall to lock in a profit or to stop a loss, even if you intend to buy the very same securities again when they start moving up.

Look at the chart: If the price starts in the lower left-hand corner of the page and is rising towards the top right-hand corner, then the price is trending up. Conversely, if the price starts in the top left-hand corner of the page and is falling towards the bottom right-hand corner, then the trend is falling.

Markets don't go up forever; they tend to be cyclical in nature. One line of thought says 'buy in November, sell in May then go away' because this time frame tends to closely represent the yearly cycle. Other traders hold the view that one in four years tends to be a bad year and so they look for a four-year cycle. Do your research; see whether these or other patterns fit the securities or the market you wish to trade.

Take Responsibility

If you give responsibility for managing your investing and trading to others, or if you buy and sell securities on the advice of experts and they turn out to be wrong, you can lay the blame at their feet. Ultimately, though, nobody cares more about your money than you. Outside managers and experts may have a fiduciary responsibility to behave in a prudent manner with your money, but except for cases of gross negligence, they can lose it all and walk away, sometimes pointing the finger of blame at yet another expert. If your bank manager, broker, trust fund manager, mutual fund manager or Uncle Fred proposes that you sink some money in a security and the chart shows that the price is on a downward trajectory, simply say no. It's astonishing how otherwise intelligent and sensible people yield to the supposed superior expertise of their money managers when a 12-year-old kid can see that the security is tanking. 'It'll come back', they say. To which you should reply, 'Okay that's fine; let's wait until it does. We'll know that when it bottoms and starts to turn around and we'll get it a whole lot cheaper. Timing does matter.'

Take responsibility for your investments. Undertake technical analysis courses from a reputable training organisation. These courses should not cost a fortune; if they do, look elsewhere. Also, consider joining a registered technical analysis association. These organisations often provide access to tonnes of material, such as newsletters, journals, videos on trading techniques, extra training, annual conferences and so on.

You can also get charts that shows the basic trend of just about any security, in any market, for free, at a dozen Web sites. Look in the financial pages of the major Web sites — for example, Yahoo!7 or ninemsn — to find information on individual securities. You don't need to become a fully-fledged market technician to observe whether a price is rising or falling! And don't buy into a falling price or sell when a price is still rising.

A great way to increase the speed at which you can wise up on the art of analysing securities and understand the basis behind trading decisions is to join an association of like-minded people. In Australia you can join the ATAA (Australian Technical Analysts Association) at www.ataa.com.au. In New Zealand the ATAA equivalent is STANZ (the Society of Technical Analysts New Zealand) at www.stanz.co.nz.

Avoid Euphoria and Despair

Technical traders apply indicators to charts to get an 'objective' reading of market sentiment towards the security. In practise, the degree of objectivity varies. Some indicators, especially patterns, can be interpreted in more than one way. Certainly the decision rules based on indicators can vary. Any single chart can offer a number of equally valid ways to trade the security, depending on your risk preference, choice of time frame, selection of indicators and patterns and so on. But one condition links all the variety of potential decisions — that the decision be made on the empirical evidence on the chart and not on some emotional impulse of the trader.

It's human nature to bet a larger sum of money when you've just had a win, perhaps on less evidence than you normally require to 'take' a trade. Likewise, traders often become timid after taking a loss and pass on trades that by any technical standard offer a fabulous profit opportunity.

This is why technical traders use indicators and try to use them as systematically as possible, even the ones who modestly shy away from claiming to have a 'trading system'. A good trading regime employs trading rules that impart discipline to every trading decision in a conscious effort to overcome the emotions that accompany trading. One definition of a successful trader is the trader who feels neither euphoria nor despair over trading outcomes. To damp down emotion is a clear objective in all technical trading. Better to get mad at the indicator that lets you down than to kick the cat. Trading is a business, and business should be conducted in a non-emotional manner.

If you find yourself paralysed by fear that your investment may go sour, your best move may be to get out of the market altogether (especially if you're losing money). Stepping back allows you to take a view of the market or your particular stock in a more rational and less stressed manner. Your next trade can then be taken with a clear mind.

Making Money Is Better Than Being Right

When you ask brokers and advisers for the single biggest character flaw of their customers, they all say the same thing: 'The customer would rather be right than make money'. This fault can rear its ugly head in any number of circumstances, although one stands out: Refusing to take a loss and get on with the next trade. Either the trader didn't have a stop-loss rule in the first place (a situation you can avoid by checking out Chapter 17), or he refused to obey it. To take a loss says to him that he's wrong about the direction of the security, and he takes it as a personal affront.

Clearly the rule that you must set a stop-loss is a cousin of 'the trend is your friend' and several other rules of good trading noted in this chapter, but refusing to take a loss and get on with the next trade has the deepest psychological roots. Some people have an unusually hard time facing losses, and because they can't take a small loss, they end up taking big ones, which only reinforces the fear and loathing of losses. Soon you're not trading systematically, but on emotion, and worse, the single emotion of fearing losses. If you start falling into this morass, get a trading-system designer to help you develop a system that takes very few losses. Or, get a trading coach or get a psychiatrist. Don't get emotionally trapped by the experience or you'll start thinking that the market is against you. Trading, like business, isn't personal. The market doesn't care whether you even exist, let alone whether you're right about any particular trade.

The old saying, 'It's better to be safe than sorry' applies equally as well to trading as any other venture. If you find yourself taking big losses, then you need to determine what you're doing wrong. Are you trading against the trend? Maybe you don't have tight enough stops in place to minimise losses? Any time you feel that the market turns against you, your best action may be to step out of the market until you figure out what you're doing wrong.

Don't Let a Winning Trade Turn into a Losing Trade

You can have a fine trading system with excellent indicators properly back-tested for the securities you're trading but still be a lousy trader if you don't have sensible trading rules. A good trader differentiates between indicators (which only indicate) and trading and money management rules (which manage the risk).

How can a winning trade turn into a losing trade? Many ways. First is the failure to use a stop-loss. Then there's changing horses in mid-stream — adjusting perception of risk while the trade is in progress by looking at a new indicator that's not back-tested and not part of the trading plan. Finally, you can trick yourself into thinking that the market 'owes' you the highest price it already attained. Your gain at the highest point during the trade was (say) $3,000 but now it's only half that. You think that if only the price will go back to test the old high, you'll exit there. But so is everyone else, hence the price may never get there as the smart money, is selling into the rally. This will put pressure on the price which eventually fails. The problem is that you're not looking at an indicator that tells you the price is likely to retest the old high — you're telling the market that it should go back to retest the old high because that's how much money you want to make. This is how you start to see what you want to see on the chart rather than what's actually there.

If you find yourself with a massive windfall profit but you're not certain the trend has peaked, consider selling down say 50 per cent and allow the rest to run, only selling the remainder when you're certain that the trend has peaked. This way you protect your initial investment and some of the profit, should the trade go bad suddenly.

Don't Curve-Fit

Just because an indicator 'fits' your chart of historical data doesn't make it a workable indicator for the future. Market characteristics change over time. What works today may not work tomorrow. A good technical trader back-tests indicators using realistic assumptions. If you over-analyse indicators so that they're a perfect fit for the past, they'll almost certainly fail to work in the future. Acknowledge that it's okay to have numerically more losing trades than winning trades as long as the gain/loss ratio is more than 1:1. In the same vein, if you're buying someone else's trading system, be sure that it's not just some bright idea that would've worked in the past but is so complex and detailed that it won't work on a broader range of conditions.

Likewise, don't use too many indicators — they won't all provide a buy or sell signal at the same time. Use two or three that you feel comfortable with and understand. Instead of trying new indicators to get a good match for a particular security, try different securities against the indicators that you are comfortable with. Trading securities is all about judgement — your judgement — based on what you see on the charts and what the indicators are telling you. Fiddling with parameters so that the indicator fits your particular chart is a recipe for disaster.

Trade the Right Amount

Position-sizing is a thorny subject on which statistics experts disagree. Is there a single best portion of your capital stake to bet on any one round of trading? Yes, although you may not want to do the fancy maths to arrive at the precise number. Still, you know that in poker, if you have four kings, you should bet more than if you have a pair of sevens. Likewise, in securities trading, you should know whether you have a good hand or a bad hand and know when to fold. This information comes from your indicators.

The more confirmation of a buy/sell signal you can get, the safer it is to place the trade. For example, if you have only one indication that the trend is turning your way, you can bet small, and add to the trade as confirmation comes in. Or you can just wait for all the indicators to provide confirmation. Either method is 'right' but only one method is right for your risk appetite.

Diversify

Diversification reduces risk. The proof of the concept in finance won its proponents the Nobel prize, but the old adage has been around for centuries: 'Don't put all your eggs in one basket'. In technical trading, the idea is relevant in two places:

- ✔ **Your choice of indicators:** You improve the probability of a buy/ sell signal being correct when you use a second and non-correlated indicator to confirm it. You don't get confirmation of a buy/sell signal when you consult a second indicator that works on the same principle as the first indicator. Momentum doesn't confirm relative strength because it adds no new information. They both use the same arithmetic construction, so they give you the same information. Widen your horizon beyond a few indicators, and seek indicators that use different concepts instead of torturing old indicators to come up with better parameters.

- ✔ **Your choice of securities:** You reduce risk when you trade two securities whose prices move independently from one another. If you trade a technology stock, you achieve no diversification at all by adding another technology stock. Instead, you may get a better balance of risk by adding a consumer products company or a utility. For example, if you trade BHP shares, you get no risk reduction by adding Rio to your portfolio. The two resource stocks move in tandem because they're highly correlated to one another.

Don't bet the bank on one or two securities. Instead, have a range of securities spread across a number of sectors. That way if one goes bad your losses will, hopefully, be minimised.

Chapter 19

Ten Rules for Working with Indicators

*I*ndicators measure market sentiment. You use them to help make trading decisions as rational as you can. Your goal in using indicators is to go with the flow — to trade in the direction of the trend.

Listen to the Price Bars

Price bars contain a lot of useful information. It does take patience to understand them. Indicators are faster, but they only take the data in the price bar and reformat it. Think of the bar as a miniature indicator in its own right. For example, when you have a series of higher highs and suddenly the next bar closes lower and at the low of the day, then the market price is sending you a message in a bottle — this uptrend is now over.

Every bar tells an evolving story about crowd behaviour and the market. Try to listen to it. Floor traders always comment that electronic trading isn't the same as being on the floor in the thick of things — you can't hear the crowd, but you certainly observe it graphically. As an individual trader, you can't hear the crowd, either, so you have to rely on your imagination and on the action presented in the charts. (Refer to Chapter 4 for more on bar basics and Chapter 6 for candlesticks.)

Understand Your Indicator

Use indicators that make sense to you in terms of crowd behaviour and market trends. What works for some other trader may not work for you. You need to use an indicator that you trust and that really reflects your trading style and risk appetite; you can't trust an indicator if you don't understand how it reflects market action. In other words, don't use an indicator mechanically because some self-styled expert says it's a great indicator. The world is full of great indicators. Get your own that reflects you!

Dozens of indicators are available. Think of technical analysis as a giant department store full of indicators. One department or another has an indicator that's ideal for you.

If maths isn't your strong suit, don't let it hold you back from using maths-based indicators. Technical analysis is about measuring the behaviour of human beings in markets in a form that you can use to time your trades for higher profits and lower losses. You don't need to know how an indicator works in order for it to convey market sentiment to you, just as you don't need to be a mechanic to drive a Ferrari. Seek to know how to 'drive' your indicator, not necessarily how to construct it — though this can help.

Use Support, Resistance and Chart Patterns

Support and resistance are valid concepts that all technical traders respect. You can graphically pinpoint support, resistance or chart patterns using any number of techniques, including drawing trend lines on the chart. You can estimate support and resistance using bands and channels, or using momentum and relative strength indicators. To preserve your capital, it's a good idea always to know the support or resistance level of the security you're trading in order to cut your losses when it's broken. (Refer to Chapters 7 and 8 for more information on support and resistance.)

Use the Breakout Principle

The breakout concept is a well recognised idea that most technical traders use in one form or another. A breakout tells you that the crowd is feeling a burst of energy and are in general agreement on where price is going.

Whether you're entering a new trade or exiting an existing one, it usually pays to trade in the direction of the breakout. It also pays to study the character and conditions under which real breakouts occur so that you don't get caught by false breakouts. (Chapters 8 through 10 cover breakouts in more detail.)

Watch for Convergence/Divergence

When your indicator diverges from the security, watch out because this suggests something's happening. You may or may not initially be able to find out why, but divergence always spells trouble for the prevailing trend. Convergence usually, but not always, is comforting. (This rule refers to convergence and divergence of indicators versus price, not the internal dynamics of indicators such in the case of the MACD indicator, as we discuss in Chapter 10.)

If your security is trending upward and the momentum indicator is pointing downward, be cautious, because this could mean the trend is about to turn (down). A price-indicator divergence is a discrepancy that weighs against the trend. In this case, the uptrend is at risk of pausing, retracing or even reversing. If you're risk averse, you should exit. Look for divergence between price and volume, too. Logically, a rising price needs rising volume to be sustained. If the price is spiking upward but volume is falling and following, you then don't really have bullish sentiment.

Choose a Trading Style

This is another way of saying 'know thyself'. What type of market do you like trading? Do you like trends or swing trading? If you like trading with trends, then trend-following indicators will appeal to you. Trend-followers stay in a trade for a relatively long time and minimise the number of transactions they make. On the flipside, if you like to trade on every price movement, then swing trading indicators will suit you because they change much faster, more often and result in more trades.

In practice of course, many traders use both trend-following and swing trading indicators, and it sets up a contradiction that needs to be managed. When you have both types of indicators on the chart, you may get analysis paralysis. The swing trading indicator says 'Sell' while the trend-following indicator says 'Not yet'. They both can't be right for the trading style you're after. When you choose a trading style — either the trend-following indicator or the swing indicator — try to stick with it over the life of the trade.

Back-test Your Indicators Properly

You're free to use the standard indicator parameters that come packaged with software that you may buy, or are offered on Web sites. Experience shows that the standard parameters are useful and reliable over large amounts of data and across different markets — that's why their inventors chose them.

For this reason, some traders never feel the need to perform their own back-tests. They prefer instead to put their effort into improving other aspects of their analysis — for example, in bar or pattern reading. But if you *are* going to back-test indicators to refine the parameters, do it correctly. Use a large amount of price history in testing an indicator — and don't make the indicator fit history so perfectly that the minute you add fresh data the indicator becomes worthless. This is called curve-fitting and it's a waste of time. It's better to observe price behaviour and estimate the range of sensible and reasonable parameters than to find the perfect number. The perfect number for the future does not exist.

Acknowledge that Your Indicator Will Fail

Indicators are often wrong. Bad things happen to good indicators. Support lines do get broken only for a day instead of signalling a new trend as a breakout is supposed to. Confirmed double bottoms that look textbook perfect on the chart do fail the very next day instead of delivering that delicious 40 per cent profit. And moving averages generate whiplash losses even after you've added every clever and refined filter known to man.

It's a fact of life — indicators fail some of the time. Don't take it personally when the indicator lets you down and causes you to take a loss. Indicators are only arithmetic, not magic.

There Are No Silver Bullets

Technical traders have invented at least 100 separate patterns and another 300 maths-based indicators. They can be combined in an infinite variety of ways over an infinite number of time frames with an infinite number of qualifying conditions. So it's possible that somebody has discovered a superior combination of indicators. But none of the indicators is a secret and no indicator combo is going to be right all the time. Remember that markets are always oscillating between ranging and trending conditions, and traders all have different (and some times contradictory) agendas. Don't expect the perfect solution for all times — there's no secret silver bullet.

As in all things, *caveat emptor* and shut your ears to the guy trying to sell you an indicator if he says 'It never fails!'. Of course it fails. If it never fails, why would he sell it to you? And why should you have to pay for an indicator in the first place? You don't. Every indicator ever invented is easily available in books, magazines and on the Internet. The secret to successful trading doesn't lie in indicators. It lies in consistency and discipline.

Be Original (If You Dare)

It's okay to use an indicator differently from the way the inventor intended it to be used, or the way everyone else uses it. Remember that the indicator is a technique that can always be refined. Some of the simplest trading ideas are often the most effective. For example, try out a long-term indicator in a short-term time frame, or vice versa. 'Disobey' the standard way of interpreting indicators — if you want. Under the right conditions and in the right time frame, doing the opposite of the conventional wisdom can sometimes make more profit than the conventional application. It's weird but true, for example, that triple smoothing an indicator can make it more responsive to the price rather than less responsive, a counterintuitive outcome if ever there was one. Be brave, be creative and most of all think about ways to improve your performance — not how to best imitate someone else's.

Appendix

Resources

• •

A search for material on technical analysis is immediately overwhelming. Books, software, Web sites, training courses — it's positively intimidating. A lot of the information you find is full of jargon and mathematics, and some of it is downright crackpot.

Relax. You don't need all this stuff. Plenty of technical traders use a single, easy-to-master technique to achieve their financial goals. We know one trader who made his first million after reading one book (Edwards and Magee's *Technical Analysis of Stock Trends* — see the 'Library Essentials' section later in the chapter). Others try all the ideas and methods, and don't want to miss a trick.

Why spend time and money on research? Because you never know when you may come across an idea that strikes a resounding chord in you — the *Eureka!* moment, when you say to yourself: I can do this.

The Bare Minimum

The most flexible and easy to use software is AmiBroker (www.amibroker. com). AmiBroker is feature-rich, fast and reliable. It comes with all of the standard preset indicators and its programming language is flexible enough to allow you to program anything you dream up. Back-testing is a breeze and it has portfolio management capabilities. AmiBroker reads a myriad data feeds, including the free Yahoo! quotes. Best of all, though, is the price — it's by far the best value for your dollar.

Insight Trader (www.insighttrader.com.au) is an excellent Australian charting package. It's been around for 15 years and is very popular with Australian traders. Insight Trader reads its own propriety data format, as well as the popular MetaStock format, and has excellent portfolio management features. Insight Trader users can scan securities for predetermined technical and fundamental criteria, but the package is not as flexible as AmiBroker.

MetaStock by Equis (www.equis.com) is quite user friendly. It comes with preset indicators and a user guide. At the Equis Web site, you can review a range of data feeds (some of them free) or browse through their online bookshop.

Your Trading Edge (YTE) magazine (www.yte.com.au) is a bimonthly Australian-produced publication for traders in futures, options, forex, stocks and commodities. The articles range from trading strategies to market analysis and commentary. Not to be missed are the regular articles by the grand lady of technical analysis, Dawn Bolton-Smith.

Get a free copy of the magazine *Technical Analysis of Stocks and Commodities* by visiting www.traders.com. This magazine has an excellent annual review of charting software, system suppliers and so on. Also available is a CD-ROM of all the past articles, which you can search by subject.

Also look for *Active Trader* magazine (www.activetradermag.com) and *Stocks, Futures and Options* magazine (www.sfomag.com)

Australian Professional Technical Analysts (APTA)

The Australian Professional Technical Analysts (APTA) group, online at www.apta.org.au, serves professional technical analysts in the Australian markets. In addition to providing a forum for the sharing and discussion of ideas, APTA generates opportunities for networking and provides a focal point for all people interested in the professional application of technical analysis.

Many members have years of experience in the application of technical analysis, both in Australia and overseas in many different market types, including equities, futures and foreign exchange trading.

Australian Technical Analysts Association (ATAA)

The Australian Technical Analysts Association (ATAA), at www.ataa.com. au, welcomes anyone interested in technical analysis, whether for private trading or investing. The ATAA conducts meetings each month in eight Australian cities and hosts an annual conference. A journal is published bimonthly containing many articles on technical analysis and trading.

The ATAA also offers a Diploma in Technical Analysis to members who pass the required courses, which are run in association with the Financial Services Institute of Australasia (FINSIA), online at www.finsia.edu.au.

Society of Technical Analysts of New Zealand (STANZ)

The Society of Technical Analysts of New Zealand (STANZ), at www.stanz. co.nz, supports individual traders and investors who wish to manage their own funds.

STANZ provides monthly meetings with presentations from local and international speakers, the monthly STANZ newsletter, and a video and DVD library.

International Federation of Technical Analysts (IFTA)

The International Federation of Technical Analysts (www.ifta.org) was incorporated in 1986 and is a global organisation of market analysis societies and associations. IFTA is an international non-profit professional organisation with member societies in more than 26 countries.

The International Federation of Technical Analysts (IFTA) offers certification to professional Technical Analysts around the world through the Certified Financial Technician (CFTe) and the Master of Financial Technical Analysis (MFTA) programs.

IFTA also holds an annual conference and publishes an annual Journal.

Financial Services Institute of Australasia (FINSIA)

The Financial Services Institute of Australasia (FINSIA) fosters high standards of professional practice in the financial services industry by encouraging career-long participation in higher education, vocational education, and continuing professional development.

FINSIA (www.finsia.edu.au) offers two courses in technical analysis:

- **Technical Analysis:** This subject introduces students to the key concepts in technical analysis and develops skills in the construction, interpretation and application of charts for a variety of markets. Practical examples are used with traditional bar chart analysis and trends following and momentum indicators.
- **Specialised Techniques in Technical Analysis:** This subject introduces students to some of the most important and widely used specialised techniques in technical analysis, such as Japanese candlesticks, point-and-figure charting, the Gann, and Elliott wave.

Software and System-testing

Software packages for general charting and specific applications number in the hundreds. In addition to those we mention in the section 'The Bare Minimum' earlier in the chapter, these are the software packages we know personally.

- **TradeStation:** www.tradestation.com
- **Jurik Adaptive Moving Averages:** www.jurikres.com
- **NeuroShell Trader:** www.neuroshell.com
- **Triangles and System Performance:** www.tsagroup.com
- **Advanced GET:** www.esignal.com
- **BullCharts:** www.bullcharts.com.au
- **Bull's-Eye Broker:** www.archeranalysis.com
- **CycleTrader/WaveTrader:** www.cycletrader.com.au
- **El Wave:** www.adest.com.au
- **Genesis:** www.genesisft.com
- **Incredible Charts:** www.incrediblecharts.com
- **Market Analyst:** www.market-analyst.com
- **Netquote Charts:** www.netquote.com.au
- **Proview:** www.proview.com.au
- **ShareFinder:** www.sharefinder.com.au
- **STEX Charting:** www.stex.com.au
- **Technifilter Plus:** www.technifilter.com

Library Essentials

We like these books and use them over and over again:

- ✔ Colby, Robert, *Encyclopedia of Technical Market Indicators,* 2nd edition (McGraw-Hill)
- ✔ Kaufman, Perry, *Trading Systems and Methods* (Wiley)
- ✔ Murphy, John, *Technical Analysis of the Financial Markets* (Prentice Hall)
- ✔ Schwager, Jack, *Technical Analysis* (series: Schwager on Futures) (Wiley)

Introductions

- ✔ Achelis, Steve, *Technical Analysis from A to Z* (Probus)
- ✔ Bedford, Louise, *Charting Secrets* (Wiley)
- ✔ Gifford, Elli, *Investor's Guide to Technical Analysis* (Pitman)
- ✔ Guppy, Daryl, *Chart Trading* (Wiley)
- ✔ Guppy, Daryl, *Share Trading* (Wrightbooks)
- ✔ Hull, Alan, *Charting in a Nutshell* (Wiley)
- ✔ Kamich, Bruce, *How Technical Analysis Works* (Prentice Hall)
- ✔ LeBeau, Charles, and David Lucas, *Technical Traders Guide to Computer Analysis of the Futures Market* (McGraw-Hill)
- ✔ Meani, Regina, *Charting: An Australian Investors Guide* (McGraw-Hill)
- ✔ Meyers, Thomas, *The Technical Analysis Course* (McGraw-Hill)
- ✔ Pring, Martin, *Technical Analysis Explained* (McGraw-Hill)
- ✔ Krastins, Ivan, *Listen to the Market* (McGraw-Hill)
- ✔ Schwager, Jack, *Getting Started in Technical Analysis* (Wiley)

Classics

- ✔ Edwards and Magee, *Technical Analysis of Stock Trends* (Saint Lucie Press)
- ✔ Hamilton, William, *The Stock Market Barometer* (Fraser)
- ✔ Lefevre, Edwin, *Reminiscences of a Stock Operator* (Wiley)

✔ Mackay, Charles, *Extraordinary Popular Delusions and the Madness of Crowds* (Harmony Books)

✔ Nelson, S A, *The ABC of Stock Speculation* (Fraser)

✔ Rhea, Robert, *The Dow Theory* (Fraser)

✔ Schabacker, R W, *Technical Analysis and Stock Market Profits* (Harriman House)

✔ Wilder, J Welles, *New Concepts in Technical Trading Systems* (Trend Research)

Special areas

✔ Aby, Carroll D, Jr, *Point & Figure Charting, The Complete Guide* (Traders Press)

✔ Arms, Richard W, *Volume Cycles in the Stock Market* (Dow Jones-Irwin)

✔ Arms, Richard W, *Trading without Fear* (Wiley)

✔ Bensignor, Rick, *New Thinking in Technical Analysis: Trading Models from the Masters* (Bloomberg Press)

✔ Bollinger, John, *Bollinger on Bollinger Bands* (McGraw-Hill)

✔ Bulkowski, Thomas, *Encyclopedia of Chart Patterns* (Wiley)

✔ Chande, Tushar, and Stanley Kroll, *The New Technical Trader,* and Tushar Chande, *Beyond Technical Analysis* (Wiley)

✔ Connors, Laurence A, and Linda Bradford Raschke, *Street Smarts* (M. Gordon Publishing Group)

✔ Crane, John, *Advanced Swing Trading* (Wiley)

✔ Davey, Catherine, *Contracts for Difference* (Wiley)

✔ Dorsey, Thomas J, *Point & Figure Charting* (Wiley)

✔ Douglas, Alex, Pontikis, Peter, and Larry Lovrencic, *FX Trading: An Australian Guide to Trading Foreign Exchange* (Wiley)

✔ Farley, Alan S, *The Master Swing Trader* (McGraw-Hill)

✔ Granville, Joe, *Granville's New Strategy of Daily Stock Market Timing for Maximum Profit* (Prentice-Hall)

✔ The Hirsch Organization, *Stock Traders Almanac* (Wiley; updated yearly)

✔ Hurst, J M, *The Profit Magic of Stock Transaction Timing* (Traders Press)

✔ Hyerczyk, James A, *Price Pattern & Time: Using Gann Theory in Trading Systems* (Wiley)

- Millard, Brian, *Channels & Cycles: a Tribute to J.M. Hurst* (Traders Press)

- Morris, Gregory L, *Candlestick Charting Explained* (McGraw-Hill)

- Nison, Steve, *Japanese Candlestick Charting Techniques* (Wiley)

- Peters, Edgar, *Chaos and Order in the Capital Markets* (Wiley)

- Prechter, Robert, and Alfred Frost, *Elliott Wave Principle* (New Classics Library)

- Pring, Martin, *Martin Pring on Market Momentum* (McGraw-Hill)

- Sperandeo, Victor, *Trader Vic — Methods of a Wall Street Master* (Wiley)

- Steidlmayer, J Peter, *Steidlmayer on Markets* (Wiley)

- Sweeney, John, *Maximum Adverse Excursion* (Wiley)

On technical trading

- Balsara, Nauzer, *Money Management Strategies for Futures Traders* (Wiley)

- Chu, F J, *The Mind of the Market* (Fraser Publishing)

- Collins, Art, *When Supertraders Meet Kryptonite* (Traders Press)

- Davis, Ned, *Being Right or Making Money* (Ned Davis Research)

- Du Plessis, Jeremy, *The Definitive Guide to Point and Figure* (Harriman House)

- Elder, Alexander, *Trading for a Living* (Wiley)

- Elder, Alexander, *Come into My Trading Room* (Wiley)

- Elder, Alexander, *Entries & Exits — Visits to Sixteen Trading Rooms* (Wiley)

- Hill, John, George Pruitt, and Lundy Hill, *The Ultimate Trading Guide* (Wiley)

- Huff, Darrell, and Irving Geis, *How to Take a Chance* (W.W. Norton & Company)

- Johnston, Stuart, *Trading Options to Win: Profitable Strategies and Tactics for Any Trader* (Wiley)

- Paulos, John Allen, *A Mathematician Plays the Stock Market* (Basic Books)

- Rotella, Robert, *The Elements of Successful Trading* (New York Institute of Finance)

- Schwager, Jack, *Market Wizards: Interviews with Top Traders* (HarperBusiness)
- Tharp, Van, *Trade Your Way to Financial Freedom* (McGraw-Hill)
- Toghraie, Adrienne Laris, *The Winning Edge* (Traders Press)
- Vince, Ralph, *The Mathematics of Money Management* (Wiley)
- Williams, Larry, *How I Made $1,000,000 Trading Commodities Last Year* (Windsor Books) and *Long-Term Secrets to Short-Term Trading* (Wiley)

Training Courses

Try the Web sites of the exchanges, which offer training courses as well as data and other material. Most broker sites also have good courses for paying clients. On the whole, you should be able to get excellent training for a reasonable price.

- www.adest.com.au
- www.daytradinguniversity.com
- www.decisionpoint.com
- www.marketwise.com
- www.moneybags.com.au
- www.pfgbest.com
- www.pristine.com
- www.tradingontarget.com
- www.tradingschool.com

Technical Analysis Web Sites

We can't list all the excellent Web sites, which number in the thousands. At many of the sites listed here, you have to pay a fee to get the best material.

- www.adest.com.au
- www.aer.com.au

- ✔ www.aeroinvest.com
- ✔ www.asx.com.au
- ✔ au.finance.yahoo.com
- ✔ www.barchart.com
- ✔ www.bigcharts.com
- ✔ www.billcara.com
- ✔ www.candlecharts.com
- ✔ www.chartfilter.com
- ✔ www.chartpattern.com
- ✔ www.chesler.us
- ✔ www.clearstation.com
- ✔ www.dorseywright.com
- ✔ www.egoli.com.au
- ✔ www.elder.com
- ✔ www.elliottwave.com
- ✔ www.ez-pnf.com
- ✔ www.firstpacific.net
- ✔ www.incrediblecharts.com.au
- ✔ www.investopedia.com
- ✔ www.investorweb.com.au
- ✔ www.maridome.com
- ✔ www.pring.com
- ✔ www.prophetfinance.com
- ✔ www.recognia.com
- ✔ www.reginameani.com.au
- ✔ www.stockcharts.com
- ✔ www.theinvestingsite.com
- ✔ www.traderclub.com
- ✔ www.tradingmarkets.com

- www.tradingroom.com.au
- www.tsagroup.com
- www.turtletrading.com
- www.wealth.us
- www.weblink.com.au
- www.yte.com.au

Data Providers

Try the Australian Securities Exchange (www.asx.com.au) or broker Web sites as well as the data providers listed here.

- www.almax.com.au
- www.beyondinvest.com
- www.boursedata.com.au
- www.datahq.com.au
- www.databull.com
- www.esignal.com
- www.justdata.com.au
- www.keyquotes.com.sg
- www.netquote.com.au
- www.premiumdata.net
- www.proview.com.au
- www.quote.com
- www.thenextview.com

Index

• *C* •

• *U* •

• *V* •

Notes

FOR DUMMIES®

Business

Small Business FOR DUMMIES
1-74031-109-4
$39.95

Share Investing FOR DUMMIES
1-174031-146-5
$39.95

Personal Finance FOR DUMMIES
1-74031-004-7
$39.95

Business Plans FOR DUMMIES
1-74031-124-8
$39.95

Buying & Selling Your Home FOR DUMMIES
1-74031-166-3
$39.95

Investing FOR DUMMIES
1-74031-041-1
$39.95

MYOB Software FOR DUMMIES
0-7314-0541-2
$39.95

GST and BAS FOR DUMMIES
1-74031-033-0
$39.95

Reference

Gardening

Superannuation - Choosing a Fund FOR DUMMIES
1-74031-125-6
$29.95

Sustainable Living FOR DUMMIES
1-74031-157-1
$39.95

Job Hunting FOR DUMMIES
1-74031-030-6
$39.95

Gardening FOR DUMMIES
1-74031-007-1
$39.95

FOR DUMMIES®

Technology

1-74031-086-1
$39.95

0-74031-160-4
$39.95

1-7403-1159-0
$39.95

1-74031-123-X
$39.95

Cooking

Pets

1-74031-010-1
$39.95

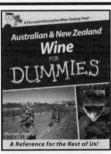

1-74031-008-X
$39.95

1-74031-040-3
$39.95

1-74031-028-4
$39.95

Parenting

Health & Fitness

1-74031-103-5
$39.95

1-74031-042-X
$39.95

1-74031-143-4
$39.95

1-74031-140-X
$39.95

Health & Fitness Cont.

1-74031-122-1
$39.95

1-74031-135-3
$39.95

1-74031-054-3
$39.95

1-74031-009-8
$39.95

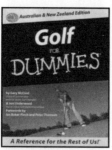

1-74031-011-X
$39.95

1-7403-1173-6
$39.95

1-74031-035-7
$39.95

1-74031-146-5
$39.95

1-74031-059-4
$39.95

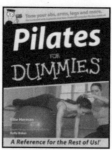

1-74031-074-8
$39.95

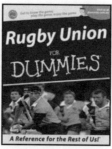

1-74031-073-X
$39.95

1-74031-094-2
$39.95